A CULTURAL HISTORY OF GARDENS

VOLUME 6

A Cultural History of Gardens
General Editors: Michael Leslie and John Dixon Hunt

Volume 1
A Cultural History of Gardens in Antiquity
Edited by Kathryn Gleason

Volume 2
A Cultural History of Gardens in the Medieval Age
Edited by Michael Leslie

Volume 3
A Cultural History of Gardens in the Renaissance
Edited by Elizabeth Hyde

Volume 4
A Cultural History of Gardens in the Age of Enlightenment
Edited by Stephen Bending

Volume 5
A Cultural History of Gardens in the Age of Empire
Edited by Sonja Dümpelmann

Volume 6
A Cultural History of Gardens in the Modern Age
Edited by John Dixon Hunt

A CULTURAL HISTORY OF GARDENS

IN THE MODERN AGE

Edited by John Dixon Hunt

Bloomsbury Academic
An imprint of Bloomsbury Publishing Plc

BLOOMSBURY
LONDON · OXFORD · NEW YORK · NEW DELHI · SYDNEY

Bloomsbury Academic
An imprint of Bloomsbury Publishing Plc

50 Bedford Square	1385 Broadway
London	New York
WC1B 3DP	NY 10018
UK	USA

www.bloomsbury.com

BLOOMSBURY and the Diana logo are trademarks of Bloomsbury Publishing Plc

Hardback edition first published in 2013 by Bloomsbury Academic
Paperback edition first published in 2016 by Bloomsbury Academic

© John Dixon Hunt 2013, 2016

John Dixon Hunt has asserted his right under the Copyright, Designs and Patents Act, 1988, to be identified as Editor of this work.

All rights reserved. No part of this publication may be reproduced or transmitted in any form or by any means, electronic or mechanical, including photocopying, recording, or any information storage or retrieval system, without prior permission in writing from the publishers.

No responsibility for loss caused to any individual or organization acting on or refraining from action as a result of the material in this publication can be accepted by Bloomsbury or the authors.

British Library Cataloguing-in-Publication Data
A catalogue record for this book is available from the British Library.

ISBN: 978-0-8578-5034-8 (HB)
978-1-8478-8265-3 (HB set)
978-1-3500-0994-3 (PB)
978-1-3500-0995-0 (PB set)

Library of Congress Cataloging-in-Publication Data
A catalog record for this book is available from the Library of Congress.

Series: The Cultural Histories Series

Typeset by Apex CoVantage, LLC, Madison, WI, USA

CONTENTS

	LIST OF ILLUSTRATIONS	VII
	GENERAL EDITORS' PREFACE	XI
	Introduction *John Dixon Hunt*	1
1	Design: On the (Continuing) Uses of the Arbitrary *Anita Berrizbeitia*	13
2	Types of Gardens *Peter Jacobs*	37
3	Plantings *Dennis McGlade and Laurie Olin*	63
4	Use and Reception *Udo Weilacher*	93
5	Meaning *John Dixon Hunt*	117
6	Verbal Representations *Michael Leslie*	141
7	Visual Representations *Michael Jakob*	161

8 Gardens and the Larger Landscape   181
   David Leatherbarrow

   NOTES   207
   BIBLIOGRAPHY   225
   CONTRIBUTORS   249
   INDEX   253

ILLUSTRATIONS

CHAPTER 1

Figure 1.1 Plan of a residential garden	16
Figure 1.2 Mathur/Da Cunha/Leader, diagram, Freshkills Competition proposal	19
Figure 1.3 Georges Descombes, Tunnel Footbridge, Lancy, Switzerland	32
Figure 1.4 Rebstockpark, Frankfurt, Germany, Master Plan by Laurie Olin and Peter Eisenman	34

CHAPTER 2

Figure 2.1 The "Sitio"	42
Figure 2.2 Squatter's gardens	46
Figure 2.3 An indigenous garden cemetery, Bathurst Island, Australia	47
Figure 2.4 Modern sculptures overlooking the Holy city, by Isamu Noguchi	52
Figure 2.5 The temple garden of Tofuku-ji, Kyoto	56

Figure 2.6 "Garden of Australian Dreams" 57

Figure 2.7 A metaphor of grocers shelves lined with produce, Quebec 59

CHAPTER 3

Figure 3.1 Hestercombe, Somerset, England 69

Figure 3.2 Iford Manor, Wiltshire, England 71

Figure 3.3 Hidcote Manor Garden, Gloucestershire, England 72

Figure 3.4 Great Dixter, East Sussex, England 73

Figure 3.5 Millenium Park, Chicago, Illinois 74

Figure 3.6 Abby Aldrich Rockefeller Sculpture Garden, Museum of Modern Art, New York City 79

Figure 3.7 Le Jardin en Mouvement, Parc André-Citroen, Paris, France 80

CHAPTER 4

Figure 4.1 Fritz Schumacher, Stadtpark Hamburg, Germany 98

Figure 4.2 Wagenfeld, Leipacher und Boyer, Luisenpark Mannheim, Germany 105

Figure 4.3 Atelier Stern und Partner, Irchel Park Zürich, Switzerland 106

Figure 4.4 Niki de Saint-Phallle, Tarot Garden, Garavicchio, Italy 109

Figure 4.5 Latz + Partner, Hafeninsel Saarbrücken, Germany 111

Figure 4.6 Dani Freixes and Vicente Miranda, Parc del Clot, Barcelona, Spain 112

Figure 4.7 Zulauf, Seippel und Schweingruber, Oerliker Park, Zurich, Switzerland 114

CHAPTER 5

Figure 5.1 Bryant Park, New York City, as redesigned by the Olin Partnership 124

ILLUSTRATIONS

Figure 5.2 From Bernard Lassus, *Jardins Imaginaires.*
Les Paysagistes-Habitants — 126

Figure 5.3 The Geological Observatory, Cadarda, above Lugano,
designed by Paolo Burgi — 128

Figure 5.4 Invalidenpark, Berlin, designed by Christophe Girot — 128

Figure 5.5 Along the olive terraces, Fleur de l'Air, Provence — 137

Figure 5.6 Plan of Le Jardin de l'Alchimiste, Eygalières, France — 137

Figure 5.7 Le Jardin de la Noria, Uzès, France — 138

CHAPTER 7

Figure 7.1 Paul Klee, *Rosengarten* (Rose Garden) — 165

Figure 7.2 Mahoney Charles Mahoney, Wrotham Place from the
Garden — 166

Figure 7.3 Paul Vera, The "modern" garden in the property of Charles
de Noailles, Paris — 168

CHAPTER 8

Figure 8.1 Roberto Burle Marx, Gardens of the Museum of
Modern Art, Flamego Park, Rio de Janeiro — 184

Figure 8.2 Luis Barragán, demonstration garden, El Pedregal,
Mexico City — 187

Figure 8.3 Le Corbusier, roof garden, 24 Rue Nungesser et Coli, Paris — 192

Figure 8.4 Le Corbusier, roof garden, Unité d'Habitation, Marseilles — 194

Figure 8.5 Laurie Olin and Peter Eisenman, Wexner Center for
the Visual Arts, Ohio State University, Columbus, Ohio — 196

Figure 8.6 Isamu Noguchi, UNESCO Gardens, Paris — 198

Figure 8.7 Garret Eckbo, ALCOA Forecast Garden, Laurel
Canyon, Los Angeles, California — 202

Figure 8.8 Peter Latz, Duisburg-Nord Landscape Park, Duisburg — 204

GENERAL EDITORS' PREFACE

The volumes of this series explore the cultural world of the garden from antiquity to the present day in six particular periods. Each volume addresses the same eight topics, determined by the general editors for their relevance to garden history across different times and cultures. Thus a reader interested more, say, in planting or in types of gardens could read through the chapters devoted to those issues in successive volumes. Contrariwise, either of those interests might be contextualized by a volume's discussion of other aspects of the garden in a given period. There is therefore both a horizontal and a vertical way of using these volumes. Further, each volume includes both its editor's introduction, which rather than abstracting or summarizing the other contributions, surveys the period from a fresh vantage point, and a bibliography, which encompasses references from all the eight chapters augmented with that editor's additional readings.

HISTORY

These volumes are a historical enquiry and not an encyclopedia. They do not pretend to be comprehensive, either geographically or chronologically. The authors of the individual chapters have been encouraged to foreground what seem to be the most significant episodes and examples of their particular topic, leaving it to the reader to envisage how other sites that he or she knows better might further illustrate, challenge, or qualify the given analyses. But in every instance, we intend there to be some narrative of one particular theme as it exists, unfolds, or develops during a particular historical period. The definitions of these historical eras must be taken with some caution and elasticity, since a chronology of garden making does not always fit the divisions of time devised for and endorsed by other histories: André Le Nôtre did his work after 1650 but is arguably more usefully considered in a volume focused on the Renaissance than on the Enlightenment; similarly, Gertrude Jekyll and William Robinson were designing before 1920, but we understand their work better within the cultural content of the modern age.

CULTURAL HISTORY

There are of course many modes of history that have developed over the centuries. A relatively new one addresses the cultural context of human activity. "Culture" derives from the Latin *colere,* which has as some of its meanings "to inhabit," "to respect," "to pay attention to"; it emerges also in our words "colony" and "cultivation." Gardens, then, must be considered as driven by and evidence of a whole congeries of human concerns; they are not, above all, to be examined in terms of their merely visual appearance, materials, or stylistic histories. The diversity and density of human involvements with those sites we call gardens mean that the discipline of garden history draws upon adjacent disciplines such as anthropology, sociology, economic, and political history, along with histories of the arts with which the garden has been involved. So three large questions are posed: why were gardens created? How were they used or visited (there being no handy term for the "consumption" of gardens)? And how does their representation in different arts express the position and value of the garden within its culture in diverse periods? Regretfully, we were unable to extend the range of these volumes to include the garden making of China and Japan among other Eastern cultures, although inevitably the rich examples of such gardens have been invoked on occasion.

GARDENS

The range of places that can be envisaged within this category is enormous and various, and it changes from place to place, and from time to time. Yet this diversity does not wholly inhibit us from knowing what it is we want to discuss when we speak of the garden. Yet the garden is typically a place of paradox, being the work of men and women, yet created from the elements of nature; just as it is often acknowledged to be a "total environment," a place may be physically separated from other zones but answering and displaying connections with larger environments and concerns. Gardens, too, are often created, and subsequently experienced, as commentary and response: a focus of speculations, propositions, and negotiations concerning what it is to live in the world. Both the physical gardens and the ideas that drive them are cultural constructions, and their history is the topic of these six volumes.

John Dixon Hunt, University of Pennsylvania

Michael Leslie, Rhodes College

Introduction

JOHN DIXON HUNT

"Landscape is not the opposite of the town; landscape is culture"
—Peter Latz[1]

A reader of this, the sixth, volume in the *Cultural History of Gardens* might be forgiven for wondering, "What's new?" and "Why?" in the world of garden making and landscape architecture, or rather, why has so much emphasis been placed upon the new, when—with even a modicum of historical sensibility—so much of it looks somewhat familiar if not downright old hat or *vieux jeu*? Indeed, that is perhaps the main issue here—that maybe we do have to decide whether it is a question of old headwear, spruced up and worn again in a jaunty fashion, or a really new game, with new rules, players, and scorecards. A further provocation comes with the diversity and much enlarged scope of landscape architecture in the modern period: the authors of the first three chapters, for instance, are all trained landscape architects, yet even allowing for the different demands of their topics, it is difficult sometimes to remember that they are indeed writing about the same phenomena.

Designers of gardens and landscapes have always worked within a quartet of conditions—conditions, that as the first chapter here makes clear, are both challenges and constraints. This quartet consists of (1) the materials to be used, (2) the type of site and how that determines design, (3) some dialogue between invention (doing something new) and repetition (reproducing previous work or even representing nature), and (4) the demands of a client, private or public (such demands being rarely compatible with the other constraints). Every age has seen gardens and landscapes created within these same parameters, which in their turn are the result of the cultural conditions of a given time and place; it is the differences in these conditions and their interactions that determine the outcome and results. The history of modern gardens and landscapes has seen an enormously enlarged scope and many changes in each of those four categories.

The materials now available to contemporary garden makers include plastic, concrete, aluminum, and all sorts of composite bricks and stones; the plant palette, too, can be more varied, more adaptable, and more contrived (scientifically) than ever before, yet Dennis McGlade and Laurie Olin also show that despite such new resources, the palette used is sometimes very limited. Garden types, as the second chapter sets them out, are probably more numerous and certainly more specifically characterized and programmed than in previous periods. The dialogues (traditionally explained as) between nature and culture are of continuing significance and are endlessly invoked, yet our concepts of nature are continually shifting and certainly very diverse (e.g., the Amsterdamse Bos or even Parc Bercy in Paris seem "natural" enclaves to some people, while others see them as urban contrivances). Different and changing cultural standards allow no secure or stable categories or perspectives (e.g., the innovative use of former steel works by Peter Latz to create the park of Duisberg Nord in the 1990s now strikes its many users as having produced an absolutely familiar parkscape). And while the categories of clients throughout the modern period may seem little changed from the recent past, ranging from rich individuals and institutions (whether corporate, municipal, or state) to private households, the process of commissioning, designing, and then building gardens and landscapes is fraught with, on one side, the extreme professionalization of designers and, on another, by the assumption of many people and constituencies that they must have a voice in public work.

Another conspicuous element of modern gardens and landscapes is how very much diversity is apparent in their forms and styles. If we think back to earlier gardens, we probably have some idea—however imprecise, however implausible—of what they looked like and what we might say about them. We would identify an "English landscape" naturalism during the eighteenth century, even though in practice there were radically different modes of this within England itself, and many more as the style spread across Europe and traveled to the United States and Australasia. We also could conjure up a medieval type, or a typical baroque design, ignoring the Islamic versions of the former or the ideological differences that underpinned, say, a Catholic French and a Protestant Dutch garden of the late seventeenth century. Such notional ideas, however, though obviously flawed or even fallacious, seem impossible in the modern period; indeed, even during the nineteenth century it becomes much harder to isolate some defining characteristic amid an increasingly eclectic repertoire of styles and programs. Perhaps the public park from Munich to Birkenhead to Seattle does offer itself as a plausibly compelling identikit of the period. Even so, the genealogy of that type can be traced from the eighteenth century (Stowe, Ermenonville, Worlitz) right up into the twenty-first century (Downsview, Fresh Kills, Seattle's Olympic Sculpture Park).

But the twentieth century frustrates any similar attempt at even a caricature of its typical garden, as the illustrations selected by authors for their contributions to this volume attest. Moreover, the artistic history of the twentieth century is rife with innovation and experimentation in art and design that also defy schematic categories. Partly and obviously, we may be too close to all this work to identify a convincing pattern or type, to hear a tune in all the noise (to adopt Valentine's formulation from Tom Stoppard's *Arcadia*). But more crucially, the last eighty years have seen a huge diversification of gardens and gardening. Peter Jacobs's survey of the types of modern garden makes clear how the very idea, the forms, and above all their functions have exploded. Professionals, amateurs, commercial makers, and suppliers of garden materials to ever-increasingly garden-inclined and do-it-yourself (DIY) populations simply refuse, as Matthew Arnold said of Shakespeare, to abide our question.

This is perhaps *the* cultural phenomenon to register about the modern period: its exponentially large range of work. Nonetheless, it can be interesting to try to open up some of the complexities and variety of both built work and its conceptual projections throughout the modern period and in various societies. The work of two practicing landscape architects can be reviewed, both of whom are extraordinarily prominent in their own countries, are acutely attuned to how their work responds to cultural patterns and obligations, and, being extremely articulate, have tried to reach out to a larger audience to explain their determinedly vanguard work: Martha Schwartz in the United States and Bernard Lassus in France.[2]

Schwartz's professional career famously took off with her facetious laying out of the Bagel Garden in Boston in 1979, and her subsequent publication of its mock design project in the pages of *Landscape Architecture*, the journal of the American Society of Landscape Architects, the professional body of American landscape architects. What is most interesting about that event is how much its fame and influence were achieved, as she acknowledges, "almost entirely through the power of an image and the media";[3] the influence of photography and the media in spreading the word about fashions and styles of the modern garden is huge. The wonderful, fresh jokiness of the bagel garden, partly because of its widespread publicity, has come to be taken seriously even by Schwartz and extrapolated into a whole design practice and aesthetic that can be branded, at least by her commentators who refer to "The Schwartz look."[4] Yet, the violently opposing responses to the Bagel Garden then and subsequently reveal the fissures that have opened in our society's understanding of gardens. That work brought into focus one basic and paradoxical cultural attitude: that we cannot rely any more on earlier, tired notions of nature—hence the bagels, if you like, instead of plants from the garden center (what if it had been those purple cabbages?). With the bagels and with almost all of her subsequent work, Schwartz delights in challenging our expectations about "nature," saying our wishful thinking that nature is "all around us" is "meaningless,"[5] and being careful that her interventions do "not . . . blend into nature."[6] Yet, contrariwise, she still needs the concept of a normative nature, if only to play against, along with the very materiality of what the rest of us still call "nature," even if in her hands, it is high-jacked from its customary contexts. Deliberate artifice presupposes, indeed must rely on, its converse.

The reach of modern garden design beyond natural, growing materials is one of its distinctive marks; as David Leatherbarrow suggests, nontraditional garden effects and associations, whether aluminum, or the detritus of technology and industry, are the larger landscapes into which the modern garden has to be inserted or which it draws into its purview. Schwartz may substitute the virtual for the actual—colored vinyl and steel canopies at the Broward County Civic Arena in Ft. Lauderdale (1998)—but such gestures work best if we register their irony, and in this case, the irony only works if the poles and disks not only recall the trees lost to development in the Florida Everglades, but we also know they were actually substituted for living royal palms by Schwartz herself during a design process crippled by budget constraints. Schwartz needs nature, not just as an idea but as an experience, to play against her virtual alternatives; "non-plants"[7] are steel and plastic, but as she also uses real plants alongside the virtual ones, we get the point. It is therefore disingenuous of her, as of other contemporary designs, to deny or trash some lingering nostalgia for nature. Essentially modern, however, are her reliance upon irony ("saying" one thing but meaning another), the speed with which her installations can be engineered (as opposing to waiting for "nature" to grow) and her appeal always to "High contrast" of all sorts.[8] Where she eludes being categorized as typically modern is her refusal of any ecological virtue: "designing ecologically does not determine form or style" and "eco-led narratives tend to marginalize cultural issues."⁹

Bernard Lassus, too, disdains the notion that design can be ecological: ecological purity—the restored water meadows of the Escher valley—is but the degree zero of design.¹⁰ From his early observation of vernacular gardening discussed in *Jardins Imaginaires. Les Paysagistes-Habitants* (1977) to his recent work for the COLAS headquarters, Lassus has pursued a dual purpose, in itself a strange but typical modern amalgram. On one hand, his gardens and landscapes admit imagination and even fantasy—"admit" in two senses: that the designer recognizes and deploys fantastic elements (the *dramatis personae* of Disney films in the vernacular sites; cut-out steel trees and plastic flower tubes at COLAS), but equally visitors can bring their fantasies into play on his sites. On the other, he escapes from the comfortable forms and materials of conventional site-work—the two COLAS gardens may be designed with a view to minimum maintenance, but their colored ironwork cutouts, plastic flowers and transparently scenographic illusions commit him to a wholly new aesthetic. In them, as in most of his career, he has discovered in structuralist dualisms a truly modern context for designer and landscape visitor alike. Not just, if at all, to play off one element at the expense of another—nature/culture, tactile/visual, virtual/actual, homogeneity/heterogeneity, solids/cracks or faults, measurable/immeasurable, vernacular/elite—but to ensure that their dialogue or encounters elicit new experiences where each element is enhanced and transformed by the ensemble. The physical achievement and haptic experience that this creates recovers for the imagination what he terms an "immeasurable," lost in the modern shrinking of space. Like Schwartz he works through contrasts, between the speed of the autoroute or the anonymity of the company headquarters in the faceless *banlieu*, on one hand, and our irrepressible need for locality and nature, on the other, even if the *here* and now turns out to be imaginary. There has to be a there there—landscape's endemic version of the Gertrude Stein's modernist taunt.

Lassus and Schwartz are in some ways, surely, at the radical end of modern garden making and landscaping. Their example is not one readily imitatable or followed by others. Yet their work opens up some of the cultural challenges of recent garden making and landscape architecture, and it nonetheless determines the scale of other work in relation to them. It also sets high artistic standards. For both began their careers as artists, and both have been annexed to contemporary art movements—Schwartz willingly to performance and installation art ("we must look to art . . . and art history"¹¹), Lassus out of an early apprenticeship to Fernand Léger and (less enthusiastically) to land art.[12] Those involvements have sharpened their sense of their landscape work's modernity, distancing them deliberately and effectively from historical garden design. Modernism's refusal of precedence or antecedence is one of the defining cultural attitudes in design; even those, like Dan Kiley, who seem to embrace the geometries and formulae of classicism, have gone out of their way, it seems, to protest their independence of them. When Lassus or Schwartz do evoke historical precedent, it is via transformation or distortion: Lassus's huge *tapis vert* stretched across the autoroute at the rest area of Nîmes-Cassargues; Schwartz turning French topiary and Japanaese sand gardens into a plastic rooftop extravaganza for the Whitehead Institute for Biomedical Research, or upending the traditional role of sculpture in gardens with banal commercial garden ornaments, like the gilded frogs at the Rio Shopping center in Atlanta, Georgia, or the Westphalia park with 51 Garden Ornaments.

Both Lassus and Schwartz are also wholly typical of the modern field in their response to the manifold kinds of spaces that our lives call into play— "backyards, highway corridors, shopping-mall parking lots, city and suburban streets, railroad corridors, strips, plazas, courtyards, waterfronts"[13]—the list is Schwartz's, but add corporate headquarters, new towns, derelict housing estates, toxic wastelands and abandoned ports, a routine *square* in a less than fashionable Parisian arrondissement, and the repertoire is also Lassus's. And they participate—not exceptional at all in this—in the circulation and promotion of their designs via imagery in magazines and their own publications. If we might argue that this modern reliance on the circulation of designs for self-promotion began with Humphry Repton in the early nineteenth century— pillaging his unique red books for individual clients in order to put into wider circulation published versions of his designs, then our age of mechanical reproduction has increased enormously the public's ability to access ideas and projects. It was the endless reiteration in magazines of the iconic Donnell garden by Thomas Church that ensured the success of a Californian lifestyle centered on the garden, the swimming pool, and the barbecue pit and bar.

How built sites would be used and treated by others is not neglected by modern landscape designers and their critics, but it gets conspicuously less attention. The sexy processes of design too often trump consideration of even design implementation and certainly of its quotidian use. The consideration by Udo Weilacher, himself a landscape architect, of the uses of and responses to new designs in Germany and Switzerland in this volume, however, shows how worthwhile such a topic might be. We know a lot about new gardens and landscapes from their initiation—designers are good at self-advertisement, but far less concerned about the sites as they are used and inhabited after they have been built. The rapidity of changing practices among professional landscape architects (their move from *atelier* to corporate corporation; the digital revolution and its displacement of manual drawing; the embrace of often arcane theoretical positions from outside the discipline) has tended to eclipse the longer existence of sites after the event of their "completion": we read endlessly about the design of Parc La Villette, far less about how it is being used and, in use, reshaped. The site, after all, should be what the business of place making is all about, yet Berrizbeitia argues that site seems "but a locus for [designers'] creativity," in effect ignoring its subsequent existence or, if you like, the creativity of the folks who actually get to use and enjoy it. So Weilacher's final examination of the public's expectation of public parks, in the face of both design ambitions and planning codes, is a necessary element of our total picture.

It may often seem, indeed, that modern designers are so bound up with their own concerns that the afterlife of their built works gets scant attention. That afterlife consists in the use and reception of designed sites by publics whose concepts or assumptions of space may not be available in advance to designers, at least in the fullest range of possible ideas and reactions. One way in which to gain access to that conspectus of ideas and assumptions is to study how gardens and landscapes are envisaged *outside* of the processes of their design and implementation. So one reason for including chapters on the representation of gardens in both visual and verbal arts is that how we respond and how we experience the garden—whether actual or imaginary—are as important an aspect of garden culture as how they are designed and built. Both writers and visual artists make a fundamental contribution to this *idea* of the garden, though it is not always easy to make connections between the range of built work and the ideas of landscape exposed or elicited in other arts.

The chapters by Michael Jakob and Michael Leslie suggest that the perspectives of visual artist, filmmakers, poets, and novelists are neither always as optimistic nor as upbeat as the professional discourse of design usually suggests. For many modern artists and writers, gardens are the loci of doubt, skepticism, ambiguity, even chaos and evil that we tend to assume cannot coexist with the green thoughts of the garden's green world. It is as if, counting on long-held and sentimental affection for green places, modern artists have deliberately called that bluff: the garden, they insist, is nothing like what the gardening magazines tell us; beautiful untouched swathes of natural scenery are still the site of horrendous human violence. Of course, designers are highly unlikely to commit themselves to making places that evince gloom, doom, worry, and perhaps fear; we do not plan to visit a park or garden because it will challenge our confidence and pleasure in space and place. Nor do people who themselves garden do so to express despair or other negativity: in a well-heeled and certainly well-gardened suburb of Philadelphia, there is one front garden entirely covered entirely with black plastic—perhaps the closest anyone comes to disdaining garden's pleasures in a practical way. Parc La Villette's deconstruction of traditional landscape was intended to and may indeed still give some of its visitors pause; but the grid of red follies is still great fun, and the exploration of its scattered garden incidents enjoyable.

If the garden and the park continue to hold out the possibilities of personal freedom and democratic pastimes, if both amateur and professional designers continue to provide for the fun of play and the opportunities for healthful exercise, for benign communion with nature and for many other, often sentimental associations, it must also give us pause to consider how often these same sites and their virtues are presented skeptically, even negatively, in the visual and literary arts. We expect art and literature to provide us with subtle and probing analyses of our worldly situations, and since the garden has never been anything but a place of contested values (nature versus culture, just to start with) it should come as no surprise that it emerges in poems, novels, films, and paintings with a richer and more intricate, often darker, character than is suggested by actual creations. And maybe we do, and should, return to those real places with more sensitive appreciation of their complexities.

If we were, for example, to take the truly rich assemblage of work selected for the Tate Gallery exhibition on the "Art of the Garden" in 2004, or to revisit several anthologies of writing (particularly poems) about gardens, the agenda of themes is revealed to be extensive. The gardens in visual art can be messy, muddled, and unkempt; places of dubious privilege; the sites of domestic activity like laundry, but also of dysfunctional families, and sex; floral abundance and yet (Ian Hamilton's Finlay's inscriptions) stern admonitions. In an astonishing number of examples, the gardens are utterly emptied of people, with sometimes a quite sinister effect, yet sometimes such emptiness only suggests that the garden has managed to flourish by itself. Modern poetry of the garden is no less inclusive and sometimes disturbing. Patrick Hare unveils the "Deceit in the Park" (that's why we are locked out after 9 P.M.); Kelly Drake's Sicilian *hortus* has had its sculptures "smashed . . . beyond the malice of the weather"; Alasdair Aston's "Everything in the Garden is Lovely" ironically celebrates the blight, grubs, poisonous plants and even the death of the gardener.[14]

What the imagery from other media also hints at are the constraints, at once ideological and bureaucratic, within which our thinking about gardens is constructed. The twentieth and increasingly the twenty-first centuries have witnessed an increased scientific and popular concern with environmental and ecological issues, which has had an impact on much design, transforming how sites are conceived, implemented, and received, and at the very least the broadcasting of ecological messages has made more people aware of their own demands of and interventions in the natural world. The later twentieth century also saw a whole rooster of legislative rules and regulations devised to mediate between designers and the communities in which their work would be built—handicapped access is an important example, but so too are directives ensuring better ecological processes for such mundane matters as storm drainage and erosion. Too, more and more people are engaged in monitoring design through community activity, participating frequently in the consultations that designers now undertake with communities, or, in the face of what they see as overbearing and insensitive projects, protesting when they are not listened to or when they are not so involved.

Anita Berrizbeita traces how the shifts and maneuvers through which professional landscape architects address the physical transformation of sites generally involve some element of the arbitrary (or its resolute, and not always convincing, denial). She concludes with the wry observation that nothing much has changed in the modern landscape despite the sequence of many different iterations of practice and principle that designers have engaged in *(plus ça change, plus c'est la même chose)*. Such a conclusion, or—more importantly—the processes she surveys and analyses that lead to such a conclusion, seem to have no strong or convincing cultural explanation. Perhaps the very role of the arbitrary, which she isolates as a central theme, is by definition essentially modern, since in the larger artistic world of modernisms "chance" has been much valued; we may think of surrealism's celebration of the unexpected, yet also wonder just how much landscape architecture has really been able to embrace chance in its processes. What is claimed to be a new insistence that we should rely upon the random transformation of materials (and perhaps usage) over time has become extremely important to contemporary practitioners; but it is hardly a novel idea (Alexander Pope in the 1730s believed that "time would make [Stowe] grow . . . "[15]).

Earlier histories of gardens have been much preoccupied with what designed sites meant to their contemporaries and how such places expressed or shaped contemporary ideas. That perspective was considerably advanced in the mid-twentieth century through the attention given to garden cultures by art historians and literary scholars, a staple of whose work was the identification and explanation of meaning in visual and verbal arts. Modern gardens—or at least modern garden commentators—tend to cleave to that nostalgia for meaning, but their grasp of the topic is slipping; some, indeed, would wish it away.[16] Writing of Dan Kiley's Fountain Place in Dallas, Texas, Yoji Sasaki noted that "the margin necessary to allow the expression of meaning . . . no longer exists."[17] It's a somewhat gnomic remark, but I take its metaphoric reference to pages printed with text inside empty margins to imply that Kiley's work fills out the whole surface of the page, leaving us no place in which to register our reactions to it, that its sheer physical presence bleeds off the page and leaves no white spaces even for his own commentary. Transferring the metaphor to the site, then, presumably means that Kiley leaves no room for anything but the physical performance of his fountains and walkways; even the sidewalk (its actual margin) does not yield such opportunity, even though the boundary condition of Fountain Place is part of its identity and success.

Then there is Sasaki's phrase, "expression" of meaning, implying that there is always meaning but that its expression is totally off the page, let alone marginalized; there is also the implication of verbal articulation, discursive expression, though the thought that one might draw or sketch in the margins is not admittedly excluded. The remark along with its subject, Kiley's wonderful plaza, suggests a series of key questions about the modern focus upon meaning: why has the "need" arisen to make the attribution of meaning to landscape architecture such an issue in recent decades? Indeed, why is there any need to search for meaning at all? Why can we not let a built work (as we say) "speak for itself"? (An interesting metaphor, another discursive assumption, which leads to another question.) Does meaning have to be discursive—that is, expounded in words? Are there other ways of articulating meaning? Perhaps even what is the meaning of meaning in these contexts? Who decides what (if any) meaning pertains to a site—the designer, its critics, its uses and visitors, its historians? Do we in fact really mean to talk about meaning? Is that really what we look for in a landscape site? At all? Or primarily?

These are larges issues, some of which are addressed in the chapter on meaning here, but mostly the questions signal certain shifts in modern sensibility towards the garden as an art form. Ever since the late eighteenth century, landscape architecture has needed to establish itself as a serious member of the pantheon of the fine and design arts, and it has accordingly felt the need to discover ways to proclaim that it is more serious and intellectual (more meaningful) than its connections to horticulture would imply. Yet, at the same time, this desire to establish its credentials has now come up against a decisive aspect of modernism that—broadly speaking—values formal qualities above all else and requires each medium to rely only on its own inherent resources—thus paintings are about a flat surface and the arrangement of pigment on it (not about story or event out there beyond the canvas). Or, as explained by the famous dancer Isadore Duncan, "if I could tell you what it [my dance] means, there would be no point in dancing it." Struggling against formalism and the limiting scope of its specific materials, landscape architecture found itself in a quandary: if it reached out to grab meaning as a way of making itself both visible and respectable again, it risked losing modernist credentials. That explains, I think, some of the difficulties this topic has encountered.

But concerns with what landscapes and gardens might mean are also importantly about how these places relate to all our other interests and involvements. One critic who has tackled the question of meaning, Bob Riley, argued that gardens were a "special expression" of the multitude of meanings people have discerned in the natural world.[18] Leaving aside the intriguing question of expression (surely it is we who express those feelings, not the garden[19]), he is surely right to see the garden as the site where men and women imagine or identify many concerns and see them somehow focused in the garden, even though some of their concerns do not even have anything specifically to do with gardens or that the gardens that are sought for are not always what we would expect them to be. Indeed, the very need to write "gardens and landscapes" or "gardens and parks" in connection with recent history, accepting that the garden by itself is no longer the prime site of professional practice or human significance, signals how much the modern designer is faced with finding landscapes that reflect, respond to and even shape social ideals and needs. David Leatherbarrow's exploration in this volume of how gardens relate to the larger landscape also sees their range of reference as ever widening and unbounded. And what we may once have felt were the materials and associations endemic to gardens have now come to entertain an often arbitrary-seeming agenda that is both within and beyond the control of designers.

A cultural history of the modern garden, then, is open-ended and necessarily ongoing. The historical narrative is likely to become more knowledgeable and more analytical simply because the impact of society on design seems to matter more than ever and is being monitored with greater sophistication. How the profession and the expectations of those for whom it ultimately works—the users of gardens and landscapes—will change over the next decades is imponderable. Back in 1941, Fletcher Steele mused about the modernist potential of his profession: writing under the title of "Private Delight and the Communal Ideal," he anticipated that "[i]f there is to be any alteration in the function of the landscape architect, it will come with a change in human order itself."[20] And on the relationship of that human order to place making, the late Dieter Kienast, a Swiss designer, was confident that the garden is indeed "the last luxury of our time," because it cherishes what is "rare and valuable in our society: time, devotion, and space"; as well, it utilizes the skills of the age—"spirit, knowledge and handicraft."[21]

CHAPTER ONE

Design: On the (Continuing) Uses of the Arbitrary

ANITA BERRIZBEITIA

To design in landscape architecture entails working within limits set by, principally, four criteria. First, landscape architects work within limits set by the materials they use, whether natural—water, plants, and ecology—or man-made—steel, concrete, plastic, and so on. Second, they work within established formal and spatial codes and conventions, adapting them to specificities of site, of the program, and, most importantly, of cultural context. Third, they organize and coordinate a complex web of productive facilities and activities, including the possibility for future growth and expansion. Finally, they work within the constraints determined by the political context, whether private clients, the government, or a community, which requires responses to often unpredictable rules and demands.

During the twentieth century, each of these constraints emerged individually as a key design criterion, provisionally relegating all others to secondary importance. These shifts in design focus displaced the primacy that had been historically given to aesthetics as the general basis for design in landscape architecture. Further, they motivated the creation of new design methodologies that moved away from the purely compositional (characteristic of design practices of the beginning of the twentieth century) toward research-oriented, and data-driven, practices (by the last decade of the twentieth century). Today, design has become a highly institutionalized cooperative process in which all aspects of a project are hyperrationalized by numerous consultants, community members, clients, and, not least, landscape architects themselves. The pressure to legitimize all aspects of a project is widespread and accepted. From project descriptions in the design literature, to lectures, to public presentations, to competition entries, designers present their proposals as a series of seemingly objective responses to site, program, circulation, sustainability, accessibility, and economics, among others, giving the impression that not only is theirs the "right" solution but also that the particular design is inevitable, the only objectively justifiable one, with no traces of subjectivity, no presence of the arbitrary.

This chapter traces the evolution of design as responses to changing cultural conditions, and it does so through charting changing notions of what constitutes the arbitrary in design. For one of the distinguishing features of twentieth-century design, from Eckbo and Rose in the 1930s to the recent neo-rationalist practices of the so-called landscape urbanists, is the universal objection to the arbitrary. With the rejection of the classical tradition[1] in landscape architecture in the late 1930s began four decades of theories that strove to systematize design processes, to establish design protocols, and to take away all that was considered arbitrary. Design education, too, became based on the assumption that the arbitrary is bad. To this day, we demand that our students suppress all personal opinions on taste, and teach them the various ways one can think through a project, rationally. Just about the worst thing one can tell a student, or one can hear about design, is that the work is arbitrary. However, during the last three decades of the twentieth century, the arbitrary reappeared in landscape architecture, this time recast not as an entirely negative attribute of design but as the necessary element that enabled designers to release the boundaries of the discipline from the restrictions left by the positivistic practices of the preceding decades. With the freedom supported by this new cultural climate of the seventies came the open recognition that to design means to make choices, choices that, beyond satisfying the programmatic, ecological, and functional requisites of a project, point to discursive aesthetic sensibilities and renewed formal practices.

The word *arbitrary* can mean several things in landscape architecture. First, a work is arbitrary because it has followed a flawed design methodology. Here, as in the dictionary, it means "existing or coming about seemingly at random or by chance or as a capricious and unreasonable act of will."[2] When the set of decisions that lead to the work are vague, or when the reasoning behind those decisions is not clearly apparent in the forms, the work seems motivated by the arbitrary. Second, a work may be arbitrary because of its formal vocabulary. The designer is using forms in an uncritical way, following conventions, or latest fashion. In this sense, it is also related to eclecticism, a form-for-the-sake-of-form attitude that uses design vocabularies indiscriminately. Third, a work is arbitrary when its forms are not grounded in the ecological and physical realities of the site. Fourth, a work is arbitrary when its program does not relate to the social realities of the communities it serves. Fifth, a work is arbitrary when the materials it uses are made to perform in ways that do not relate to the natural properties of the medium itself (for example, a tree is made to grow into topiary form) or is pretending to express something it is not (as in fake rustication to make something built in the twentieth century appear to have been built in the nineteenth).[3] These diverse definitions did not originate all at once. Thus, for example, when landscape architecture was aligned with the social vocation of early modernism—the era of the great public beaches, parks, playgrounds, and highways—all aspects of a project not determined by function or program were considered arbitrarily conceived. Similarly, the environmental urgency that began during the 1960s has put enormous pressure on designers to conform to site, native ecologies, and sustainability, all else (form, history, and program) falling into the category of arbitrary. We can even understand the history of twentieth-century design by charting the shifting location of the arbitrary in the various theories and practices that advanced the discipline throughout the century.

II

In both their writings and projects of the 1930s and 1940s, Garrett Eckbo, Dan Kiley, and James Rose challenged the purely compositional approach to landscape architecture in favor of a rational approach based on program, scientific developments in horticulture, and the spatial and formal possibilities afforded by new materials, such as aluminum and reinforced concrete. One can clearly understand their challenge within the context of what was considered the design bible,[4] Henry Hubbard and Theodora Kimball's *An Introduction to the Study of Landscape Design*, published in 1917.[5] A comprehensive volume on esthetic theory in landscape architecture, the introduction was largely based on Édouard André's *L'Art des Jardins: Traité Général de la Composition des Parcs et Jardins*, published in Paris almost four decades earlier in 1878.

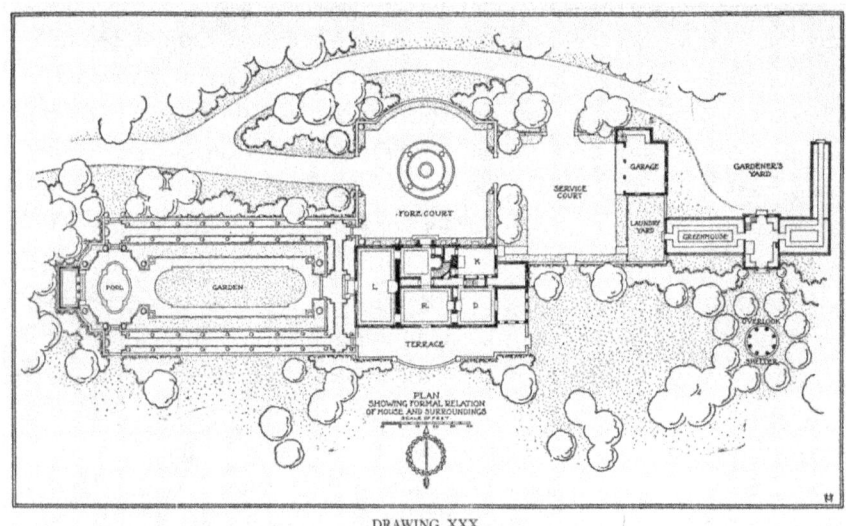

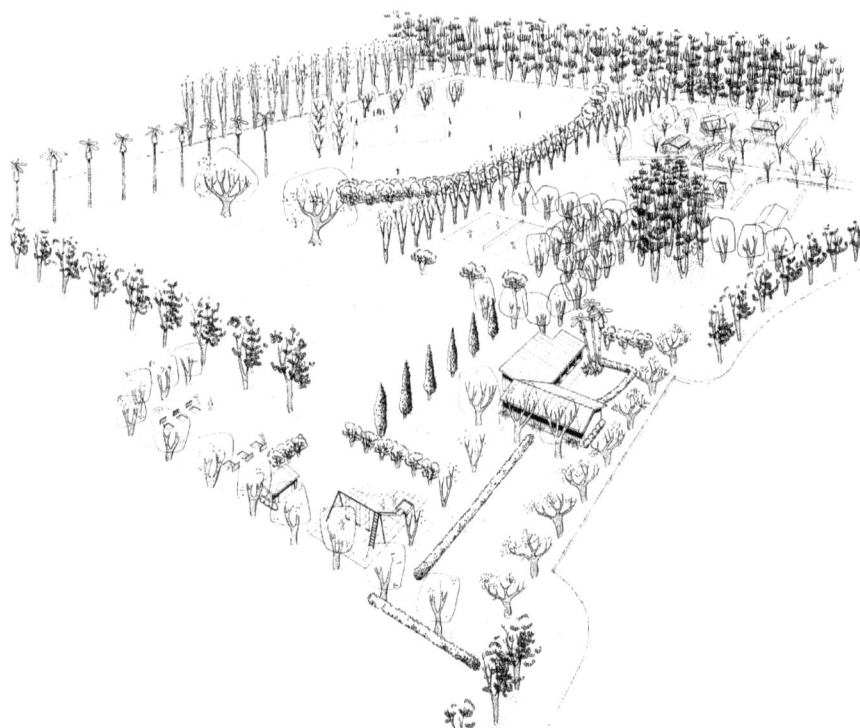

FIGURE 1.1: Plan of a residential garden, from Hubbard and Kimball, 1917 alongside, Garrett Eckbo, Ceres Camp, community recreation space. San Joaquin Valley, 1940. Farm Security Administration.
Source: M. Treib and D. Imbert, eds., *Garrett Eckbo: Modern Landscape for Living* (Berkeley: University of California Press, 1997), 125.

Hubbard and Kimball provided guidelines for design and for the interpretation of natural landscapes through visual frameworks, leaving aside as secondary all programmatic, ecological, and site criteria. For Hubbard and Kimball, there were two primary forms of spatial organization. The first involved the creative manipulation of a received language and was the result of a process of *invention*. The second, subtler and, in their minds, a higher art, was the result of a process of *imitation* of nature. The first appealed to the intellect and was fundamentally characterized by "repose, restraint, refinement, and formality."[6] The second, by contrast, was characterized by the use of variety and contrast, which "made a studied appeal to the emotions through the human associations aroused."[7] These two were basic and universal typologies: all design throughout the history of landscape architecture fell into one of the two categories, regardless of the time and place of origin.

Because the ultimate goal of landscape architecture was to "produce an effect of pleasure in the mind of the beholder,"[8] Hubbard and Kimball also provided a list of such possible effects. In addition to the beautiful and the picturesque, it includes sublimity, desolation, melancholy, gaiety, and mystery. The most extensive part of the book is, not surprisingly, devoted to the rules of landscape composition. Beginning with forms of order—repetition, sequence, balance (symmetrical and occult balance), it then goes on to describe the individual characteristics of objects within a landscape composition (shape, size, scale, distance, texture, color, light and shade, atmosphere and atmospheric perspective, and landscape compositions).

Hubbard and Kimball were keen observers of the natural landscape, and clearly recognize it as a fundamental source in design. However, their understanding of nature seems largely visual; nature is nothing other than a source catalogue for effects in design. Thus, they describe the difference between character and style as the difference between naturally produced harmony, through the action of landscape processes, and designer induced harmony, through composition. According to Hubbard and Kimball, landscape processes can be perceived esthetically, even though the "observer has no knowledge of what forces produced it."[9] Examples of landscape character are the prairie, the tundra, sand dunes, sequoia groves, sierra mountain meadow, the bushy pasture, the English pasture, and so forth. Similarly, in their chapter on natural landscape forms, hills, valleys, plains, rivers, shores, rock, and so on are visually analyzed and thus assimilated into their vast formal dictionary of landscape. The book is, on one hand, an impressive and overwhelming document for the breadth and thoroughness of descriptions of everything that has to do with landscapes, from natural to urban, from small garden to estates to suburban developments, from urban parks to National parks and reservations, from paths to complex circulation systems, streets, and utilities. On the other hand, by processing everything through the same aesthetic framework, in spite of vast differences in scale, program, and client, the book became, for the next generation of landscape architects, a rigid and narrow vision of design. More fundamentally, although Hubbard and Kimball adapted André's treatise to the realities of American conditions—the rising pressure for suburbanization and the romantic appreciation for the American wilderness-the *Introduction* represented the approaches of a still largely traditionalist culture that was fixed on the achievements of the nineteenth century, and slow to absorb the effects of industrialization on American society during the first decades of the century.

Eckbo, Kiley, and Rose criticized this tradition as arbitrary on many levels. Calling the approach a "mechanical, pre-conceived formula for design,"[10] Eckbo, for example, called for a release from "subservience to arbitrary authoritarian "formal" axial patterns" and from "subservience to nature and its naturalistic imitation and reproduction."[11] Throughout their writing and to develop their argument, Eckbo and Rose made analogies between concepts that had developed in architecture almost two decades earlier and the specificities of the medium of landscape. First, they took the idea of economy of means ("less is more") to break away from the two typologies of the classical tradition advanced by Hubbard and Kimball. In the free plan of modern architecture, with its interlocking volumes that worked as dynamic flow-through spaces, achieved via the most efficient use of walls, they saw the opportunity to invent a new planting spatiality. They rejected the traditional use of plant massing found in naturalistic design, and proposed freestanding lines of trees that gave spatial value to both sides of the plant. "One result of the application of science to environmental control is to free us of mass, and its attendant staticity. For example, in one small particular, when plants are used as specimens, rather than as mass, fewer plants are required for the same control and division of space. This is partly the result of using all sides of the plant—instead of only the one side used in massing—as a design element . . ."[12] Further, the sense of transparency characteristic of the modern sensibility would also be achieved in landscape architectural space through the elimination of the understory (shrub) layer in planting, and limiting the use of plant forms to below and well above eye level, achieving a sense of division without obstructing views through. Rose described this new type of landscape space as "informality without the loss of form,"[13] a remarkable phrase that cut through the dominant binomial categorization of landscape space.

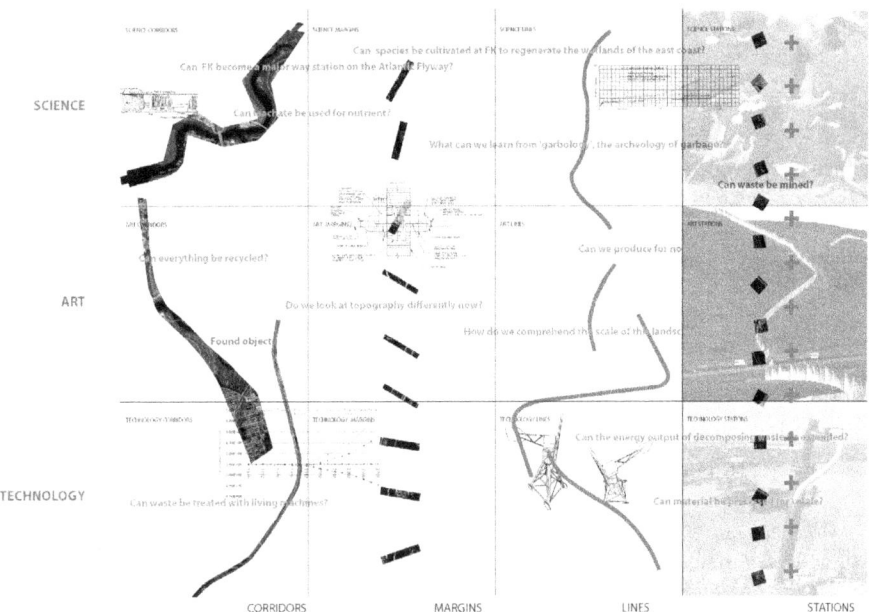

FIGURE 1.2: Mathur/Da Cunha/Leader, diagram, Freshkills Competition proposal, 2002. Courtesy of the designers.

Second, they took the modernist idea that the medium is the message to look closely at the materials of landscape, especially plants. In traditional design, plants were assigned to shapes, after the ground had been compartmentalized according to a pattern or a massing had been established according to a scenic or other composition, but they did not themselves dictate form. Eckbo, Kiley, and Rose proposed that plants, like building materials, had inherent qualities that were the object and subject of design. "To use plants intelligently, one must know, for every plant, its form, height at maturity, rate of growth, hardiness, soil requirements, deciduousness, color texture, and time of bloom. To express this complex of inherent quality, it is necessary to separate the individual from the mass, and arrange different types in organic relation to use, circulation, topography, and existing elements in the landscape. The techniques are more complicated than in the Beaux Arts patterns, but we thereby achieve volumes of organized space in which people live and play, rather than stand and look."[14] Here we see the rejection of an art-for-art's-sake sensibility in the use of plants and the introduction of program and social use of space that, paired with the right plant type, became the basic building blocks of their designs.

But more fundamental than the formal criticism, Eckbo, Kiley, and Rose called for new *design processes*. Beaux Arts methodology was concerned first with the act of imposing order on the site, rather than searching for existing order in the site. Each category of project demanded predetermined types of solution. The first decision a designer took was to assign a type to the project, the choice of which was given by the program, whether a public park, a private garden, a memorial, a ceremonial place, and so forth. Once this decision had been made, the designer would work the type into the site, negotiating abstract geometries into the irregularities of the topography, beginning with the first moves, the placement of the axis (or of axes) or the direction of views. Eckbo, Kiley, and Rose maintained that this was a wrong, arbitrary process of design. Design, they proposed, begins with analysis of program and site, architecture and people, not with composition of patterns in the ground. "It is fundamentally wrong to begin with axes or shapes in plan; ground forms *evolve* [emphasis added] from a division of space,"[15] and "[f]orm is a result not a predetermined element of the problem."[16] That this was not just a matter of a new generation rejecting the old is evident in Rose's assertion that one could conceivably have a symmetrical composition in modern gardens, as long as symmetry was arrived at through due process, and not as a preconceived solution to the project.[17] In other words, they proposed a fundamental shift in design approach, from bringing order into the site, to finding order and expressing that order in the site. Here are the seeds of ideas that remain with us today, that each project must be considered anew, and that objective site, program, economic data, and not aesthetics, are the determining factors of design.

During the post-World War II years, a climate of optimism and economic expansion made itself felt in a prevalent positivism in design. Landscape architecture borrowed from the "exact sciences" to develop design methods that depended on increasingly technical information as basis for decision making. In addition, the growing complexity of project types that landscape architects undertook, made practices evolve from an *atelier* model, centered on the artistic talents of a single designer, to a corporate model, one that revolved around the collaborative effort of multidisciplinary teams. Hideo Sasaki's 1950 essay "Design Process" and Kevin Lynch's *Site Planning* (first edition 1962) became new and paradigmatic approaches to the design and planning of landscapes.[18] Although different in scope, they both share the objective of systematizing design, of eliminating the mysterious aura surrounding the art of landscape architecture, and thus turning it into a rational sequence of decisions that were backed up by increasingly technical criteria. Sasaki proposed a simple sequence that began with three types or research—verbal, visual, and experimental, including formal experiments—followed by analysis—study of programs and circulation, and their relationships to each other—and ending with synthesis, the articulation of all factors into a design. For Sasaki, delaying design decisions to the end of the process had the benefit of eliminating the arbitrary. In his words, "[t]he design-form which finally evolves from the critical thinking process will not likely be arbitrary or pre-conceived. Rather, it will be a functional expression consistent with structure and materials used, with little concern as to whether it is 'modern' or 'traditional.'"[19] Similarly, although with a much longer list of procedures to follow in order to accomplish due process, Kevin Lynch offered a rational basis for design and planning. Lynch also acknowledged that the process itself is cyclical (unlike Sasaki's, which reads as linear), requiring many feedback loops until a solution begins to emerge.

New design processes require new methods, and it is during this time that the use of diagrams becomes ubiquitous in design practices and teaching. Diagrams are drawings that isolate elements of a project in order to explain how they work, what they do, and their relationships to other elements in a plan, without describing the elements themselves. During the late 1950s, Kevin Lynch began to describe cities diagrammatically, a collection of elements (paths, edges, districts, nodes and landmarks), focusing on what these elements did for the organizational and functional aspects of the city, instead of focusing on what they looked like.[20] His later volume *Site Planning* is heavily illustrated with diagrams that explain how things work, in an effort to demonstrate the conceptual shift from compositionally based to rational decision making. Diagrams became an effective and widespread design and presentation tool that reached an advanced degree of sophistication and visual richness in recent practices. In Bernard Tschumi's and Rem Koolhaas's proposals for the Parc de la Villette in Paris, the diagram and the plan coincide, representing the maximum expression of an anticompositional approach to design, in favor of frameworks that guide, without fixing, the future development of the landscape. Indeed, both Tschumi and Koolhass have stated that theirs was not a design but a method that was, in principle, applicable to any site.

With Eckbo, Sasaki, and Lynch the arbitrary in design is eliminated through careful attention to program, the needs of the users, and site (although by twenty-first-century standards, a very basic understanding of site). Prioritizing program over ecology, however, became arbitrary in the eyes of Ian McHarg, who conceived of "non-ecological design as capricious, arbitrary, or idiosyncratic, and is certainly irrelevant."[21] For McHarg, as is well known, nature is understood as process only, not image to be imitated, and it is the single source of valid criteria for design. He invented what is called the suitability diagram, in which he ranked aspects of a site in a scientific way to determine the siting criteria. It must be said, though, that the shift in scale from residential and urban scales, considered in the Hubbard and Kimball and the Eckbo, Sasaki, and the Lynch writings, to the regional scale in McHarg's necessitated the invention of a new approach, and thus, McHarg's writings are not directly comparable to theirs. However, McHarg insisted that one could apply his approach to urban areas and to smaller sites, simply by breaking down the scale of the mapping, building a finer-grained database, and by asking a different set of questions.[22] If process explained nature, it also explained form, at least the forms of nature. For McHarg, form was the expression of process in an organism. Process here means the evolution of the organism toward optimal fitness, and form, the communication of that process. In other words, if forms had earlier been an aesthetic concept, something that brought out an aesthetic response, for McHarg, it was, on the contrary, a source of information. McHarg did not see form as something to figure out visually or spatially, he saw it as an entry into a completely different set of questions. Whereas a designer, upon seeing a form, would ask how it is made, McHarg would ask why does it have that form.

III

In the work and texts examined thus far, the formal always appears as evidence of the arbitrary. Nevertheless, during the last two-and-a-half decades of the twentieth century, the next generation of landscape architects, all trained in the tradition of modernism, returned to the *deliberate* use of form, accepting the need for some degree of the arbitrary in design. Compare the definitions of formal and arbitrary in Tables 1.1 and 1.2.

The cultural conditions that supported a return to the arbitrary (although never labeled as such) began to emerge during the 1960s, with all the interrelated political, social, economic, and cultural changes that occurred across Western society. Within design culture, more specifically, came the realization that the great contribution of the modern movement was not a new and better world, but a new formal style that, now devoid of ideology, became open to a scrutiny that questioned what had become the obligatory correspondence between form and function, ecology and naturalism, analysis and design. The design methodologies that had developed held that a systematic adherence to the requisites of program, ecology, site, and context would inevitably yield (or result in) a design and, thus, that landscape architects would not be burdened by the need to make arbitrary choices among different formal organizations. The evidence, though, suggested otherwise. After all the analysis, the countless diagrams, and ecological assessments, what came out was work that repeatedly

TABLE 1.1: Attitudes toward, and location of, the arbitrary in critical theories and practices 1938–1969.

Date	Writings + Practices	Attitudes towards and location or assumptions of the arbitrary
1938	"Freedom in the Garden" by James Rose, *Pencil Points* "Plants Dictate Garden Forms" by James Rose, *Pencil Points*	Located in pre-determined formalism
1939–40	"Articulate Form in Landscape Design," James C. Rose, *Pencil Points* "Landscape Design in the Urban Environment" Garrett Eckbo, Daniel U. Kiley, James C. Rose, *Architectural Record* (May 1939) "Landscape Design in the Rural Environment" Garrett Eckbo, Daniel U. Kiley, James C. Rose, *Architectural Record*, (Aug 1939) "Why Not Try Science?" James C. Rose, *Pencil Points*, (Dec 1939) "Landscape Design in the Primeval Environment" Garrett Eckbo, Daniel U. Kiley, James C. Rose, *Architectural Record*, (Feb 1940)	Located in static formality, the predominance of visual criteria, and lack of social and recreational program.
1950	*Landscape for Living*, Garrett Eckbo, "Design Process" by Hideo Sasaki	As above; also advocated systematic design methodology as way to eliminate the arbitrary.
1962	*Site Planning*, Kevin Lynch	As above, advocating systematic design methodology with feed-back loop to further refine design process and eliminate the arbitrary.
1967	"An Ecological Method for Landscape Architecture," Ian McHarg, in *Landscape Architecture*	Located in the absence of ecological criteria in design
1969	*Design with Nature*, Ian McHarg	Also introduced ecological inventory as method to determine suitability of sites for development.

TABLE 1.2: Attitudes toward and location of the arbitrary in critical theories and practices, 1969–2012. Halprin, who first describes the value of the aleatory and of chance in design in his *RSVP Cycle*, begins a new attitude toward the arbitrary.

1969	RSVP Cycles, Lawrence Halprin	Located now in holistic design approach that included ecology, representation, narrative, intuition, alternative mappings, and chance in order to break away from unimaginative pragmatism
1976–onward	Peter Walker begins practice of minimalist gardens	Types of garden are no longer associated with use, but can be combined in unexpected ways in order to make the landscape visually more powerfully.
1980s	Michael Van Valkenburgh begins experiments with landscape phenomena in garden projects and competitions	Uses formal vocabulary as frame and measuring device for the expression of phenomena.
1983	"Postmodernism Looks Beyond Itself," George Hargreaves, *Landscape Architecture*	Criticizes modernist space as essentially arbitrary, one that revolves "around an internal organization system, in an idealized and invented space."
1984	Competition for the Parc de la Villette, Bernard Tschumi, OMA/Rem Koolhaas	In their collage method of designing landscapes, all congruence between the layers is lost.
1986	"Jardins élémentaires," Michel Desvigne; introduced gardens that measure erosion and deposition.	Manipulates natural phenomena to transform it into an aesthetic experience, countering a prevalent "natural determinism."
1988	*Il Territorio Transitivo. Shifting Sites,* Georges Descombes; a series of projects that engage the history of the site and reveal its complexity.	Site is not a binding concept, but a locus for creativity.
	Byxbee Park, Palo Alto; Guadalupe River Park, San Jose, California, Hargreaves Associates: Two public parks that engage phenomena and hydrological cycles, while using the same formal vocabulary	Forms are available and can be used in many types of site, regardless of the specificities of ecosystems or cultural conditions.

1989	Mill Race Park, Columbus, Indiana; MVVA Engages the flood cycles of river as event.	Engages phenomena in the service of form and personal experience.
1990–onward	West8/Adriaan Geuze. Begins practice of working with ecological instability at many scales, from garden to an urban scale using a strong formal and abstract language.	Ecological practices do not necessarily have to embrace a naturalistic image.
1991–94	Landschaftspark Duisburg-Nord, Latz + Partners. Adapts preexisting industrial uses into new programs for public space	Shatters all expected congruence between program, materials, ecologies, and spatial configurations.
1998–onward	Recent landscape architectural practices, such as Field Operations, StoSSLU, and others, that use digital technologies to model new ecological concepts such as gradients, flows, emergence, and adaptability	Forms that are the result of an aleatory process, such as those that come from digital techniques, are not necessarily devoid of content. Abstract, formalistic digital manipulation can be an effective tool for producing forms that better address contemporary ecological and programmatic concerns.

fell back into what Peter Walker called a neo-Olmstedian vision.[23] Analytical methodologies by themselves, could not sufficiently address questions of formal vocabularies, of representation, of conceptual translations. Lawrence Halprin's *RSVP Cycles: Creative Processes in the Human Environment* (1969) is a seminal text that questions conventional inventories of sites, those based only on the physiographic characteristics of a place, to the exclusion of all else. Halprin argues that the pre-condition for design is the creative, not just the rational, analysis of a site, one that goes beyond scientific inventories to accommodate other forms of perception of space, such as dynamic patterns of movement. He also insists on the need for translation, a series of analogies that mediate between analysis and design that themselves constitute the form-giving process. Most important, he recognizes the value of chance in design.[24] Like Halprin's, the work of American earthwork artists demonstrated that thoughtful, rigorous site analysis can result in innovative and provocative formal language in the landscape. In taking on the subject of landscape and the perception of phenomena as the content of their work, they provided a powerful model against the reductive and functional design language of postwar modernism in American landscape architecture. Also during this time, the introduction of texts on phenomenology, structuralism, critical regionalism, and, later in the 1980s, cultural geography presented new approaches and frameworks for the interpretation and representation of landscapes.

From these diverse aesthetic and intellectual currents would spring a new generation of landscape architects. In their work, the arbitrary emerges differently, for it is not a complete arbitrariness as implied by an uncritical acceptance of style without regard for site, ecology, or program. Rather, it is a partial arbitrariness, by which I mean the use of forms that, while addressing thoroughly the rational and pragmatic demands of a project, *exceed* these in order to engage other representational or formal agendas. In terms of design method, partial arbitrariness refers to that moment in the design process that is determined by intuition and by a designer's personal sensibility. It implies choices that are not entirely traced to analytical procedures.[25] I insist on the notion of a partial arbitrariness, as opposed to a complete arbitrariness, because it is not objectively possible to deny the importance of the work discussed earlier and its continuing legacy. Most of the knowledge, the methods, and the technologies perfected then continue to be used, although not as the sole content of the work. Nevertheless, accepting a measure of the arbitrary is precisely what allowed landscape architects to break away from what became a rote, deadening, and unimaginative pragmatism to exceed the functional requirements of program, to engage ecology conceptually and not just technically, and to think about site in more complex terms. Accepting a measure of the arbitrary allowed landscape architects to expand the boundaries of the discipline, to reclaim the right to generate their own design processes and sensibilities, and to express something more unpredictable and immeasurable through other forms of research and analysis. What follows is a demonstration of different modes of the arbitrary in landscape architecture at the end of the century and the messages it has sustained.

After two-and-a-half decades of successful practice with Hideo Sasaki, Peter Walker criticized the bland, recessive landscapes of corporate America that by the 1970s had become largely based on criteria from outside—from behavioral sciences, social sciences, engineering, ecology, in other words, disciplines that were external to the design professions and that were restricting their autonomy as cultural practices and discourses in their own right. Walker countered the prevailing norm with a proposal to return to the language, the internal and historical codes, and the conventions of landscape architecture. A return to language would recover landscape architecture's own frameworks of knowledge, and landscape itself would become once again "visible," as medium and as discourse. His was not a postmodernist interest in making symbolic references to the past, but an interest in the "expression of the objective, a focus on the object in itself, rather than its surrounding context or interpretation."[26] Walker had been collecting minimalist art since the early seventies and began exploring the connection between landscape architecture and contemporary art in his own work and in design studios at the Harvard Graduate School of Design.[27] His substitute intent was to eliminate students' preconceptions, to expand the boundaries of their thinking, and to teach the skill of translating from one discipline and one medium to another. To assume the thinking, if not the image, of minimalism provided students with a repertory of formal mechanisms that were innovative and powerful in their expressive potential. Fundamental for Walker was motivating students to push beyond program, ecology, and site, beyond analysis, into the realm of what had been previously considered the arbitrary, in order to achieve expression.

Walker had assumed this approach in his own work and the Tanner Fountain (1985) in Cambridge, Massachusetts, remains a perfect example of this new attitude toward design. Having received the charge from the university to site and design a fountain commissioned by a donor, Walker begins by questioning the traditional, and expected, format of an urban fountain. The donor had requested that the fountain not be left an empty basin during the winter, when it is turned off, and that people could interact with it. Walker then made the decision that the fountain, understood since the Renaissance as a purely decorative object—to be watched from a distance and not entered—in the urban landscape would become its opposite, a space to be occupied. Of the fountain itself, Walker has stated, "We finally decided that the edge was the thing, and that we would have no internal recognizable geometries. You get an ambiguous relationship between the object and the field. We moved the fountain to the edge and let it buzz. The fountain is made of insignificant objects placed in a significant way."[28]

Walker constructed this ambiguity by countering a perfect circle, sixty inches in diameter, with a set of decisions that undermines the integrity of the pure form, offering an alternative reading of it as porous field. The circle is made by 159 boulders that, from a distance, seem spatially condensed to form a figure with a closed boundary, an object. Up close, the figure turns into a field when it becomes apparent that the asphalt pavement of the surrounding paths has been allowed to enter it, bringing with it people, dogs, and passersby, thus turning it into a space. However, the circle as self-contained object reasserts itself again, this time by remaining indifferent to changing conditions on the ground. Whether asphalt, grass, or existing tress, the boulders remain obdurate in their placement and orientation and in holding the legibility of the figure as a perfect circle. As representation, the boulders themselves act symbolically (objects of contemplation with a variety of nonprescribed meanings) and functionally, as seats, stepping-stones, and gathering space.

In a similar operation of substitutions in which types are mixed in seemingly arbitrary ways, Roberto Burle Marx addressed the ambiguity fountain/space in his design for one of the courtyard gardens at Parque del Este in Caracas (1956–1961). Here, Burle Marx did not follow the traditional spatial configuration, which distinguishes between the perimeter, devoted to circulation, and the symmetrical space of the center, typically occupied by a fountain. Instead, these relationships are reversed: water, traditionally presented as a jet in a central fountain, is displaced to the perimeter and is presented as a surface on the walls as it cascades from trays and as reflecting pools on the floor. Circulation is displaced from the perimeter of the space to the center. Furthermore, the walls of the traditional patios, conceptually a definitive boundary, are here dissolved and dematerialized into light, deep shadows, water, reflections, and sound. Finally, the traditional domestic and refined scale and texture associated with the courtyard garden are replaced by an abstract, graphic, tough urban language. The patios are, in effect, the conjunction of the domestic courtyard of the Spanish and Portuguese colonial house, the urban plaza, and the promenade of the modern house and of the English landscape garden.

Pietro Porcinai's design for the garden at the Villa il Roseto (Fiesole, 1961–1965) is also a transformation of a historic type in garden design, in this case, the garden compartments of Renaissance Italy. Traditionally, the space set aside for these gardens was subdivided into a series of regularly shaped compartments for the display of flowers and herbs. Edged by hedges at an approximate height of twenty-four to thirty inches and a width of two feet, the pattern was intricately and tightly laid out, such that the hedges saturate the space of the terrace. Although early representations of some of these gardens show paths through the compartments, presumably to look at the herbaceous plants being cultivated, later, the hedges became the primary material, and evolved into very complex designs of intricate scrolls and geometric configurations. These were neither to be occupied (they were not spatial), nor were they pure ground (they did not lay flat on the surface like the French parterre does). Porcinai intervenes in the spatial and the material relationships of such hedges, and in so doing, he transforms the reading and associated programs of the traditional terraced garden. First, he increases the width of the hedges such that they are transformed from (thin) partition to horizontal surface. Second, he pulls the shapes apart so that the hedges become spatial, inhabitable spaces. Trees, planters, lawns figured as circles, and furniture now occupy the new spaces in an informal and unpredictable layout, admitting within its compartments the programs of modern living.

These landscapes have in common a design method that entails a meticulous analysis of the historic type and its associated program. This analysis may include the historical processes that led to the emergence of the type, and its evolution to the present, the social uses given to it, the materials associated with it, the characteristic spatial organization, its design—literally proportions, size, scale, and texture—and relationship to others of similar kind. This thorough investigation into the nature of the type and its program is not to copy it, but to *intervene* in it. The process of dismantling the type into components is a prerequisite to making precise, deliberate, substitutions, not only in the parts themselves but also in the relationships that hold the parts together. The result is a reconstituted landscape, in different but recognizable form. In its new form, it engages the user on many levels. Visually, it "objectifies" the landscape; that is, it brings it into the foreground instead of it receding as background for architecture or events; socially it provides new and unexpected uses and experiences, and conceptually it expands the range of associations and experiences available in design. By placing traditional forms in new social and programmatic contexts, these designers tell us that type is no longer associated with a singular use, that type is a free choice made by the designer.

The arbitrary pairing of type and program is also seen in Martha Schwartz's Jacob Javits Plaza, where a domestic garden type is mixed with a public plaza type. Here, she shatters our expectations of material and function by presenting all of the plaza's elements in unexpected relationships to each other. The bench has the shape and length of a scroll in a parterre; the grass is turned into a massive object, only to be rendered as partly hollow by the presence of steam; and the light poles contribute a functional and a spatial role.[29] With this project and many others that characterize Schwartz's early work, where she uses "found" materials like bagels, Necco candies, tires, sheets, Astroturf, or Plexiglas, she proves capable of turning any material, or any form, into landscape. Schwartz develops this stance from her interests in pop art, from which she learned that a change in scale decontextualizes and transforms an object, making it useful in unexpected situations. Here we see the watchful eye of the designer roaming and scanning the world around her, fully open to possibilities, discovering potential in any material or form. More than telling us that there is no prescribed connection between form and program, she tells us that material associations and restrictions in landscape architecture are made increasingly looser through the use of new technologies and fabrication techniques. Further, Schwartz demonstrates the resiliency and adaptability of forms themselves which, when placed in new relationships with others, enable the emergence of new types or categories of space and experience.

The resilience and adaptability of forms has been effectively verified in the many parks and public spaces built along the Ruhr valley as part of the extensive reclamation of industrial areas for public use. Sites previously used for industrial purposes were transformed into recreational parks without removing the existing industrial infrastructure. These parks make visible layers of history, juxtapose native and exotic ecologies, offer the visitor unprecedented experiences of the industrial sublime within a landscape setting, and break all expected congruence between program, materials, ecologies, and spatial configurations. These sites are replete with the arbitrary. The examples are many, Landschaftspark Duisburg-Nord by Latz + Partners being by now the canonical one.

In 1983, the year he founded his firm, George Hargreaves published a short essay calling for an end to the purely formalistic approach of modernist landscape architecture, which he characterized as being of two types, the "asymmetrically geometric", and "the fluid amorphous," both of which revolved "around an internal organization system, in an idealized and invented space."[30] Formalistic this time around meant work that had no resonance with the surrounding site, with ecological ideas and that, although it responded to social program, had become as mechanical, predictable, and imposed as the work the early modernists had criticized forty years earlier. Hargreaves was also critical of the polarities that had developed in the discipline that positioned design in opposition to ecology and science. During the next decade, Hargreaves Associates built works that were conceptualized as dynamic, open-ended landscapes that bridged ecology and design. For these achievements, Hargreaves has been described as a "poet of process," achieving nothing less than "a kind of alchemy in which the dross of post-industrial landscape is transformed into something approximating gold . . . combining a strong sculptural language with a sensitivity to both environmental process and social history . . . "[31]

The language of sculpted landforms that became one of the firm's signatures is the result of a highly complex design process that brings together many types of information to bear on the final form of the earthworks. Hargreaves was interested in the potential of his landforms as measuring devices, registers of wind erosion, deposition, gradients of moisture, and, in the case of the Guadalupe River Park, flood control. However, he was equally interested in the forms themselves as visual objects. As Julia Czerniak pointed out, these landforms are as much instrumental as they are representational.[32] They do not mimic natural processes; these shapes do not exist anywhere as natural landforms.[33] Hargreaves is a gifted designer and astute businessman who would not risk all (that is, his self-image as an artist and the visual integrity of his landscapes) to undirected process. As can be seen in the beautiful clay models his office produces, from which the projects are faithfully built, the designs stand out as finished formal works before natural processes, such as erosion and emergent vegetation patterns, begin to transform his initial sculpting of the land. By pairing a form-for-the-sake-of-form attitude with an ecological agenda, Hargreaves disrupts the expected correspondence between naturalism and ecology and shows that forms support ecological processes but that they do not themselves need to mimic ecological processes. Further, these forms were used as primary design elements in very different places: Palo Alto, California (in a suburban setting); San Jose, California (in a tight urban setting); Louisville, Kentucky (laced between a highway and river); and in Lisbon, Portugal (also in a suburban setting). This recurrence of similar forms across sites, programs, and ecological regions points to their self-consciousness as pure language, their arbitrariness with regard to site. The same formal vocabulary can be used in many and different types of sites, regardless of the specificities of ecosystems or cultural conditions. They do not need to be invented anew for each site. The task of the landscape architect is to recognize the territory where a particular form is most effective.

All landscape architecture, by necessity, begins with site research. Congruence with site, along with ecology, reduces significantly all potential arbitrariness. Curiously enough, though, landscape architecture is not in every instance about site in the same way, which suggests that *site is not a binding concept* but a locus for creativity. Concepts of site have evolved substantially during the course of the twentieth century. For example, the chapter devoted to issues of site in Eckbo's *Landscape for Living* is very short and the concepts presented are very rudimentary, compared to frameworks recently developed.[34] With Sasaki and Lynch, the tools to analyze sites were diverse but always based on quantifiable, scientific data, including social and economic data, in addition to standard physiography. McHarg focused on the ecological structure of sites, eliminating all cultural, historical, and experiential analysis. Site-specific art gave landscape architects the frameworks to break away from rational data as the only tools to interpret sites and the inspiration to express their perceptions in innovative ways. Also, unlike the more conservative practices of "place-making" and regionalism, site specificity did not seem to claim to be essentialist, historically bound, or totalizing about a place.[35] It only engaged one, sometimes a few, aspects of it, such as scale, topography, the earth's position in relation to other planets and stars, or the ephemerality of color and light.

In other words, it was essentially arbitrary in terms of choice of subject, or the means of revealing that subject. It was never intended to blend in, to be materially or formally conciliatory toward what was there. From this work, landscape architects learned that sites are not just received, they are construed and constructed in spite of the constraints posed by their stubborn material logic. The range of approaches to the question of site is now so diverse that merely to achieve congruence with the physical attributes of the site is considered too simplistic (as represented by certain ecological practices that seek to "hide" the hand of the designer). Today's sites, layered with many types of occupation and material histories, are rarely as simple as what is visible on their surface.

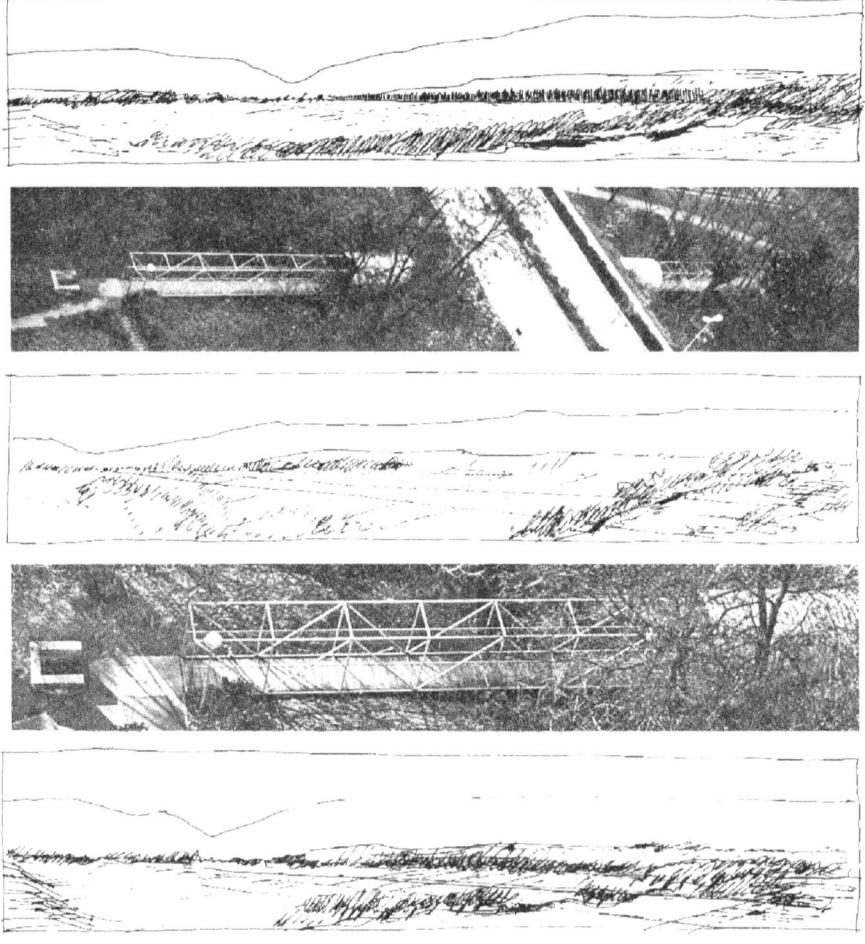

FIGURE 1.3: Georges Descombes, Tunnel Footbridge, Lancy, Switzerland, 1985–88. *Source*: G Descombes, *Il Territorio Transitivo. Shifting Sites*, ed. Giordano Tironi (Rome: Gangemi Editore, 1988), 25.

Michael Van Valkenburgh Associates' restoration of Alumnae Valley at Wellesley College reveals site as a complex subject with no easy answers. The project entailed the reclamation of a low-lying 13.5-acre wetland that had been filled and for the last 100 years served as utility yard for the campus, holding a gas manufacturing facility, a power plant, a parking lot for 300 cars, and industrial shops. Its original topography and hydrology had been disrupted to such an extent that it was impossible to bring them back in their original form or function. Its vital connection to the larger campus watershed, which it helped drain into adjacent Lake Waban, had been severed by a roadway. Its ground had also been seriously contaminated. Bringing back the valley as a social space (with paths and places for contemplation) and as an ecologically functioning wetland was not straightforward. Toxicity of the ground was at dangerous levels, and it entailed capping, which raised the valley floor six feet above the original grade. Raising the valley floor in turn disconnected the wetland from the lake. This required a conceptual shift from a joined lake-wetland system to a perched marsh (an intermittent wetland), making it necessary to pump water uphill into it during times of drought. The marsh is thus maintained as such artificially during dry periods, calling to question the sustainability of this solution over the long term, and its arbitrariness as an ecosystem that can no longer be maintained on its own, without the aid of technology to carry out its natural functions of drainage and purification. Likewise, the series of drumlin-like mounds in the center of the valley, arbitrary in that wetland valleys never contain drumlins, were nevertheless necessary to dispose of excess fill from the excavations of the foundations for the campus center and to cap contaminated soil.

If the introduction of a techno-marsh and the mounds into the valley seems forced, even arbitrary, it nevertheless addresses two other important aspects of the place: its geological past and its hydrological ancestry.[36] In addition, it provides students and faculty with new places for strolling, contemplation, and closer access to the lake. Its relationship with the original site is, thus, tenuous in some ways, not in others. The project is full of choices that balance history, budgetary constraints, ecology, regulations and technology. The result combines a *retrospective* with a *projective* attitude toward the site that cannot be completely rationalized in terms of objective data. Breaking away from the purely pragmatic allows the landscape architects to recover and maintain aspects of the site's history, but without completely reconstructing the past.

Finally, the contemporary practice of landscape architecture emphasizes the design of frameworks, rather than forms, and stresses strategic organizations, dynamic infrastructures, open-ended programs, concepts that can evolve and

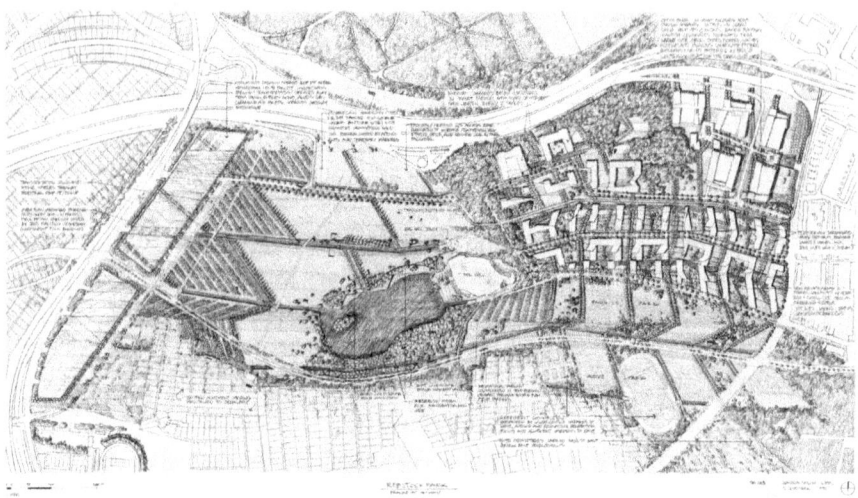

FIGURE 1.4: Rebstockpark, Frankfurt, Germany, Master Plan by Laurie Olin and Peter Eisenman. Coutesy of Laurie Olin.

"learn" from community input, from ecological instability, from disturbance events, and so on. This focus on the adaptive aspects of landscape, of program, and of space, has conceptual roots in recent ecological theory, which rejects the climax model of ecosystem evolution in favor of a nonequilibrium model, in which ecosystems are continuously responding and adapting to unpredictable events. In this framework, landscape architects do not design with an end result in mind, but instead design a process and let it unfold, with some measure of predictability but without fixing all aspects of the design.

The tools to model the spatial dynamics of evolution and adaptability are given by digital technologies, since traditional modes of representation—plan, section, perspective, collage, are unsuitable to represent the effects of time in a landscape. Digital technology has provided a repertory of forms that is unlimited, and particularly suitable for generating forms that better represent new ecological concepts such as gradients, flows, emergence, and adaptability. Digital technologies are helpful also for generating form in flat, "formless sites, such as postindustrial or barren agricultural lands, where there are no traces of previous ecological systems or historical uses. However, generating these is a process that is as formalistic in its origins as the previous compositionally based designs. Designers begin by choosing an image that is digitally manipulated to create effects that are analogous to those produced by natural processes, or that generate patterns of structure and difference on a site.[37] The output, and here is the difference, is aleatory and unexpected. It is not possible to imagine, much less predict, what the outcome of the work will be. The process leads the way. From here the conceptual leap is sometimes formal; that is, the forms that result from the digital experiment are transferred to the site and are then modified further to adapt to local conditions of topography, moisture, orientation, and circulation. Sometimes the leap is metaphorical as when designers isolate and extract from the image information that describes relationships between the parts. These relationships are then used to drive, by analogy, the organization of the project. These are heuristic devices, procedures meant for deriving a design from a long process of trial and error that involves testing, revising, learning from, and, if necessary, rejecting the initial choice, only to begin again until the best form for the project is found.

The design of ecological structure, then, requires formal translation, the formalistic. Landscape architects recognize and discover the potential embedded in new digital forms that can be applied to the conceptualization and eventual construction of the environment. From this method of design we learn that forms that are unexpected and the result of an aleatory process, the arbitrary, are not necessarily devoid of content. In this situation, what matters is that the form chosen be evaluated against multiple criteria—technical, empirical, and aesthetic—to determine its suitability and its effectiveness. Underlying the extreme rationality in contemporary landscape architectural discourse are, nevertheless, the partially arbitrary, the landscape architect's intuition, highly acute visualization skills, and the creativity to discover in a borrowed, initially arbitrary, form its ecological, social, experiential, and metaphorical potential.

CHAPTER TWO

Types of Gardens

PETER JACOBS

The garden is first and foremost the physical expression of a conscious act to create beauty, to provide refuge, to explore natural process, to design a social gathering space, or to achieve some combination of these objectives. In the broadest of cultural typologies, the wilderness, the landscape, and the garden characterize three settings that capture distinctly different ideas of nature. Each relates to social agency and the attitudes and values we attribute to the natural world that surrounds us.

Wilderness suggests the absence of human intervention, the raw nature to which Thoreau referred from the top of Mount Ktaadn when he exclaimed, "Here was no man's garden, but the unhandselled globe. It was not lawn, nor pasture, nor mead, nor woodland, nor lea, nor arable, nor wasteland."[1] In contrast, landscape is all of these. It represents that aspect of nature that has been harnessed, at least partially, for productive, recreational, visual, or spiritual use. The contemporary idea of landscape focuses on the functional needs of human settlement: for food, water, energy, minerals, and forest products, as much as for our aesthetic needs.[2] Gardens, finally, are those settings where the human spirit, vision, and aspirations are expressed by and through design. The places we call gardens are conceived and implemented with social intent and aesthetic purpose. Put simply, a garden does not happen by accident or happenstance. Rather, it is a purposeful attempt to express an idea or attitude with respect to nature, society, or both.[3]

Gardens and gardening, the object and the process, are intimately connected aspects of our love of nature and our desire to associate with it. Gardening has always been an important genesis of the search for beauty, recording the changing cultural norms associated with our interpretations of this elusive quality. It is, as well, an intensely personal occupation that serves as a setting for reflection, relaxation, and socialization, where friends and neighbors can share successful secrets in sustaining the life and ambiance of the garden. The interaction of gardening and gardens in their landscape and cultural settings frame the idea of the garden, informing the broad choice of a modern garden typology.

The specific approach to the modern garden adopted in this chapter reflects an amalgam of social and cultural factors. Each of the five proposed themes is informed by the early-twentieth-century writings of authors such as William Robinson, Frank Waugh, and Gertrude Jekyll, and, later, the works of Fletcher Steele, Sylvia Crowe, Humphrey Carver, and Christopher Tunnard, to name only a few. More recently, an explosion of professional magazines, academic journals, and countless books devoted to the garden have increased the popular understanding and appreciation of the rich variety of modern gardens.[4]

The first of the modern garden types is based on gardeners and the gardens that result. The modern garden can be conceived by professionals, by amateurs, by the homeless, and those whose food and health depend on its produce. Many of the most iconic of modern gardens have been designed by individuals who have devoted their lives to shaping the garden as an expression of society, as the locus of social commentary, or as a means of exploring natural processes. These gardens reflect different formal and programmatic characteristics in different cultural settings, within a spatial and societal context as across a number of regions and societies worldwide. Some of the most evocative examples are private gardens, but others, helping to shape and give character to human settlements, are in the public domain.

The second type focuses on the civilizing nature of gardens and the variety of roles these gardens play within the structure of modern civic life. These gardens display the public face of community—whether as a park, a square, or a plaza; as a system of trails and pathways; as a network of green spaces associated with urban infrastructure; or as an opportunity for creative change in marginal urban places. All contribute to the perceived quality of community life, however that quality might be defined in differing social formats.

The third modern type concerns the support that gardens offer to the institutional structure of our communities. Increasingly, modern gardens have been conceived to highlight the civic activities and corporate aspects of contemporary society. Not surprisingly, the form and even the function of these gardens vary with cultural context and landscape setting. The push and pull of the forces of globalization and those of local settings can be expressed in the provision of services related to tourism, for instance, where the gardens associated with worldwide hotel chains compete with those designed to support ecotourism.

The fourth type celebrates the ability of gardens to recall and to commemorate important individuals and collective events. Commemorative gardens are an expression of our history and the cultural values that we associate with it. These include our garden cemeteries, memorials, and heritage sites, as well as those gardens where we celebrate special community events. We might also include in this type those modern gardens that for cultural reasons are deemed to be in need of conservation, which has become a special focus of modern garden theory and practice (recent modern work is disappearing faster than are older gardens, perhaps because they were conceived with an agenda too targeted on contemporary concerns).[5]

Finally, conceptual gardens are gardens of the mind, experiments that are often purposefully free of the constraints dictated by time, money, or client—innovative gardens whose only relevance is the joy of exploring new frontiers in one of the oldest of human endeavors. These experiments may capture the narrative and metaphorical power of gardens, both imaginary and experimental, generating ideas that reflect where society has been and where it might be headed.

The very relationship of gardens, landscape, and wilderness continues to change over time, and according to physical setting and cultural context. Indigenous populations in the arctic have few if any cultural referents to the garden, while many urban societies across the globe have almost no sense of wilderness. Increasingly, both rely on an understanding of these concepts through their virtual presentation in other media, which has become a minor industry in the modern period. Nor would the transient gardens of the homeless, the suburbanite, or the urban apartment dweller share the same form, materials, or program. Hence, the modern garden types suggested in this chapter do not constitute an exhaustive list. In the spirit of Umberto Eco's modern essay *L'oeuvre ouverte*,[6] they should be considered as a network of types that interact with each other to transform the original set, adding new garden types in response to changing conditions.

GARDENERS AND THEIR GARDENS

The first garden type is built around the people who have established the core practices and forms of the modern garden. Generally, the most ubiquitous and intensely cared for gardens are those that we associate with our homes and neighborhood communities. Not surprisingly, there are as many different types of modern gardens as there are social groups to interpret them and physical settings in which these gardens can be found.

Many of these gardens continue to be patterned after historical styles associated primarily with the traditions of France and England, but others are influenced by the cultures of Asia, notably Japan and China, or by oriental traditions derived from Persia, Spain, and India. Still others have emerged from the creative forces of nineteenth-century urban reform movement exemplified in the United States by the vast practice of Frederick Law Olmsted and in Europe by a host of planners and designers.[7] Notwithstanding these cultural sources, however, the modern garden type is distinguished by its commitment to starting afresh, to reexamining the principles and practices of the ancient gardening arts, and to contributing fresh layers of insight to the humus that has preceded their efforts. This renaissance is invariably accomplished by inspired and committed gardeners, be they professional or amateur, who have labored in their own gardens; or for clients who have commissioned their professional expertise; or for groups and individuals who seek to improve their community settings and their own well-being.

Masters' Gardens

Masters' Gardens are personally conceived, built, and maintained by renowned landscape architects, artists, and garden designers. These gardens serve as experimental laboratories that allow for the development of new ideas and strategies in garden design, the use and maintenance of plants, or for innovative social and artistic activities. They are usually the product of relatively modest constraints and reflect the evolving philosophical and practical interests of each of the designers. Over time, many of the innovations derived from these experiments are transferred to private and public settings and are integrated into popular gardening practices.

Throughout her life, Gertrude Jekyll used her garden at Munstead Wood, England, to experiment with new approaches to organizing and combining plants. The combinations of colors, textures, and form that she used in border plantings were particularly successful with regard to foundation plantings and entry paths to homes on relatively small lots. The design strategies and plant groupings she developed at Munstead Wood were enormously popular and, through her many publications, influenced the small individual gardens of the emerging middle class in England as well as Europe and North America. Her influence has permeated the modern garden movement and found expression in a variety of forms and settings.

Many superb gardens developed during the twentieth century have been conceived and built by inspired amateurs, gardeners who have the time and passion to develop their own tableau of paradise. Christopher Lloyd, a younger contemporary of Jeykll, also experimented with plant materials at Great Dixter, England, throughout his life. Vita Sackville-West and Harold Nicolson in the gardens at Sissinghurst in England, and Francis Cabot in his garden, Les Quatres Vents, at Cap à l'Aigle, Quebec, developed superb garden complexes. The first is devoted to a wide variety of plant materials arranged and organized with respect to all manner of color and form, while the second emphasizes the various historical periods and garden cultures found in the history of garden design. Although these gardens do not focus on the tenets of modern style and form, they are resolutely modern in their study of natural process and the interpretation of garden cultures.

James Rose, Dan Kiley, and Garrett Eckbo were among the first to substantially rethink the basic principles of the art and program of the modern garden and the larger landscape in North America. Their approach developed not as a set of formal principles but as a professional manifesto.[8] Rose explored his sense of joy and pleasure in the design of his personal garden, and his understanding of the natural virtues of juxtaposing sun and shade, rock, water, and plants using a minimalist and modern design vocabulary. Kiley's gardens feature the judicious choice of plant materials, subtle changes in level, and strong visual order organized within a structure of spatial grids. Eckbo created hundreds of gardens in California where he explored the play of light and shadow, climate and space, among which the Burden and Gladstone gardens (1948) recall the figures and forms of the early modernists Kandinsky and Moholy-Nagy. Later in the Alcoa Forecast Garden (1959), Eckbo explored the use of new materials in the garden, substituting aluminum screens for the more tradition use of wood or hedge materials. Latter still, the Donnell garden designed by Thomas Church in 1948, also in California, emerged as one of the principle icons of the modern landscape garden movement in North America.

Little Sparta, by Ian Hamilton Findlay, addresses other modern concerns. Created over forty years on an abandoned moorland croft in the Pentlan Hills south of Edinburgh, Findlay's garden served him as a laboratory for experiments that he then could drawn on for interventions across Europe; particularly concerned with the use of the garden for social and political commentary, he transferred to it many of his early experiments in concrete poetry—engraved stone markers, miniature naval vessels, or the stone conning tower of a nuclear submarine emerging beside a pond. The garden became, in his words, an attack on, not a retreat from, cultural concerns.

Similarly, near Rio de Janeiro in Brazil, Santo Antonio served as an incubator of design ideas and a refuge for the Brazilian landscape architect Roberto Burle Marx. A wide variety of plants, culled from the many excursions he and his colleagues conducted throughout the tropical forests of Brazil, was brought to the greenhouses and nurseries on his hillside property. There he could observe their behavior outside their native habitats prior to introducing them in his own and other civic and residential gardens. Santo Antonio includes a number of garden sites where Marx experimented with the form, colors, textures, and settings of the enormous variety of plants, artifacts, stones, and water systems found in Brazil. In and of themselves, the gardens reflect the evolution and enormous influence of his approach to modern garden design. Santo Antonio combines the two tendencies that have dominated much of the discourse and practice of garden design in the twentieth century: the garden is at once an artistic display and a showplace of natural process. It is an expression of the very nature of nature in Brazil, an affirmation that the indigenous plant materials of the Amazon are every bit as valid an artistic expression as were the more tradition "exotic" plants of Europe. The gardens throughout the site marry art and nature, tradition and modernity as very few others have managed to achieve.

FIGURE 2.1: The "Sitio" served as Roberto Burle Marx's experimental design laboratory, as well as sheltering his collection of native plants, pottery and paintings. Photo: Peter Jacobs

Commissioned Gardens

Commissioned gardens are those designed by landscape architects and garden designers in response to a client's program, interpreted through the eyes of the designer. This garden type ranges over an enormous number of conditions, but distinguishes itself from the first group insofar as a person or persons, other than the garden designer, generates the set of conditions to which the garden is intended to respond. Many of these gardens occur in the countryside where space permits extensive development of the garden program; others are intensely urban, responding to the constraints of limited space and the hard edges of the city. The commissioning of gardens has varied over the course of the century, with a distinct movement from private homes and estates to civic and public settings. The best examples of these projects have become icons of modern landscape architecture and garden design.[9]

The influence of European models, modern or much older, has been profound, reflecting the tastes of owners who had visited or lived in Europe, as evidenced by several key examples in the United States: Vizcaya Gardens, built for the industrialist James Deering near Miami, Florida; Beatrice Farrand's design of Dumbarton Oaks in Washington, D.C.; and Fletcher Steele's Naumkeag, in Stockbridge, Masachusetts. Dumbarton Oaks was a product of an active involvement and partnership between Farrand and the Bliss family, but it reflects the taste of the clients and their travels. The gardens that surround the residence are reminiscent of Italian traditions, yet for other parts, Farrand developed an early modern design strategy linking the formal gardens to the forest backdrop of the estate with informal paths and clearings. Similarly, Fletcher Steele's design of Naumkeag, in Stockbridge, Massachusetts, borrows the distant landscape of the farming community and began to question many of the traditional garden conventions of the nineteenth century, exploring a more modern vocabulary of garden design. Steele was one of several designers who were much influenced by the attempts in early-twentieth-century France to involve gardens in the mainstream of modern art.[10]

Gardens that were obviously informed by and conformed to the tenets of modernism began to emerge as a general phenomenon just prior to and following the World War II. A.E. Bye, using a limited vocabulary of low junipers on the hills and ground covers in the swales, emphasized the gentle undulations of the Shapiro property on Long Beach Island, New Jersey. The property is presented as an abstract, minimalist tableau. Thomas Church introduced a decidedly modern design idiom at the Donnell property, using the famous free form swimming pool and focal sculpture to draw the eye to the distant California landscape. The Irwin Miller garden in Columbus, Ohio, is perhaps the most formal of the mid-century modern gardens, a masterpiece designed by Dan Kiley.

Commissioned gardens in the second half of the century have expanded, worldwide, to include public civic and private corporate sites. The client is no longer limited to an individual or a family and may include corporate directors, community groups, or institutional and cultural boards. Garden programs have changed as well to reflect the concerns and needs of the different client groups. In many cases, the garden program is designed to display a progressive social attitude, to receive civic or corporate visitors, or to serve as the setting for all manner of cultural activities. The design of the home garden that so preoccupied the early modernists shifted toward a concern with the planning and design of residential developments by the mid-century, and then to the broader concerns of educational, civic, cultural, and corporate spheres in the later years. The evolution of these decidedly modern garden types is addressed in the third group of garden types.

Collective Gardens

Collective gardens are found wherever space is shared, either in public urban spaces that are allocated to them or the collective landscape settings that are used by residents of suburban housing communities. Under the auspices of the Public Works Authority, Eckbo developed a modern model of collective garden settings for the farming communities in the southwest of the United States.[11] Other examples of the community gardening movement existed in projects such as the Radburn Community by Clarence Stein and Henry Wright and in the Levittowns that emerged after the World War II.

Not all of the explosion of suburban housing and new town communities was successful. Too often, repetitive anonymous apartment buildings were grouped in housing projects such that it was virtually impossible to establish any sense of identification or belonging to an individual's housing unit and its location. One interesting response to such anonymity was Bernard Lassus's proposal to paint landscape and garden scenes on the facades of the repetitive, anonymous, low-cost housing blocks in Uckange and Thionville, in France, deriving their imagery of natural scenery from interviews that revealed community preferences and personal memories. Crime rates dropped, and a sense of identity and belonging emerged.[12]

Yet, other collective garden types have evolved within the context of second residences, vacation homes, or permanent homes for those who do not require close proximity to the workplace. The landscape pattern of the Sea Ranch community, developed by Lawrence Halprin, attempts to preserve the natural features and forms of the California coastline; demarcation of individual properties is suppressed in favor of the lines of hedgerows that are an historic part of the landscape setting, and the whole coastal complex is organized as an integral part of a natural garden setting. Similarly, the Pedregal community designed by Luis Barragan in Mexico City emphasizes the landforms and rocky desert setting into which individual properties are nested.

The community garden movement is another form of the collective garden. A wide range of professional and popular publications supports the movement, many filled with technical information that addresses the propagation and maintenance of plant materials as well as providing information on new, or rediscovered, species of fruits and vegetables unavailable in local grocery stores. The contemporary concern for the loss of biodiversity and the limited choice of varieties of all manner of foodstuffs, coupled with the equally important concern with the use of chemicals in the growing process have informed the movement. The poster child of this concern and sometimes its battleground is the garden lawn.[13] Of all the components of the garden setting, the lawn has attracted more time and money, more chemical and biological treatment, and more social emphasis than have all others. The lawn has become synonymous with the suburban garden, the athletic circus, and a loss of plant diversity.

The community garden serves as a major resource of flowers and food for families throughout Europe and North America, and in some cities, the soil and fertilizer, and even the tools required to tend the gardens, are subsidized. Urban food co-ops have experimented with the use of lightweight soils on roofs and with hydroponic gardens to produce food, while all manner of marginal urban land in Africa and Asia is exploited to feed an ever-increasing urban population. Many of these "gardens" are stitched together with whatever materials may be available, frequently to support urgent functional needs for those with limited resources.

Diana Balmori and Margaret Morton's study of the "transitory" gardens of homeless squatters in New York City illustrate how gardens are built from scrounged plant materials and furniture to complement whatever settings may be available in the vacant lots that they occupy. In the same city, Green Gorillas organize gardens, parks, and playgrounds in low-cost housing areas of the city where common civic spaces are anything but the norm. All of these garden types provide a source of aesthetic pleasure and perhaps, most importantly, a setting for social interaction in relatively peaceful settings. As such, they support a modern civil society.

FIGURE 2.2: Squatter's gardens attest to the desire of the homeless to find garden refuge on sites that have been abandoned, using materials that have been scavenged.
Source: M. Morton, *Transitory Gardens, Uprooted Lives*, ed. D. Balmori and M. Morton (New Haven, CT: Yale University Press, 2003), 23.

Vernacular Gardens

Vernacular gardens emphasize the regional character of the landscape setting, local cultural practices, and the visual forms associated with them. Revisited as a source of professional and academic interest, studies by J. B. Jackson in America and projects by Michel Corajoud in France, illustrate the continuing use and transformation of historical vernacular garden settings and their ability to adapt to changes in the social, political, and economic life of their respective community. They can be found in the floating markets and gardens of Xochimilco Ecological Park designed by Mario Schjetnam in Mexico; behind the stonewalls of Montreuil, France; and in the courtyards of urban Africa.

FIGURE 2.3: An indigenous garden cemetery radiates the sense of a sacred forest site on Bathurst Island, Australia. Photo: Peter Jacobs.

They are associated with farmsteads, suburban homes, trailer parks, and the tightly knit backyards of urban row housing.

Another set of vernacular gardens can be associated with indigenous peoples in settings as diverse as the Amazon, the Arctic, the Sahara, and the mountain chains of Asia. These gardens are rarely conceived in the same spirit, or for the same reasons, as those associated with modern, industrialized settings of the world. In some cases, such as in the Canadian Arctic, the very concept of a garden is unknown. Yet, even there, various forms of marking the landscape and of celebrating the spirit of place are an important expression of cultural practices. It is open to question whether they may be counted as gardens, as is the modernity of traditional practices that have lasted for centuries.

GARDENS THAT CIVILIZE

The metaphor of the garden has been used to indicate how cities might be humanized through the judicious design of urban parks and gardens, emphasizing how city form and natural process can be wed.[14] Complex and extensive urban design strategies, however, do not typically address the core social, natural, or aesthetic values of the garden, although gardens designed as focal points within these strategies do.

Civic gardens highlight the care and commitment that towns and cities provide their citizens as much as the tourists and neighbors who visit them. A long tradition of Victorian public gardens extends well beyond Europe to North America, Australia, India, and Asia. This tradition was expanded in the early twentieth century to include all manner of parks and playgrounds primarily associated with urban communities. Modern civic gardens informed by this tradition now include a wide variety of parks, squares, and plazas; networks of green spaces that support the infrastructural needs of the ever expanding urban footprint; and the increasingly creative use of marginal urban land for recreational, experimental, and other productive uses.

Public Parks and Gardens

Public parks and gardens, informed by their social, moral, and hygienic roles in the mid-nineteenth century, now celebrate the recreational, cultural, and natural values of the twentieth century. The restoration of Bryant Park in New York City, the Palais Royal, the Tuilleries in Paris, and the network of civic parks developed in Barcelona for the Olympic games are all examples of a commitment to social, artistic, and environmental quality. A growing number of projects have been conceived around the reuse and rehabilitation of former industrial sites and building complexes that are no longer viable for their original intended uses. The urban setting is full of such sites, usually seriously degraded but centrally located. Others are located adjacent to water, clays, or other material sources critical to an initial industrial endeavor. Perhaps the best-known example in North America is the Gas Works Park in Seattle, Washington, designed by Richard Haag between 1971 and 1988. The Brickworks project on a tributary of the Don River in Toronto, designed by Michael Hough, is another, but the incidence of such remaking of toxic or degraded sites seems a major focus of contemporary work.

The traditional focus on mastering the use and distribution of plant materials characterizes much of the early work of the modern garden. Jens Jensen was one of a number of landscape architects who argued for the use of indigenous plants and the design of natural setting for social and educational activities in public park settings. These preoccupations have been expanded within the idiom of the modern garden to include concerns with the conservation of energy, the reuse and purification of water, and the use of the wild garden as a means of conserving plant species.

Process gardens that link art and nature, such as Allan Sonnfist's Time Landscape located in a public square in lower Manhattan are intended to illustrate how nature progresses over time in the absence of human intervention.

Gilles Clément's "garden of movement" is another such experiment to embrace the growth and change of a wide variety of plant material as they shape and reshape the garden. At his home in the south of France Clément enjoyed the necessary conditions and opportunities, free of typical client constraints, to explore his ideas with respect to natural process and the changing forms that result from design that grows out of the habits and behavior of plant communities rather than the imposition of a plan to which these communities are expected to conform. This approach to garden design found public expression as the "Gardens of Movement" in the Parc Citroen in Paris, France.[15]

Civic squares are the hardware equivalent of the software associated with parks and playgrounds in the city. They serve as places to gather for community events, to celebrate civic festivals, and cultural activities. Rosa Klias has designed a number of successful civic squares and gardens in São Paulo and Belem, Brazil—sophisticated solutions to complex urban programs and social issues. Williams Square in Dallas-Fort Worth, Texas, celebrates the history and settlement of the region, whereas Berri Square, in Montreal, suggests a narrative for the ongoing development of the city. Examples of smaller mineral gardens include the network of squares and plazas in Barcelona, and the Jacob Riis Park designed by Paul Freidberg or the Paley Park designed by Robert Zion in New York City. Isamu Noguchi's California Suite plaza celebrates the landscape of California in an enclosed courtyard garden setting, whereas Don Vaughn's Ambleside Fountain, located on an inlet in Vancouver, stresses the geology of the stone shoreline and humans' shaping of it. Tanner Fountain, designed by Peter Walker is an important example of this garden type. Composed of rocks, grass, asphalt and steam, the fountain and its setting respond to the social dynamic of the communities of the "town and gown" in a very small space at the core of Harvard University in Cambridge, Massachusetts.

Garden Trails

Garden trails are located along the canals, rivers, historic trails, and even marginal industrial sites in and adjacent to the urban core. These are linear urban gardens, frequently associated with the movement systems that animate the city. The Battery Park promenade by Laurie Olin in New York City or the Sherover promenade overlooking Jerusalem by Halprin and Shlomo Aronson are two such urban pathways, strategically situated and framed by linear plantings that complement the views and activities of the dense pedestrian traffic drawn to them. Similarly, Gideon Sarig weaves a delightful walking path through the historical neighborhoods of Tel Aviv, uniting the district of early Bauhaus architecture with adjacent historic and contemporary architectural districts in the city. At a larger scale, Roy Mann has emphasized the historic, social, and recreational potential of walking trails along the rivers and canals of numerous North American cities, and the entire shoreline watershed of the metropolitan region of Toronto has been examined for its potential contribution to the restoration and regeneration of the natural systems that flow through this vast urban region. In Ljubljana, one of the most delightful of urban trails, designed by the architect Jose Plecnik, follows the river in the urban core. Conversely, squatters use the river's edge as a preferred location of rich produce gardens in many cities throughout Latin America.

The potential of these open-space systems or linear gardens to support viable urban development has been stressed in writings by Thomas Mawson, Lewis Mumford, and O.C. Simonds, whereas Lawrence Halprin's network of pathways and fountains that weave their way through the expressway in Portland represents a modern pioneering experiment, embracing movement through the city. In a similar vein but entirely different context, Walter Hood developed a series of "garden ideas" in the form of social gathering spaces that were located in an inner city neighborhood underneath the ubiquitous expressway in West Oakland, California.

Infrastructure and movement systems create massive changes in the natural systems and landscape structure of the regions affected. One has only to think of the Three Gorges project in China or the James Bay project in northern Quebec to realize the power and extent of modern intervention in transforming wilderness and the landscape. Fernando Chacel saw this challenge of landscape change as an opportunity to explore landscape rehabilitation and restoration in the forests of Brazil. His concept of "ecogenesis" has been transferred to new urban gardens in the residential districts of Rio and to the rehabilitation of the devastated coastal shorelines.[16]

Framed by discrete shoreline paths, indigenous plants suggest the wilderness of the Amazon, the landscapes of the Jacarepaguà coast, and the gardens of Roberto Burle-Marx.

Conserving Gardens

Conserving gardens subject to revision, disinterest, or outright loss has become a growing challenge and source of concern. The rediscovery of historic settings, whether that of utopian or period communities, or of properties that were once the site of important events, or the homes of notable personalities, has spawned research on the garden styles, materials, and plant life of generations past. The "Jardin des Retours" on the Charente River in France is one such example, where Bernard Lassus created gardens that reconstitute and reinterpret the history of the site and the region, whereas in his competition entry for the restoration of the Jardin des Tuilleries, Lassus clearly expresses the view that the history of gardens has no privileged era but rather is best expressed as a series of garden layers built one on the other.[17]

There is a growing concern that a number of the icons of modern civic gardens, such as Dan Kiley's plaza at Lincoln Square in New York City or Arthur Erickson and Cornelia Oberlander's design for Robson Square in Vancouver have been, or might be, lost to new development proposals or to the ravages of simple neglect. Halprin's Skyline Park in Denver, Colorado, has been largely destroyed; Heritage Park in Fort Worth, Texas, is utterly neglected.[18] The idea that the modern movement is an historic one that affects gardens, particularly those of the fifties and sixties, as much as it does painting, sculpture, and architecture of the period, is gathering credence. Modern restoration of historic garden sites, such as that of Bryant Park in New York City, restored and redesigned by Laurie Olin, has added new layers of garden design to those conceived in previous eras, enriching both.[19]

GARDENS THAT REFLECT SOCIAL SETTINGS

Gardening is one of the most important of global industries. Measured in terms of gross national product, it ranks right after armaments, drugs, and tourism, and well before agriculture, mining, and forestry. It is one of the most important recreational activities in the developed world, and a critical source of food in urban centers. It is equally an activity that accurately reflects the culture within which it is practiced. A wide variety of garden settings has been used to represent specific cultures and historic periods. Modern interpretations of the Japanese and Chinese garden traditions have been exported throughout Europe and North America. Conversely, a number of the modern "Western" gardening models are now found on institutional, university, and corporate sites of Asia. The lush colors, modern forms, and rich variety of plants that characterize Latin American gardens have seeded themselves throughout the world, as have the more restrained and ordered projects derived from the modern Scandinavian tradition.

Civic Gardens

Civic gardens associated with public institutions and events are frequently found in settings such as zoos, botanical gardens, and especially outdoor sculpture gardens. Important examples of the latter include the Museum of Modern Art Courtyard and sculpture garden in New York, the roof terraces of the Oakland

Museum in California by Kiley, and the Billy Rose sculpture in Jerusalem designed by Noguchi. Extensive sculpture parks in the vicinity of large cities, like Storm King gardens in New York State or the Parco di Celle near Pistoia, Italy, use former agricultural land or old picturesque woodland to enhance the visitor experience. Gardens serve as focal points in the larger complex of zoos, marine lands, and botanical gardens devoted to displays of nature in all its forms. Examples include the Cacti botanical garden in Arizona by Jones and Jones, the geology park in Tel Aviv, Israel, by Gideon Sarig, and Henri Bava's Garden "Aqua Magica" for a horticultural exhibit in Bad Önhausen, Germany.[20] A third version of this garden type relates to places where people gather in outdoor amphitheatres to hear music or the attend plays. The Shakespeare theatre garden in Stratford, Ontario, designed for socialization prior to the play and during intermissions, features an unusual collection of plants that might have been found during Shakespeare's time. A music garden in Toronto interprets the structure and dynamic of music using forms and plants that recall the bass and treble staffs and the rhythm and movement of classical music. The Getty campus, by the Olin Partnership and an inserted garden by Robert Irwin, emphasizes a delightful mixture of color and form using native materials to provide a setting for the rich collection of museum exhibits.

FIGURE 2.4: The masterful reading of the Jerusalem landscape is reflected in the rhythm of the stone line berms that frame the modern sculptures overlooking the Holy city, by Isamu Noguchi. Photo: Peter Jacobs.

Educational Gardens

Educational gardens at sites for schools, colleges, and universities incorporate many characteristics of the garden setting, sometimes but not invariably on a rather large scale. Michael van Valkenberg's careful treatment of the Smith campus in Massachusetts is an example of a careful reading of the nineteenth-century values developed in Olmsted's initial plan for the campus, augmented by the artful integration of modern movement systems and open spaces that reflect the needs of contemporary campus life.[21] In other cases, natural features such as hills, rivers, and ravines are used to structure the campus, frequently with careful attention to the regeneration of native planting materials, as in the case of York University, Toronto, designed by Hough. All manner of schoolyard gardens have been generated by parents, teachers, children, and landscape architects in attempts to reduce hard paving and to introduce nature as a living educational and social laboratory. The Washington Environmental Yard, by Robin Moore, is an excellent example of a participative approach to the design of a garden, while the adventure playgrounds proposed by Lady Allen of Hurtwood emphasize the importance of free play. Both are types of modern gardens, not in terms so much of style but in their social and programmatic concerns.

Corporate Gardens

Corporate gardens and the culture they represent have not hesitated to align themselves with the power of the garden and its ability to evoke growth, beauty, and peace. Many of the first corporate gardens of the twentieth century were part of social utopian experiments in Europe and North America. These gardens were in some cases collective community gardens; in others, they were associated with worker's cottages. During the economic depression of the 1930s, Eckbo saw the need to bring modern thinking to bear on the historical issues of poverty and poor living conditions. A new and modern corporate garden emerged after the World War II, as cities expanded and new industries and manufacturing plants sought the more extensive and less expensive landscapes of suburbia. These corporate gardens were part of the attempt to situate industry in garden settings and to provide workers with a pleasant and productive setting as much as to establish an image or brand that contrasted with the grimy and unhealthy working environments of the past. Hideo Sasaki developed his practice in the Boston metropolitan region by organizing the landscape and garden settings for the corporate headquarters of many of the new electronic companies that emerged in the 1960s.

The gardens of Pepsico Corporation in Purchase, New York, designed by Edward T. Stone and Russell Page, and the John Deere Corporation designed by Sasaki and Associates outside Detroit, Michigan, are also important exemplars of this new garden format. The former offers a spacious sculpture garden open to the public. The corporate garden was also used to highlight the natural resources that supported the hydroelectric and forest industries. The Bloedel gardens designed by Haag, for instance, are located within the forest setting from which the giant forest company derived its basic resource.

Tourist Gardens

Tourist gardens and tourism have become a vital part of the global economy, contributing to the debate on the local or global imperatives that preoccupy the world of politicians and economists. The brand-name hotels found that wherever people travel for business or pleasure competes with the growing world of "ecotourism" that emphasizes the particular and specific characteristics of the local landscape and culture. The gardens associated with the former tend to generic examples, frequently of very high design standards, that feature swimming pools, waterfalls, colorful plantings, and vast lawns: the firm of Belt Collins in Hawaii has developed a worldwide expertise in this garden genre. The gardens of the latter group emphasize local plants, social activities, and cultural habits of the particular landscape in which they are situated. The traveling process is itself a subject of garden art most notably in the design of new airports and ground-based terminals. The arrival at the new airport in Jerusalem features a series of terraced gardens, by Aronson, that serve as a symbolic transition to the landscape and culture of the Holy Land. Contemporary gardens have been designed at airports from Denver to Dubai, in part to display the natural flavor of the region, in part to signal a respite from the frantic pace of international travel.

GARDENS OF MEMORY

Gardens serve as a metaphor for nature that is cared for. They remind us of the natural cycles of life, death, and regeneration.[22] Garden cemeteries, especially those attached to religious buildings, sacred places, or preternatural settings, are the most obvious examples. Memorial gardens are common in areas that have suffered the ravages of war, although relatively few celebrate our quest for peace. Still others focus on a particular cultural heritage or distinguished heritage site that emphasizes the history and traditions of a particular place and culture. Gardens have frequently been used to emphasize ceremonial routes and areas where special civil events are commemorated. The Washington Mall is one such example; Pall Mall in London is another. Large-scale civic gardens highlight many of the world's national capitals whether in Chandigarh, India; Brasilia, Brazil; or Canberra, Australia.

Garden Cemeteries and Memorials

Garden cemeteries and memorials are based on cultural metaphors of Paradise, the Garden of Eden, or peaceful settings seen as a reward for departed relatives, friends, and notable members of the community. The idea of the memorial garden is a recurring theme in modern settings. In the early part of the modern movement, a number of cemeteries were conceived as collective garden rooms with the stone markers of individual gravesites laid flat to the surface of the lawn. The social hierarchies and status of those laid to rest were submerged in the garden setting of a collective paradise. An early example of this strategy can be found in the Memorial Gardens in Montreal, by Frederick G. Todd. Other approaches focus on a Bosque of sacred trees as in the Woodland cemetery in Stockholm designed by Asplund or in the Biron Cemetery in Italy by Carlo Scarpa, where the grounds are laid out to emphasize the complex aspects of the life-cycle events of birth, life, and death. Similarly, modern gardens have emerged to prepare the pilgrim for visits to holy shrines such as the Ba'hai Shrine in Haifa. And, in a particularly daring break with tradition, Shigemorei Morei introduced the modern garden movement to Japan, most notably at the Tofuku-ji temple gardens in Kyoto.

Garden memorials commemorate individuals or a collective group that share a common experience. The memorial to John Fitzgerald Kennedy at Runnymeade near London, designed by Sir Geoffrey Jellicoe, artfully combines elements of the garden and of processional movement in a sophisticated and solemn mastery of the art of landscape design. The same can be said for the memorial to the American Vietnam veterans, designed by Maya Lin, situated at the heart of the Washington Mall, or the "Rosie the Riveter" memorial in Richmond, California, designed by Cheryl Barton, paying tribute to those who worked in a war munitions factory and a landscape that no longer exists. Processional gardens whether dedicated to the "stations of the cross" or to a range of classical gods can be found in France, Italy, and Greece as in India,

FIGURE 2.5: The temple garden of Tofuku-ji, Kyoto, Japan, by Shigemorei Morei successfully transforms and renews the centuries old tradition of garden design within a modern design idiom. Photo: Peter Jacobs.

China and Japan. Perhaps one of the most impressive of modern day memorial gardens is that dedicated to Mahatma Gandhi in New Delhi, India. The Peacekeepers site in Ottawa is designed with similar social objects in mind. Other gardens are conceived to recognize the contribution of a particular culture or society, such as the Garden of the First Nations designed by Williams, Asselin, and Akaoui, at the Montreal Botanic Gardens.[23]

Ceremonial Gardens

Ceremonial gardens are usually designed to commemorate collective activities such as military or political episodes in the life of a particular culture or nation. Richard Weller's national commemoration garden in Adelaide, Australia, is one of many examples of national gardens designed to convey the essence of the national landscape. In this case, the "Garden of Australian Dreams" suggests the conjoining of two landscape myths: the mystical system of aboriginal "Dreaming" with the great Australian dream of the bountiful garden suburb.

FIGURE 2.6: In a search for common ground, the "Garden of Australian Dreams" is designed to capture both the aboriginal and the settler's understanding of the Australian landscape. Designed by the group, Room 4.1.3. Photograph courtesy of Richard Weller, designer.

It is of interest that many of the monuments to wartime events are sculptures set on stone bases surrounded by wide swaths of stone paving, while those that celebrate peace tend to be much softer compositions of flowers, lawn, and tree. Although somewhat brutal in their conception, the war memorials of Danny Karavan in Israel conform to many modern garden criteria proposed in this chapter. Gardens that celebrate military activities are very much a part of the modern movement, found wherever war has occurred in the twentieth century. Some, such as the Nitobe Garden in Vancouver, British Columbia, are designed as gardens of reconciliation between previously hostile cultures or nations.

Peace gardens exist to commemorate friendship between nations. In 1932, the Waterton Lakes and Glacier International Parks were declared an international peace park to commemorate the mutual friendship between Canada and the United States. Only one month later and a thousand miles to the east, the International Peace Garden between the border of Montana and North Dakota was created as well. In Sheffield, England, peace gardens adjacent to the town hall were dedicated at the end of the World War II as a simple civic place accessible to all, as was the peace garden in Nathan Phillips Square facing Toronto City Hall. Both are integrated into the daily rhythm of city life.

GARDENS OF THE MIND

Gardens of the mind are conceptual gardens designed to explore possible new avenues of cultural expression or to comment on the dynamics of social and natural phenomena. These gardens need not be real, although many are—if only for a short time. A number of provocative gardens designed by Martha Schwartz, such as the Splice Garden or the Necco Garden in Boston, Massachusetts, are intended to provoke a new view of the nature of a garden and what it represents as much as how it is represented. Some are executed within the format of a growing number of garden festivals in North America and in Europe; others have been built as short-term ephemeral events similar to the practices of art installations. Other gardens are explored on paper with no intention to convert the drawing to three-dimensional reality, while still others explore the process of change and evolution in the garden through the format of exhibitions.

Festival Gardens

Festival gardens have always been an integral part of the marketing of new design ideas, new garden products, and materials. A new generation of this genre has emerged toward the later part of the twentieth century. The garden has become a subject of great interest to those whose passion may not focus on gardening, but rather on how we conceive and consider the idea of nature and of the artificial. Garden festivals at Métis, Quebec; Sonoma, California; and Chaumont, France, along with a series in the United Kingdom, provide artists, architects, landscape architects, and designers with the opportunity to experiment with all manner of garden types and garden forms. Many of these feature rubber tires, old bottles, netting, drapery, and plastic with little or no plant material used to convey images of our involvement with social conflict, love, waste, or the destruction of nature.[24] In one such project, seeds and pinecones were displayed on shelves that replicated the displays found in grocery stores, suggesting that the forest had been reduced to a simple source of commodities to be bought and sold on the open market. Claude Cormier's "Lipstick Forest" in Montreal or the "Blue Tree" in California challenges our sense of nature and the artificial in the garden. Although not a festival garden itself, the Colas garden, designed by Lassus, invents a setting built on a wooden deck with

FIGURE 2.7: The metaphor of grocers shelves lined with produce is used to suggest the pending demise of the boreal forest in Quebec, a landscape that is only valued for its ability to support the unlimited demand for its resources. NIP Paysage, Landscape Architects, "In Vitro," Metis Garden Festival, Quebec, Canada, 2001. Photo: Peter Jacobs.

perforated metal screens—designed to look like plants—partially concealing the real tree-lined boulevard below. The artificial and natural plant materials blend, and the distinction becomes somewhat moot.

Mobile Gardens

Mobile gardens reflect dynamic design strategies, like the recent mobile garden studios, housed on barges that floated down the Mississippi and Hudson rivers, creating gardens with community input at various towns and villages along the way. In the early 1980s, Jacques Simon floated a barge planted as a mobile forest down the River Seine to call attention to the loss of urban forests in the metropolitan region of Paris. Similarly, in the 1990s, Garey Abrahams proposed a barge, designed as a park and equipped with all manner of plants and garden materials that would dock at waterfront sites in disadvantaged communities along the shores of the San Francisco Bay in California. In the first case, participatory garden design was carried out with the local residents at each stop along the riverfronts; in the second, by messages warning of the continuing loss of forest cover to the spreading footprint of urbanization; and, in the third, the need to innovate new ways of providing poor communities with open space and recreation became an integral part of the proposed garden script.

Paper Gardens

Paper gardens explore social and environmental ideas of possible garden conditions that are projected on paper, and increasingly on the virtual screens of a computer. Jacques Simon used photographic collages, a precursor of today's digital PhotoShop techniques, in the 1980s to portray the possible impacts of development on the future landscapes of France. Perhaps the most influential form of paper gardens derives from garden competitions designed to ferret out new ideas, explore theoretical issues, and develop new formal vocabularies of the garden art.[25] Recent competitions have focused on the conservation of historical gardens and landscapes subject to modern development pressures and the rehabilitation of distressed gardens and parks on which floods, hurricanes, and ice storms had an impact. In individually motivated explorations, Barbara Solomon and Chip Sullivan have interpreted the history of garden design to suggest formats and structures of green architecture and landscape. The sketchbooks of Laurie Olin, Lawrence Halprin, and other modern designers contain the germ of countless garden ideas to be tested at some future time or to be cast aside as impracticable. Fantasies can be drawn much more easily then built. Contemporary garden practice relies heavily on visual simulations of garden ideas that are increasingly generated with the aid of powerful software computer programs. These visual tools will change the way we picture the garden, how we will portray them, and ultimately how they will be received.

A SHORT POSTSCRIPT

All typologies will necessarily reduce the purpose, form, and meaning of the garden experience to a selective set of references. The garden types described in this chapter represent only one of numerous possible approaches. Others could focus on the purpose and function of gardens, their formal characteristics, their position with respect to natural processes, or to the dynamic of a variety of social settings. Each of these approaches has its own internal logic, yet none exhausts the complex and multifaceted idea of the modern garden. Increasingly, gardens may not even occupy space as they are developed in a virtual world of ideas. Although the garden has always been associated with, and shaped by, plants and flowers, contemporary practice has substituted all manner of materials, in some cases excluding vegetation altogether. The garden may be in the process of disappearing as the locus of our expression of nature. Alternatively, this may be but a very temporary hiatus in an otherwise traditional commitment to garden art based on the natural world of plants. As future gardens are integrated into the mind-set of the contemporary reader, new garden typologies will almost certainly emerge.

CHAPTER THREE

Plantings

DENNIS MCGLADE AND LAURIE OLIN

Plants and their treatment have been fundamental elements of gardens for thousands of years. Although there have been places and environments devoid of plants that are also considered to be gardens, they are the exception that points to the rule, the norm, and our expectations. By the beginning of the twentieth century, many species had made the journey from botanic gardens to commercial nurseries, estates, and the public realm. Asian and American trees became common along the streets in Paris, London, and other European cities where once now found maples, oaks, paulownias, saphoras, locusts, and ashes. In parks, one came across firs, pines, cherries, azaleas, rhododendrons, viburnums, sumacs, and all manner of herbaceous and flowering plants.

Several of what have come to be thought of as national garden styles associated with different eras in history are largely characterized by a particular use of plants. One need only say Italian Renaissance garden to conjure up evergreen hedges and trees shaping a sequence of terraces and spaces, or recall an image of the broderie (embroidery) of bedding plants that combined with topiary were so characteristic of seventeenth-century French gardens, or the grand masses, clumps, and specimens of trees placed around and within vast meadows, pastures, and fields that embody eighteenth-century English landscape parks. So, too, the influx of exotic plants from foreign parts at times provided both stimulus and exhausting ubiquity: think of Tulip mania in the Netherlands following the introduction of tulips from Turkey, or the rhododendrons and azaleas that spread throughout Britain as they arrived from Asia and America.

The story of plants and how they have been selected, treated, groomed, and arranged, and how particular families and species have gone in and out of fashion, is inseparable from that of the history of gardens. What people think is beautiful, aesthetically or morally correct may have changed continually over the past 2,000 years, but the fact that we continue to take pleasure in plants, in our own time and in our own way is more than remarkable, for the twentieth century has made its own contribution to this long narrative, while frequently looking back over our shoulders to earlier times, to ancient and more-recent planting precedents.

If one considers the sequence of world events, art movements, and the lives of influential individuals in garden and landscape planting in the twentieth century, several things stand out. The careers of many of the innovators and exponents of the informal cottage garden, herbaceous borders, and natural planting movements ended between World War I and World War II. A generation of designers who were to set new trends, dominate the press and popular imagination, and lead the landscape profession were born during the Great Depression came to maturity during and just after World War II or the end of the Korean War. Their good fortune was to work in an era of mass communication and relative affluence among a vast middle class. Wars, and taxes that were levied against corporations, individuals, and estates from the beginning of the century through the 1950s, however, altered life styles and changed how people chose to spend money, especially regarding servants and private staff, which had a marked effect on garden design and maintenance. Gardens became smaller. Planting design became simpler. Fewer varieties of plants were used in simpler arrangements. Most of the garden chores were done by owners, with the more menial, janitorial, and mechanical work that did not require much, if any, horticultural expertise contracted out to maintenance firms.

Further, it can be noted that there have been no significant movements in art since the 1930s that have altered how people conceive and employ plants to compare with the impact of modernism before World War II. The site or land art of the last quarter of the century in its various manifestations, while having an impact on landscape design in general, cannot be said to have had any significant effect on planting design. This may be because plants and their "designed" arrangements can be quite fugitive and vulnerable to change by both the cultural and natural forces that fall upon them. Plants grow. Their form can change as they grow to maturity. Their shapes can be disfigured by disease and by animals. They die. Other plants may invade the space if not weeded out; some twentieth-century land artists have even incorporated the mutability of plants into their works, but many made works of inert material that will remain for quite some time into the indefinite future.

Every garden in every age, if it is to include living plants that the designer intends to keep living and growing, must be grounded in the fundamental and timeless requirements that all plants in all gardens have required—appropriate sunlight, water, soil, and climate suitable to the plant in question. Like the legs of a table, these four horticultural requirements have supported pleasure gardens throughout the ages, regardless of style, historical period, or geography. Plant breeding, especially on the industrial scale of the last half of the twentieth century, has attempted to strengthen the tolerances of plants to a wider range of pests, diseases, climate extremes, soil textures, and chemistry. But ultimately, like the seemingly omnipotent aliens in H. G. Wells's *War of the Worlds*, these superhybrids too will eventually succumb to some event or thing for which the breeders did not account. Plants are alive. It is amazing how many people seem to forget this. Designing with plants is designing with life.

The dawn of the twentieth century was the beginning of a new age in gardening. It saw the demise of serious garden design dominated by the aristocracy and the very wealthy. It was the century of the upper-middle, and even middle-middle class garden, as a focus of serious garden design, theory, and horticulture. At the beginning of the twentieth century, the debates about suitable styles for garden design and therefore the use of plants in them, as well as the debate around using natives versus exotic species, were fresh. As the century closed, these debates were still with us, but those advocating the use of native plants seemed to be in ascendance by the end of the millennium. Within the native plant movement itself is the even newer debate as to what makes a plant "native." Fossilized ginkos were found in the Pacific Northwest of the United States, but no living trees; ginkos were introduced to the west from China in the seventeenth century. The native people of North America cultivated corn for centuries, but it is considered native to Mexico. Is there a cultural dimension to the notion of what constitutes a native plant?

The views and opinions of William Robinson (1838–1935), who bridged both the nineteenth and twentieth centuries, are perhaps the foundation on which so much of twentieth-century garden debate on aesthetics and appropriateness of certain kinds of plants are based. Robinson was trained as a gardener in his youth in Ireland and was very knowledgeable about plants and the craft of gardening. He was a prolific writer of books and founder of garden magazines.[1] He was writing at a time when the growing population of the middle classes was expanding into the suburbs beyond the center of the cities and acquiring houses with yards and room to have a garden. And a garden was the chance to realize some of the ideas of John Ruskin (1819–1900), social and art critic, and William Morris (1843–96), one of the founders of the British Arts and Crafts Movement, who believed that art and beauty were founded in nature. A functional object, crafted by hand by the humble and anonymous artisan, using local materials and indigenous techniques was superior to the object made by machine. In this cultural climate, Robinson espoused cottage gardens and local plants found in the front dooryards of the anonymous yeoman farmer. There was wide popular interest in nature and wild flowers as evidenced by the number of guides to the identification of native flora and fauna written for the amateur naturalist.

However, because the industrial revolution made sheet glass relatively inexpensive, the estate greenhouse and the middle-class conservatory became more affordable. The nursery industry began to use them extensively. Glasshouses made the cultivation and widespread propagation of tender exotic plants feasible, many which of came in a riotous range of colors and forms for both flowers and foliage that were unlike most plants in the native European plant palette. Besides their colors and forms, these plants stayed in bloom during the hottest summer months when many native plants had ended their flowering. Further, they could be bedded out in the garden during warm weather months of spring through early autumn.

Robinson decried the formal, static, geometric-shaped beds frequently employed for these garish, strong-colored, tender annuals, planted in regimented rows that were the norm in the mid-nineteenth-century gardens of the very wealthy. He felt the shapes and colors an anathema to their surrounding natural settings. He found wasteful the necessity of greenhouses to grow and nurture these exotics before they could be planted out of doors. When these plantings had to be changed as the seasons changed, their beds were stripped to bare earth, which remained in full view. He found the bare soil to be unattractive, taking too long to be hidden again by the next display, and he hated planting in beds (masses of one sort of plant all lined up in regimented rows). Robinson advocated planting in borders (planting a variety of plants mixed together). His book *The Wild Garden* was widely read and influential in Germany and the United States as well as in England.

His extensive travels in Western Europe and across the United States gave him a geographic sensitivity to different plant ecologies and plant communities based on the climate, soil, and geology. This geographic sensitivity was realized in his approach to planting founded on plant associations or affinities—planting together and mixing only those hardy plants, (both exotic and native) that have similar horticultural requirements to grow.

Robinson was concerned about losing the hardy old-fashioned garden plants that proved themselves in the local climate and soils and were grown for generations. He found the native plants of the hedgerows, fields, and pastures to be beautiful in their own right, as well as those nonnative hardy plants that could grow in the English climate and soils. It is speculation as to whether his Irishness contributed to his rather democratic inclusion of native and cottage plants in gardens and to his severely dismissive attitude toward the types of grand garden filled with tender exotic plants arranged in bilateral symmetrical beds that he was employed to maintain as a youthful gardener in Ireland.

He encouraged people to grow plants and create gardens in otherwise neglected or leftover corners of the property away from the lawns and parterres, advocating planting wildflowers and ferns in irregular clumps, or "drifts" on the floor of the forest or under the hedgerow and planting bulbs in lawns in a similar fashion. He felt vines and climber roses could be trained to scramble over shrubs and up the trunks of trees, not only up pergolas and trellises. He is perhaps the first person to raise the consciousness of the gardening public to the beauty of meadows, encouraging them to think of them as another form of garden, rather than just a feedlot for estate herbivores.

He was quite ecumenical in his taste in plants, from recommending alpines for planting on the tops of walls and in rock gardens, to mixing native plants with garden hybrids and hardy exotics "naturalistically," meaning in nongeometric, unstructured, amorphous clumps and drifts. Plants that seeded themselves around the garden were allowed to stay or were selectively weeded, so that the different species and cultivars mixed with each other in a very "natural" way. The garden was not to be, or to look, overly managed, or maintained. The extensive list of plants meant that something somewhere in the garden was in bloom, fruit, leaf, or seed, providing seasonal interest, even in the dead of winter. There was to be no bare earth, no geometric bedding, and a very minimal "down" season in the garden.

The transition from the nineteenth to the twentieth century saw the decline in number of the large and elaborately designed display gardens of the Victorian Age. In Britain, intricate estate kitchen gardens and elaborate county gardens were victims of the changing tastes and the sources of a family's wealth. The gentry whose money resulted "in trade": from the industrial revolution were not as tied to the land as were the inherited aristocracy, whose family wealth originally was from agriculture and the land. Summers for the very wealthy industrialists were now enjoyed on the continent, in more exotic venues like the Riviera or villas in the Italian countryside, not at home in the country. Agriculture was becoming more international as well. Fruits and vegetables not readily available from local market gardens were imported from elsewhere in Europe. One did not need one's own talented gardener to grow otherwise exotic produce for the table.

The ranks of master gardeners and the younger garden staff and laborers were decimated by the World War I. The war also dramatically changed attitudes across society. The world of the aristocratic country house would not be the same, although for a very few of the very rich, the *Country Life* lifestyle did manage to hang on. In the United States, the Sixteenth Amendment that brought in a national income tax had much the same effect on grand estate gardening as had the levy of death duties and the war on Britain's wealthy.

Attitudes toward health and fitness that we still appreciate today were born at the turn of the century. It became fashionable to be fit and healthy, and outdoor activities like gardening played into this new active lifestyle, for the women as much as the men. The pale and wan complexion of the sedentary, tubercular beauty was very much out. The garden became as much a place in which to recreate and enjoy as to display one's wealth, especially for the upper-middle classes. The formerly neutral and static plane of lawn became the setting for tea parties, tennis, badminton, and croquet.

The gardens of Gertrude Jekyll (1843–1932) and Edwin Lutyens (1869–1944) exemplify these sorts of gardens. Jekyll was a garden designer and outstanding plants person with encyclopedic knowledge of horticulture and herbaceous and woody plants. A painter in her youth before her eyesight weakened, she was acquainted with, and was inspired by, paintings by Turner. She knew the leaders of the Arts and Crafts Movement in England and was sympathetic to their aesthetic of handcraft, rustic, indigenous materials, and use of native and traditionally used ornamental plants as might be found in rural country gardens. She knew of Monet's garden in Giverny. She was aware of Michel-Eugène Chevreul's book *The Principles of Harmony and Contrast of Colors*, printed in English in 1854. She brought a painterly eye to the arrangement of flowering plants in long flowing sweeps of color that blended and changed hue in relationship one to other. She knew color is not perceived in isolation but rather that the perception of color is effected by other adjacencies. She understood the visual effect of the soft English light in her use of color.

Jekyll knew William Robinson and was very sympathetic to much of his philosophy. She, too, was fascinated with the flowers growing in the gardens of rural cottages and loved wild flowers. She designed for seasonal interest for much of the year, emphasizing different seasons in different parts of the garden, experimenting with plant and color combinations in her own borders at Munstead Wood, Surrey. Here she planted a nut walk, a rock garden, a spring garden, and a pergola, as well as a woodland garden with ericaceous plants like heathers, rhododendrons, and azaleas, among others.

In the famous main or long border at Munstead Wood, the center portion is planted with flowers in deep, hot colors of red, orange, and yellows that transition to softer, paler, cooler versions of the yellows and oranges, eventually

FIGURE 3.1: Hestercombe, Somerset, England, 1906, by Gertrude Jekyll and Edwards Lutyens. Photo: Dennis McGlade.

ending in cool tones of mauves and blues. Color transitions were softened, and the movement of the eye facilitated, by the strategic placement of drifts of silver- and gray-leaved plants. Jekyll also used the bold, spiky, linear foliage of various yucca species to punctuate and contrast with the round foliage of Berginia as well as the finer textured plants and flowers of her borders. She also designed monochromatic borders for some of her clients.

The beds could be very wide, from twelve to fourteen feet or more. This width facilitated the planting of shrubs in the rear, fronted by a lower growing mix of plants. There was a maintenance path hidden between the tall shrubs to the rear of the border and the lower plantings in the foreground. This path was hidden by the exuberant vegetation on either side. These were labor-intensive and expensive gardens to keep in full flower. Indeed, Jekyll's planting aesthetic was widely influential, but it was not always done on such an intensive and extensive scale by her many would-be imitators because of the monetary expense and the high level of horticultural expertise her gardens required. There was usually a second nursery garden out of view in which replacement plants were grown to replace or hide those in the main beds whose prime had passed.

Annual bedding plants, arranged in drifts like the perennials, were also used in the borders to provide supplemental, late-season color, when many of the summer perennials were starting to go out of bloom. Jekyll's clients consisted of that cadre of wealthy families that strived to maintain their estates and a retinue of servants, including gardeners, even after the Great War, when trained horticultural staff were in short supply.

Geometry and the architecture of landscape did play an important part in the layout of many of her gardens, as they incorporated trimmed hedges, walls, steps, pergolas, long pools of water, and so on. The geometric structure of the gardens was sometimes provided by Lutyens's architect's eye, although he designed a few gardens totally on his own without Jekyll's collaboration. The billowing growth of the plantings contrasted with and covered much of this softened garden architecture.

The interest in and love of flower gardens with informal, loose borders of flowers of various varieties growing into each other that was so popular at the beginning of the twentieth century in the United States and Britain was not as well appreciated by Edith Wharton (1862–1937), who argued for the aesthetic of the Italian Renaissance garden and villa in her trend setting (at least for the very rich) *Italian Villas and Their Gardens*. Her emphasis was on stonework, sculpture, water, and woody plants in the form of evergreen and deciduous trees and hedges, all seamlessly integrated with the villa and equally with the site itself. Flowers had a more minor role. These gardens became very popular with the moneyed classes, in Europe as well as the United States. Harold Peto designed his own Italianate Garden at Ilford in Wiltshire, in which he placed his extensive collection of decorative, antique Italian objects and architectural fragments, perhaps too extensive for some tastes. He also designed Buscot Park in Berkshire for Alexander Henderson (Lord Faringdon), an Italianate garden more in keeping with Wharton's restrained taste.

In the United States, Beatrix Farrand (1872–1959) seemed to bridge both camps, being familiar with both Robinson and Jekyll and the niece of Wharton. At Dumbarton Oaks, the Washington, D.C., garden she designed for Mildred and Robert Woods Bliss, the gardens and plantings are bilaterally symmetrical near the house.[2] The geometry and bed layout are derived from classical and Renaissance precedents. The architectural elements of balustrades, pavements, and the decorative sculptural features are important visual components of the gardens. The oval hedge of clipped hornbeams centered on a stone fountain is garden architecture very much in the spirit of Italian gardens. The hornbeam is deciduous, but the leafless branches are so dense it reads like an evergreen mass even in the winter. As one leaves the house precinct and descends through the garden toward Rock Creek, the plantings get much looser, irregular, and

FIGURE 3.2: Iford Manor, Wiltshire, England, 1899–1933, by Harold Peto. Photo: Dennis McGlade.

appear less controlled. They transition and blend into the vegetation of the adjacent Dumbarton Oaks Park. Like all great Italian hillside gardens, Dumbarton Oaks takes breathtaking advantage of the site's topography by situating the plantings to help choreograph the experience of traversing the garden. The plantings are used to conceal and then reveal, frame, and enhance views out and over to Rock Creek and the park beyond.

The garden Farrand designed for Abby Aldrich Rockefeller in Seal Harbor, Maine, seems a synthesis of both Robinson and Jekyll, with an Asian take on the sculpture-filled Italian garden. There are the mixed perennial and annual flower borders, overflowing with blooms. These abut and are surrounded by the adjacent woods underplanted with native moss and ferns. The whole composition is set off by large Korean figurative sculptures and a wall with a round moon gate.

The Industrial Revolution had spawned many rich people who wanted gardens to display their wealth. However, these people were not necessarily interested in designing the garden and managing the maintenance of the gardens themselves. They were glad to hire the expertise they needed to impress the world horticulturally. It was even better if the garden designer brought with him or her a certain cultural and social cachet acquired by the acclaim of his or her previous body of work and the social and aristocratic caliber of other clients, hence the rise of a class of professional garden designers who could produce garden schemes that would satisfy this new garden-loving class.

But not all the rich were so hands off. The first half of the twentieth century saw many magnificent gardens designed by their "amateur" owners. Amateur gardeners created rock gardens and woodland gardens filled with rhododendrons, as well as more general pleasure and display gardens. These people brought a focused intensity to the design of their garden because it was the only one they worked on, and they continually refined and reworked the design. With knowledge of their site, its micro-climate, and its soil, their dogged pursuit of the rarest and most wonderful plants imported from exotic locales, or hybridized and selected from their on-site breeding programs resulted in some of the most gorgeous gardens ever created. The diversity of the plantings and the subtlety and nuance in their arrangement were the product of that rarest union of great taste, horticultural knowledge, and substantial income. Two of the most famous of these gardens and their gardeners in Britain are Vita Sackville-West (1892–1962) and Harold Nicholson's (1886–1968) garden at Sissinghurst in Kent and Lawrence Johnston's (1871–1958) garden at Hidcote Manor in Gloucestershire. In the United States, one family, the du Ponts,

FIGURE 3.3: Hidcote Manor Garden, Gloucestershire, England, 1907–1947, by Lawrence Johnson. Photo: Dennis McGlade.

created five gardens all within a few miles of each other near Wilmington, Delaware, and all now opened to the public. Of these two are arguably the most famous. Henry Francis du Pont (1880–1969) created Winterthur, a garden with extensive woodlands underplanted with azaleas, the color combinations of which du Pont personally selected and arranged. Nearby in Kennett Square, Pennsylvania, Pierre S. du Pont (1870–1954) created Longwood Gardens, one of the largest and finest public display gardens in the world. The other three du Pont gardens are Hagley Museum and Library, Nemours, and Mount Cuba Center for the Study of Piedmont Flora.

FIGURE 3.4: Great Dixter, East Sussex, England, Edwin Lutyens with Nathaniel Lloyd (1910–1933) Daisy Lloyd (1933–1972), and Christopher Lloyd (1930s onward). Photo: Dennis McGlade.

Another one of these amateur gardeners, Christopher Lloyd (1921–2006), lived, wrote about gardening and plants, and gardened throughout his life at Great Dixter in Sussex, the family garden he knew as a child and inherited from his mother. He was a child while Jekyll and Robinson were still alive, and Edwin Lutyens had laid out the garden for Nathaniel Lloyd, his father. It is an organic composition of varied spaces demarcated by walls, steps, and hedges. Lloyd became an inspired plants man and a master at color combinations, combining foliage, flowers, even fruit and bark to stunning visual effect. By the end of the last century, he was known and admired internationally through his writing, lectures, and books.

Because the climate of the United States is quite variable, from arid desert to rain forest, from arctic arboreal forest to semitropical dry woodland, with every gradation between, some of the plants and the garden styles of Europe did not seem to work in many regions of the continent. At the beginning of the twentieth century, certain landscape architects and nursery people began to search for plants and gardening styles appropriate to their region in the United

FIGURE 3.5: Millenium Park, Chicago, Illinois, United States, 2004, planting design by Piet Oudolf within a larger landscape design by Kathryn Gustafson. Photo: Dennis McGlade.

States, a search that is still going on today in gardens like Mount Cuba Center for the Study of Piedmont Flora, and by contemporary landscape architects like Steven Martino of Phoenix, Arizona.

Social, economic, and military events in nineteenth-century Europe led to large-scale immigration to North America, bringing not only the "huddled masses" but also educated, talented, and trained gardeners and foresters, many of whom had a marked effect on the American landscape. In 1884, one of these, Jens Jensen (1860–1951), immigrated to the United States from Denmark and settled in Chicago. An energetic, talented, and sensitive designer, he rose to design a number of large parks for the city as well as numerous estate gardens for the plutocracy produced by the burgeoning economy of Chicago. He knew Frank Lloyd Wright and designed gardens for his prairie-style houses. He witnessed the destruction of the native prairie landscape around the city as it expanded to the west. Jensen saw at firsthand in Chicago's slums and lower-class neighborhoods the grinding poverty and social injustices produced by the unrestrained capitalism at the turn of the century. He deplored the formal, geometric garden as an exotic importation of an imperial, autocratic, and class conscious Europe into a democratic, republican society and believed instead in the power of the native landscape with its gentle topography, indigenous, native plants to heal the spirit and improve the lot of the lower classes. Jensen loved the long, low, flat horizon of the Midwest landscape over which the dome of the sky seemed to him to be of equal importance. His plantings for civic parks and private estates alike were inspired by this landscape, which was a savannah composition of expansive grasslands with many wild flowers and copses of woodland.

Although he loved native plants and extolled their virtues both aesthetic and horticultural through his writings, he was not a purist. Jensen also used nonnative plants that he felt were sympathetic both visually and horticulturally to the native landscape. He used plants with horizontal branching habits like the Cockspur Thorn (*Crataegus crus-galli*) to reflect and reinforce the horizontality of the prairie, while constructing serpentine lagoons in the parks he designed, calling them Prairie Rivers. Their shorelines were planted with native emergent and aquatic vegetation that transitioned from cattails, pickerelweed, and arrowhead at the shore to lotus, water lilies, and finally open water. He created swaths of grassy prairie meadow that gently curved out of sight around copses of woodland. Shady prospects beneath the trees offered views out into these sunny meadows. Along the edges of his woodlands, lower-growing flowering trees like crabapple and hawthorns were planted, which in turn edged the meadows with lower-growing shrubs such as sumac.

Very different from that of the Chicago area, the climate of the Pacific Coast of California is Mediterranean. While rich in native species, the year-round aspect for floriferous gardens was limited because most of the native plants bloomed in the spring after the winter rains but then disappeared or went into heat dormancy for the rest of the year, as temperatures rose and the rains stopped. The landscape changed color from a few months of bright spring green to many more months of honey gold.

At the turn of the twentieth century, there was a burst of expansion of nurseries in southern California that reflected the burgeoning economy and growth of wealth and population. Irrigation technology was invented. Port cities became places where plants and seed from other Mediterranean areas in the world (coastal Chile, South Africa, parts of Australia, the Canary Islands, and the Mediterranean basin in Europe) could be conveniently introduced. Because coastal California is mostly frost free, especially in the south, fully tropical plants were also imported. Some of these imports, like various species of Eucalyptus were so successful in their new home we often think of them today as being native. Kate Olivia Sessions (1857–1940) started her own nursery in San Diego in the late 1880s, selling native plants that she propagated and collected from the wild as well as imported exotics. Sessions designed gardens and combined native and exotic plants based on their respective microclimate affinities for moisture and sun. Hugh Evans of the Evans and Reed Nursery began another famous horticultural enterprise in Los Angeles in 1936. This nursery was known for its inventory of rare, exotic, and unusual tropical and subtropical plants such as Coral trees, many species of which are now ubiquitous throughout southern California.

In Britain, the World War I not only destroyed the lives of many gardeners and their staff, as well as nursery men; it also, for the first time, made growing vegetables a patriotic act. Food shipments from abroad were interrupted by the war. Growing one's own was the way to self-sufficiency in food until the end of hostilities. Also, between the wars, the suburbs grew on both sides of the Atlantic, and many of the new houses were on larger plots of land. These largely middle-class householders had room to garden and looked for advice on how to design and manage a garden, as this was a new activity to many. The first radio program on gardening in the Britain was hosted by Marion Cran, a novelist, in 1923. With this event, broadcast journalism joined the ranks of printed media, giving the gardener another source for the information he or she craved. The Depression, however, put an end to many people's gardening efforts unless it was to grow vegetables at home or in allotment gardens to keep body and soul together.

Allotment gardens, World War II victory gardens, and late-twentieth-century urban community gardens have their roots in ancient ideas of health and the benefits of working the earth; self-sufficiency, especially in time of war; and, more recently with an interest in organic farming, a resistance to commercial produce resulting from global agribusiness and gourmet-inspired aspects of the "slow food" movement begun in Italy at the end of the twentieth century. Although kitchen gardens have been for centuries a common feature of country residences whether grand or humble, it was a German physician, Daniel Gottlob Moritz Schreber, who linked children's' health with outdoor exercise and gardens, leading to the first Schrebergartens in Liepzig in 1864. By the beginning of the twentieth century, both the concept of "kindergardens" and organized plots on public land for urban dwellers to raise vegetables and flowers had spread to Britain and America. The widespread availability in general stores and grocers of competing brands of seeds boasting new and improved vegetables contributed to these small amateur gardens through the 1920s and 1930s, especially with the economic hardships of the financial depression that affected the industrialized world.

With the scarcity of food and onset of rationing in all of the countries involved in World War II, regardless of which side of the conflict, such gardens reached their maximum extent. In 1940, in the United States, just in time for those who would start these "Victory Gardens," as they were called there, J.I. Rodale from New York City began *Organic Gardening and Farming* magazine, a periodical that became a bible for those who would eschew artificial fertilizers and chemical pesticides in favor of organic methods using compost, mulch, and beneficial insects in their gardens. With the restoration of peace, the Victory Gardens in the West gradually disappeared. They reappeared again in the early 1970s when a widespread interest in ecology and distrust of the use of chemicals in commercial agriculture, along with efforts to revive community spirit and life in the inner city of many of America's largest metropolises such as New York, Philadelphia, and Chicago. In some European countries, especially Germany, the Netherlands, and Britain, but also in Scandinavia and France, collectives of small vegetable gardens, whether created or merely tolerated by local authorities became weekend retreats, combining leisure, horticulture, and socializing for large numbers of people, often with a friendly but intense competition in growing particular large and attractive specimens of both vegetables and flowers.

In Germany before and during the World War II, the notion of using native plants took on ominous, perverse, and irrational nationalist overtones. The notion promulgated by Willy Lange (1864–1941) a landscape architect, was the pseudo-scientific idea of a botanically pure, national flora that was naturally appropriate for the gardens of the superior Germanic and Nordic races in their homeland. This botanic propaganda was wholly in line with the racial policies of the National Socialist Party, the members of which took up the botanical purism for their own hideous ends. Nonnative species were deemed inferior and were to be eliminated from the landscape, similar to the extirpation of inferior races. The "native" plants of Germany supposedly were superior to those from elsewhere, and any and all plants deemed not native to the fatherland needed be removed lest they taint the native botanic germ plasm.[3]

At the same time in Germany, and in contrast to the botany of the dark side, were the noble and creative efforts of nurseryman Karl Foerster (1874–1970). He was interested in growing and propagating a wide variety of hardy, dependable, primarily herbaceous plants for the ordinary gardener. His own garden was used for display of the plants his nursery was developing and stringently testing over many years before they were sold. His garden demonstrated the sound horticultural advice of the right plant in the right place, combining those plants originating from similar habitats with similar requirements for soil, moisture, and light levels. He favored the naturalistic, informal style of combining his plants in irregular drifts in borders. He was the first to appreciate and demonstrate the long season and visual interest of ornamental grasses, botanical favorites rediscovered by garden designers at the end of the twentieth century like Piet Oudolf in the Netherlands and Ohme and van Sweden in the United States. The gardens of these designers employ a rich tapestry of perennials in addition to trees and shrubs. Their popularity may be attributed to a reaction to the more simplistic plantings in gardens of the mid-twentieth century—gardens that had a plant palette limited mostly to shrubs and trees, with very few perennials, and the latter used in more conventional borders, not in the expansive masses of Oudolf and Ohme and Van Sweeden.

At the turn of the twentieth century, the Art Nouveau movement in France was in full swing decorating buildings and objects of all sorts, which spread to other countries. Despite its prevailing biomorphic decorative motifs based on swirls of sinuously pulled, twisted, and attenuated plants with their flowers, leaves, and stems gracefully deporting themselves in an animated languor, sometimes with a diaphanously draped young woman, it had very little effect on planting or garden design. In contrast to this the arts and crafts movement that also incorporated botanical motifs into a considerable range of products from wall coverings to textiles, furniture, glasswork, printing, and publishing did contribute to garden design in its reworking of medieval and cottage compositions and planting.

FIGURE 3.6: Abby Aldrich Rockefeller Sculpture Garden, Museum of Modern Art, New York City, United States, 1950s (with later revisions), by Philip Johnson and Robert Zion. Photo: Peter Stegner.

Other movements in fine and decorative arts had, arguably, more radical and lasting influences. The Bauhaus school, an industrial products, furniture design, arts, and architecture school whose founding is marked in 1919 in Germany, did not offer garden or landscape design, perhaps because of its focus on harnessing modern industrial manufacturing and fabricating technique to architecture and home furnishings. The institution was about architecture, building, and furnishings, not about environment, urbanism, and landscape. Nevertheless, the creation of the Bauhaus along with other more or less contemporary movements in the plastic arts, for example, Cubism, Surrealism, and De Stijl, marks the beginning of a new sensibility in design, which for gardens and their plantings meant a refutation of tradition and the historical past. None of these movements produced a distinctive garden or planting style per se. Nevertheless the painted shapes and organization of the paintings on the canvas was reflected in the plans of bed shapes, and lines of trees in the gardens designed later in the century by people like Roberto Burle Marx, such as that seen in Figure 2.1; Garrett Eckbo; Thomas Church; Geoffrey Jellicoe;

and Daniel Kiley; among others. They borrowed the shapes, visual and formal structures, and appearance, but not necessarily the theory or philosophy of the artists or artistic movements that generated them.

The art deco style was distilled in the *Exposition International des Arts Décoratifs et Industriels Modernes* in Paris in 1925. An angular, decorative geometry based on the triangle and square was one visual theme found in the exposition. It also found its way into the plans of two gardens designed

FIGURE 3.7: Le Jardin en Mouvement, Parc André-Citroen, Paris, France, 1992, by Gilles Clément. Photo: Dennis McGlade.

by Gabriel Guevrekian: the Jardin d'eau et de lumiére installed on the exposition grounds, and Villa Noailles in Hyeres, in France, a few years later. The triangles and squares were demarcated by concrete curbs and were filled with monochromatic annual flowering plants, planted with geometric precision. The monochromatic flowery infill recalls the squares and rectangles of solid color, firmly framed in a black border one sees in a Mondrian painting. Unlike a Jekyll border, these plants and their colors do not spill out of their beds, blend in to each other, mix, or mingle. In fact, some plants were totally replaced by geometry and other materials in the Robert Mallet-Stevens garden at the exposition. He placed concrete sculptures in lieu of trees, designed and executed by Jan and Joel Martel in the Jardin de l'habitation moderne.

The modern movement eschewed decoration, symbolism, and extolled the virtues of form following function. In the 1929 Barcelona Pavilion by Ludwig Mies van de Rohe (1886–1969), the outdoor courtyard has no plants at all, but rather a single, figurative sculpture writhing above a still, supernal pool of water. The exquisite proportions of the entire composition might make a Hellenistic Greek cry. The inchoate messiness of nature, in the form of the mixed canopies of the trees planted beyond in the exposition grounds, peeks over the top of the gorgeous green marble wall. The color of the wall and its irregular venation may be an architectonic reflection of the trees beyond, but the marble of the wall is static and immutable, day in and day out, visually affected only by the vagaries of the celestial light coming from above. The trees, however, move with the wind, lose their leaves, flower, fruit, grow, and die. However, the International style of architecture espoused confidence that the same typologies of buildings could be used everywhere, hence the "international" epithet; the context did not matter as the style was international. How this approach to architecture was to be reconciled with successful planting design that, by necessity, must be site responsive, if not contextual, to ensure the plants will survive and grow, was not addressed.

The modern garden as realized in South America by Roberto Burle Marx (1909–1994) retained botanical complexity without sacrificing modernity, such as that seen in Figure 2.1.[4] Marx was an autodidact working in Brazil, after spending time in Europe. He was a painter, garden designer, nurseryman, native-plant ecologist, and conservationist, who the American Institute of Architects has called the inventor of the modern garden. He worked for years with modernist architects such as Oscar Neimeyer. Like other garden designers working in places very different from Northern Europe, he looked to the landscapes and native plants of Brazil to inform his designs. The bright light and humid tropics and sensitivities to form and color that he had developed as a painter resulted in garden designs of a signature style all their own. In several instances, his paintings and his landscape plans are indistinguishable. Burle-Marx used planes of colored foliage in free-form shapes in interlocking patterns that at times meshed with his paving patterns. He employed textural contrast between fine leaved ground covers and plants with sculptural, bold tropical foliage. Trees are planted in widely spaced clumps and trimmed high to allow air movement. Water in his gardens is usually designed in still planes, or simple, falling sheets, rather than sprays or jets, which would only add more humidity to the air. Bold tropical water plants like Giant Arums (*Typhodorum lindleyanum*) emerge from the glassy surface. He also created vertical column gardens dripping with aroids and bromeliads to be placed in small urban courtyards that were inspired by the Brazilian rain forest, which contains trees bedecked with epiphytic vines, bromeliads, and orchids.

After the World War II, plantings in modern style gardens in Europe and the United States were arranged with a contemporary sensitivity that was sympathetic to the aesthetic of the modernist architecture. Symmetry was replaced by asymmetry. The simple, the clear, and the clean were preferable to the complex and elaborate or messy. The earlier Victorian associations of certain plants with certain emotions, or historical, literary, or mythological references were forgotten or ignored. Plantings emphasized foliage and form. Plants were combined according to natural associations based on their native habitat. Plants with bold foliage or interesting form were used as living sculpture. Except for these examples of botanical eye-catchers, garden plantings were not supposed to stick out in the landscape, thus implying that they were being imposed artificially on the land. The complex herbaceous border was no longer in fashion. The list of plants employed in the garden became shorter and shorter.

In England, the first public exposition to feature modern styled gardens and plantings was the Festival of Britain in 1951. It was a gallery of who was who in modernist garden design at the time—H. F. Clark, Maria Shephard, Peter Youngman, and Peter Shepheard. Echoes of the forms in Burle Marx's gardens can be seen in some of the work. Despite this tremendous endorsement of the modernist style at such a prestigious international exhibition, the contemporary aesthetic in garden design was not widely adopted by the mostly conservative English gardening public of that time, who preferred to cling to a democratized style à la Jekyll.

In North America, modernism in the garden was more widely accepted. This was partly due to a frequently noticed penchant of many Americans to embrace novelty, whatever is new and is the latest, and to disdain whatever has become normal, accepted, or traditional. A long-abiding ignorance or rejection of history and established authority summed up in Henry Ford's remark "History is bunk!" and a yearning for fresh prospects and a new horizon (frontier) has made the United States a fertile ground for change and whatever is "modern" at any given moment. Thus, after each of the great wars of the twentieth century, as American men returned and the economy shifted back to peacetime products and projects, there was a pronounced widespread interest in modern design—in clothing, automobiles, house wares, furnishings, and architecture. World's fairs and exhibitions following each of the wars promoted recent developments in science and industry. Accompanying this were the creation of a vast number of new bedroom and suburban communities across the country. A new generation of American gardens was usually sited in a suburban, rather than an urban, setting. The seamless transition from indoors to outdoor rooms became an aesthetic norm of architecture for most of the twentieth century. The outdoor room was seen to complement and extend the activity or functions of interior rooms.

Modern gardens following World War II on the East Coast were designed by James Rose, A. E. Bye, and Daniel Urban Kiley. They received considerable positive press in popular magazines and journals. The work of Rose and Bye was limited mostly to small-scale residential work. Rose was interested in creating gardens that were seamless with the house. Horticultural interest and complexity however were not his focus. A. E. Bye's gardens were planted more in the tradition of Jens Jensen, with an emphasis on native plants, subtlety placed in the context of the larger landscape. When one comes across images of some of Bye's work,[5] one is not sure if the image is a designed landscape at all. Kiley, taking on residential as well as corporate and public clients, had commissions that were more diverse and on a larger scale than the other two. Inspired equally by Mondrian's paintings as by the gardens of André le Nôtre and the Ecole des Beaux Arts with their precise architectonic layout and geometry, he extended structural grids from architecture out into the landscape, using this as an organizing device in the placement of trees, walks, terraces, while his plant palette was restrained and self-effacing.

The relatively small sculpture garden at the Museum of Modern art in New York City, in spite of its size, is the apotheosis of the grid as an organizing element in garden design. Designed by Robert Zion and Phillip Johnson, in many ways, it epitomizes the mid-century modern garden in North America. Here one finds a limited palette of plants, placed with premeditated precision in order to contrast with the orthogonal pavement grid; rectangular plant beds are determined by the pavement joints and an irregular arrangement of the copses of the trees. Against the gray and white stone and the green of the arboreal foliage, seasonal color is provided by monospecific spring bulbs and summer annuals, all in the same color—red.

It would probably be a mistake to ascribe the simplicity of the forms and minimalism of some of the most famous and admired mid-century gardens in America to reduced financial ability. The most famous modern gardens in America were almost exclusively created for wealthy people—the Museum of Modern Art sculpture garden is named the Abbey Aldrich Rockefeller Garden, owing to the patronage of what at one time was the richest family in American history. So, too, the iconic Donnell garden by Thomas Church and the Miller garden by Dan Kiley, like those produced in wealthy enclaves elsewhere, were largely a matter of a new taste and style, as they were built and maintained by leaders of industry with great resources. Nevertheless, this new trimmed down sort of garden with its limited plant palette served as a model for those aspiring to a more glamorous life who had far fewer resources and small plots of land in the new suburban landscape, a point made strongly in articles published in *House and Garden*, *House Beautiful*, and *Sunset Magazine* throughout the 1950s, 1960s, and 1970s.

The post-World War II upper-middle-class modern garden in the United States reached the zenith of its style in mid-century California. The practitioners of modern garden art there at that time created some of the most iconic contemporary gardens, arguably comparable to those of Burle Marx, but usually on a smaller scale. The Mediterranean climate along the coast, especially from San Francisco south, made outdoor living all year feasible. Winters were mild; the rainy season was short; summers were warm but with low humidity. An investment in a splendid residential garden, usable for almost twelve months of the year made a lot of sense.

Thomas Church (1902–1978), and Garrett Eckbo (1910–2001), are the two practitioners, who through their work and their writings are associated with perfecting this genre of garden in response to the California lifestyle.[6] In spite of the huge variety of plants that will grow there and that were then available to the California gardener, thanks to the efforts of the nurseries like those started by Kate Sessions and Hugh Evens, both designers sublimated planting to ease of maintenance and the precepts of simplicity and functional organization that modernism demanded. These gardens would not be maintained by a professional, full-time staff, and it was expected that the owners would do most of the work with limited contract labor. It was also assumed that the owners were probably not gardeners and that they were not as interested in taking care of their gardens as much as experiencing them as places for recreation and socializing. The swimming pool and barbeque, along with the sandbox and children's area, became the nucleus of outdoor entertaining, in lieu of the lawn for tennis, croquet, or badminton. Also, placement of plants in the California garden must be dictated by the compatibility of plant combinations to the microclimate, particularly sun versus shade, and the soils of the site overlaid with the necessity of irrigation. Because of the mild climate and availability of irrigation, year–round botanical interest could be achieved with a modest selection of the right plants. Many of the plants that grow here provide year–round interest in their leaves, flowers, fruit, stems, and/or form. An ornamental plant like Lantana has evergreen leaves and blooms almost all year. Agapanthus and bird-of-paradise, the official flower of Los Angeles, have very attractive year–round foliage and gorgeous, dramatic flowers over a long bloom period.

In his mid-century gardens, Church used shapes for some of his planting beds, pools, and pavements, and his arrangements and combination of plants seem to reflect those of Roberto Burle Marx. The plans of other Church gardens recall the zigzags of art deco. Sometimes both forms were combined in the same garden. Conversely, other gardens of his look very traditional, with bilateral symmetry and boxwood parterres. This eclecticism reflected a dispassionate, nonpurist approach to using style as any other design tool to create a garden that would work with traditional architecture and the more conservative taste of some of his clients.

Eckbo on the other hand was consistently a modernist emphasizing innovative materials in gardens such as aluminum and plastic. He also was more of a geometrician in his placement of lines of trees consisting of the same species, using them with different canopy forms for different lines, rows, and *bosques*. The canopies of his tree rows formed sculptural planes of foliage demarcating subspaces in the landscape. When Eckbo drew these tree plantings in aerial perspective or in axonometric view and when these tree lines cross or meet at right angles, they are reminiscent of the arrangement of the black lines in a Mondrian painting. He also developed plan compositions based on triangles and parallelograms with straight lines and sharp angles relieved by occasional curving lines. Irregular plantings of trees and beds of shrubs and groundcovers relieved and contrasted with these geometries in his work.

The suburban garden center was invented in the United States just following World War II. This development was concurrent with both the flight from North American inner cities by the white middle classes to the suburbs and the perfection of the California suburban garden that was then receiving national publicity in the popular press. The new garden centers offered those with the energy and finances, a resource of do-it-yourself building materials and plants to build a California-style dream garden for themselves, even if they did not live there. In the late 1960s, the *tuincentrum* also appeared in the Netherlands, invented by Dutch nurseryman Henk Drenth, which he called Tuinland (*tuin* means garden in Dutch). It was a new self-service garden center with tropicals and tender plants indoors and hardy plants outdoors. By the close of the twentieth century, commercial nurseries, along with the transport and sale of plants, had become a vast global industry. Although commerce in plants has been central to the rise of agriculture and feeding the world's population since antiquity, and the trading and sharing of seeds, and cuttings internationally has been one of the pleasures of amateurs and scientists alike for centuries, the spectacular growth of the ornamental and horticultural plant industry of the past forty years is unprecedented. As the century advanced, the nursery industry became more technically and horticulturally sophisticated as to its means and methods of propagating plants in great variety and in great numbers, quickly growing them to saleable size and air shipping them to retailers throughout the world. Suburban garden centers, and, more recently, urban garden centers, grocery stores, and big-box retailers made all these plants readily available to the amateur and professional gardener, at more or less affordable prices. Thanks to the invention and widespread use of lightweight, inexpensive plastic containers and lightweight artificial soil mixes, hardy trees, shrubs, and herbaceous plants were now available for planting throughout most of the year outdoors. The planting season was greatly extended. A wide variety of tender, tropical plants are now available all year for planting outdoors in gardens in warm climates and for use outdoors in the north during the summer and indoors during the winter.

By the late 1960s, modernism seemed to have exhausted itself. Less seemed like less. Simplicity was no longer a relief from imposed complexity, but was suspect for lack of imagination or financial resources to do anything better. Postmodernism looked to the past, to context, and to the vernacular to refresh and inspire the present with mixed results for both landscape and architecture.

From the 1960s on, there was a boom throughout both Europe and America in formerly private, historically important gardens opening for visitation for an audience with an interest in historic landscapes and gardens. Many historic gardens were revamped in their presentation of what the garden had once really looked like based (sometimes) on the latest emerging historical scholarship. This growth in historic garden openings with its concomitant growth in garden visitation corresponded to a boom in low-cost airfare for both local and international travel from the 1980s on. For the first time, large numbers of garden enthusiasts with a wide range of income and education could actually visit, and experience firsthand, the classic gardens of the ages around the world. Exploration of these historic places informed the visiting public about plants and horticultural practices that had fallen out of vogue between the World Wars, but were now seen as fresh, even contemporary because of their novelty. The garden conservancy in the United States was started in 1989 to ensure that select, important private gardens did not disappear when their owners became elderly and could no longer keep them up. Private gardens across the country were available to the public for visitation on "Open Days" for a small donation to the conservancy. In the last fifty years in the United States, there have never been so many arboreta, botanic gardens, display gardens, historic gardens, art parks and sculpture gardens, and wild flower preserves open to the public, the visits to which are enthusiastically booked by individuals as well as gardening groups, as there are today.

There has, consequently, never been so much knowledge about plants, gardening, garden history, historical styles, and garden designers, as became available in the later twentieth century to any who were interested. At the turn of the last century, there were garden books and magazines that discussed both design and horticultural practice and nurseries with extensive illustrated mail-order catalogues. By the end of the twentieth century, all of those media and venues continued, but had been joined by flower shows in many major cities, international horticultural expositions (especially in Germany and the Netherlands), art and sculpture parks and gardens, experimental garden shows (Chaumont in France, and les Jardins de Metis in Quebec, Canada), hundreds of historic, formerly private estate gardens open to the public, garden tours (local, national, and international, sponsored by botanical gardens, arboreta or plant societies), radio and television gardening programs, gardening columns in national and local newspapers. In the last ten years of the twentieth century, the knowledge base exploded exponentially with the rise, and common use, of the personal computer and the Internet. Today, there are extensive Internet sites maintained by nurseries, universities, trade associations, individuals, horticultural and botanical institutions, historic gardens, and groups of professionals and amateurs focused on particular plants or gardening methods, techniques, or philosophy.

In the 1980s, amid all these historical gardens opening to visitors, and the plethora of garden publishing and postmodern philosophizing, there was also a tremendous growth in personal wealth generated in Europe by unifying the currency of the European Union under the euro, by the incorporation of new members from the countries that formerly made up the communist east, and in England by London becoming the financial hub of the continent (though the United Kingdom did not adopt the euro). In the 1990s, computer technology and the generation of Internet commerce brought tremendous wealth to many in those industries worldwide, especially in northern California and the San Francisco Bay area. The globalization of world business during the same period further added to the wealth available to spend on gardens and plants.

The taste of these new captains of global commerce, finance, and computer technology was mostly of a traditional bent. Historicist garden designs furnished with long ignored but very traditional planting techniques became once more de rigueur—topiary, espalier, aerial hedges, pollarding, even parterres and knot gardens. The vegetable garden became a *potager*, a luxurious assemblage of organically grown comestibles with flowers and vines trained not on trellises but on *tuteurs* (stakes). Villandry was rediscovered, and anglophone amateur gardeners had to learn a bit of French. Unfortunately, the visual composition of these paradisiacal cornucopias could be easily ruined by actually harvesting their produce. Such are the sacrifices made for art!

For some, this readily available surfeit of horticulture and garden knowledge, as surfeits are want to do, especially when combined with lots of readily available cash, has resulted in a malaise or ennui. Something dramatic must happen to awaken the senses and divert one from the realm of "same old; same old" or the "been there; done that." This awakening can be achieved by a jolt of the newest horticultural technology, aesthetic pyrotechnics, philosophical theory, or a delirious mix of each. In the early years of the twenty-first century, garden expositions have attempted to do just that, at Chaumont in France and les Jardins de Metis in Quebec, Canada, among others.

In France, Giles Clément conceived Le Jardin en Movement, literally the "Moving Garden."[7] Clément observed that if one does nothing in one's garden, nature will do it. Some plants will thrive. Some will disappear or move to a different location. Plants not originally present will appear. At Parc André Citroen, on a fallow patch of land in a former industrial wasteland, he installed such a garden by planting a mix of various kinds of plants and seeds— bamboos, grasses, shrubs, perennials, and so on. The plants, though managed, were mostly left to fend for, and rearrange, themselves. There were no paths laid out but rather the visitors could wander as they pleased, with "desire line" paths appearing over time as some routes became more heavily traveled than others. It seems Clément has done the heretofore impossible. He has reconciled the old bromide "nature abhors a garden" with the world's first "no maintenance garden."

In the United States, although vernacular gardens have not really inspired the talented amateur or professional garden designers the way that rural cottage gardens did Gertrude Jekyll or William Robinson, they may have inspired certain fine artists with a populist bent. The sputtering fireworks of Jeff Koon's horticultural tour de force called "Puppy" come immediately to mind. It was a huge, inane, but still quite amusing canine topiary of wax begonias, petunias, and impatiens. Even those who would not be caught dead with something as pedestrian as a wax begonia or petunia in their garden (in favor of more esoteric and recent imports from the tropics for "summer color"), much less something so horticulturally atavistic as topiary (much loved by the ancient Romans), found this three-dimensional extravaganza amusing.

However, it would have taken the Romans half a century to grow such a big vegetational version of a dog (or perhaps more appropriately a wolf) out of myrtle (*Myrtus communis*) or bay (*Laurus nobilis*), and even then it would still have been work-a-day garden green. It took Koons's gardeners, effected by a synthesis of current technology and horticulture in the form of some hybridized tropical annuals, artificial fertilizers in solution (NPK), automated irrigation system, and stainless steel armature in the form of a cartoon dog anatomy filled with interstitial rooting medium specially formulated for the job (all unknown to the otherwise technologically and horticulturally savvy Romans), little more than a growing season of a few months to realize. Not only that, it was not landlocked in someone's private garden but could be shipped for admiration around the world. Finally, "Puppy" was in glorious polychromatic color thanks to the annuals, and stayed in color all summer, thanks again to the annuals as well as thanks to the automated irrigation and fertilizer system. Could this be the apotheosis of the garish colors, artificial forms, and labor-intensive garden displays so railed against by William Robinson at the beginning of the century? It appears that the twentieth century has come in a complete circle.

By the 1990s, postmodernism was dead, and modern as a style was revived in both garden design and landscape. Ian McHarg and Earth Day were relevant again as concerns about global warming, depletion and conservation of natural resources, and sustainable design became quite topical. Implications for planting design are many.

What are the newest garden styles and planting designs invented at the end of the twentieth century? Perhaps they are not gardens in the traditional sense that we use the term. Perhaps environmental agriculture or "technology style" is a better term for the arrangement of plantings designed to remediate sanitary and polluted runoff from the land and settlements. *Bioremediation* is the term used to describe the removal, depletion, or neutralization of poisons on a polluted site or of sanitary waste by means of plant material absorbing toxins. As more polluted industrial sites within cities are recycled for housing, workplaces, and parks, bioremediation will increase in importance and sophistication.

Gardens in the technology style might also be rain gardens and green roof plantings designed to catch, hold, and delay storm water runoff so it can recharge the groundwater. In France, a variation on the vine-covered wall was invented by botanist Patrick Blanc, who has perfected the technique of growing lush, hardy plantings on the vertical surfaces of building like the Musée Branly. This technique uses acrylic felt on which the plants roots grow stapled to rigid polyvinyl chloride, the waterproof layer at the building wall. Water and nutrients are supplied by a drip irrigation system. Green walls, like green roofs, can provide thermal insulation, acoustical dampening of sound, habitat for small animals and insects, air purification through the transpiration of the plants, and reduction in ambient air temperatures. These newer designs for planting, while perhaps being in the same functional planting camp as the reforestation and erosion control plantings from years ago, have their own intrinsic aesthetic and beauty.

In the past, sensible gardening was usually based on horticultural compatibility with the site—climate, soil, light, water. Now the selection of plants may be getting more complicated. On top of those basic four elements, the choice or selection of plants to grow has started to be predicated on selection for those that will grow without requiring undo amounts (or any) supplemental irrigation water, chemical fertilizer, and pesticides, as well as plants that will not escape and displace native species, or cross with native species producing invasive hybrids, or whose tissues will not poison native wildlife and insects.

The commonplace advice about using native plants that earlier gardeners would have counseled to address so many aesthetic and environmental problems may no longer apply. The use of native plants in a world of rapidly changing climate is problematic, in that plants, as well as other living organisms, cannot change their biology or location to conform to a region's new climate as fast as the climate in some regions of the globe seems to be changing. What is native to such new situations in a region, when that climatic situation never happened there before (or at least not for tens of thousands or millions of years)?

There is also nonsensible gardening, as there has been throughout the ages and which will likely continue on into the future. This is expressed in the efforts of determined and willful gardeners to meet the challenge of growing what they want in spite of obstacles. Aesthetic and horticultural goals are met by subduing the site through great effort and expense of technology and engineering or by sacrificing plants for short-term display, all the while winning the accolades of the crowd for such determined success. In the seventeenth century, Louis XIV's flower gardens at the Grand Trianon at Versailles could be in bloom all winter by replacing the frosty plants with fresh ones from the "stove house," the orange trees saved by temporary glasshouses built around them.[8] What horticultural caprice is comparable today—trying to grow beautiful lawns anywhere else than Ireland perhaps? Will the sophisticated scientific techniques of mutagensis and genetic engineering produce new ornamental plants with flower color or forms unknown to nature, with hardiness to withstand drought, heat, or cold that could be the salvation of the gardener in a rapidly changing environment? The term *Franken-flower* has already appeared in the popular press.

The twentieth century was *the* golden age of gardens and horticulture for the greatest numbers of people ever. The use of plants in the twentieth-century gardens and landscapes engendered large debates that revolved around issues of garden style (historical, formal, versus naturalistic), planting in beds (masses of one sort of plant) versus borders (planting a variety of plants mixed together), and whether those plants should be native (local germ plasm versus that from nearby or the region), exotic, heirloom or the latest creation of the hybridizers' art and science. The spread of interest in organic gardening was aided by the slow-food movement originating in Italy, growth in interest in conservation, sustainable design, and issues of climate change, these latter concerns appearing toward the end of the century. How science and technology as well as aesthetics and philosophy will frame the debates about planting design and plant choices in the twenty-first century is another story altogether.

CHAPTER FOUR

Use and Reception

UDO WEILACHER

Current landscape architecture, and this is by no means new, is developing in an area of conflict between nature and culture. It forms gardens and parks as dynamic spacious arrangements, vivid spaces, natural habitats that normally reflect the particularly current view of the world, its social ideal of environment and leisure, as well as the contemporary attitude to life. Spaces formed by landscape architecture do not primarily strive to appear attractive but claim to be used by human beings who come from various cultural backgrounds and who want to have the use of gardens and parks with different expectations and demands. Especially in designing public outside spaces, which, in contrast to private gardens that have only to fulfill the individual desire of a single client, landscape architects are regularly confronted with the often seemingly insoluble challenge of accommodating the most different types of user and their specific needs.

For landscape architects and their clients the completion and ceremonial opening of a new garden or park are among the most exciting moments of their professional careers. That special moment not only shows whether what the sketch on the plan promised can be actually realized, but it also reveals the first reactions of curious visitors that quickly form a public response and in its turn, therefore, being either an encouraging or depressing prediction of the future chances of development for the new open space. There are no patent remedies for popular landscape architects, not even for the provision of the famous adventure and amusing parks of our time, which are, however, deliberately not examined in this text. The most favored public parks especially are sometimes victims of their own popularity, whenever too-frequent use gnaws at their substance. Success and failure and aversion and acceptance are sometimes bound tightly together; normally, it will be years or even decades before the project, promisingly delivered to its public, succeeds in enriching the life of its users. What follows are some selected examples of these histories of success and failure of European gardens and parks in the twentieth century, considered in their developing historical contexts.

For the development of parks as a space of public use, the French Revolution was of decisive importance.[1] Europeans' attitude toward parks that exclusively had been feudal and aristocratic preserves underwent change, not least owing to the growing influence and self-confidence of the middle classes. Christian Cay Laurenz Hirschfeld, a professor of philosophy and garden theoretician from Kiel, played a considerable part in the circulation of the new idea of a usable public park and propagated as early as 1785 in the fifth volume of his *Theorie der Gartenkunst* the installation of public parks: "Public gardens should be regarded, according to sound principles of the authorities, as a necessity for any city dweller. They refresh him after the day's exertions not only through pleasant visions and sensations but also, by luring him to nature's stage, they subtly draw him away from ignoble and costly urban pastimes and accustom him gradually to inexpensive pleasures, to a gentler kind of sociability, a communicative and affable way of being . . . Here, unimpeded, everyone attains the rights to rejoice in nature."[2] This program directed at an enlightened bourgeoisie remained virtually unchanged as model far beyond the end of the nineteenth century, and it clearly shows the social usefulness people originally saw in public gardens. Public use in today's sense was certainly at that time not discussed and nearly 200 years passed until the public could actually enjoy the unlimited occupation of green lawns.

The birth hour of public parks in Germany[3] at the end of the eighteenth century is marked by the English Garden in Munich. To this day, it belongs among the most famous public parks in the country and was the first that was destined from its very inception for the public. Resulting from a decree by Elector Karl Theodor, the arrangement was originally for it to be used at the same time by the military as exercise fields and by the general public, but in the year of revolution, 1789, this dual use was no longer opportune. Therefore, the military was sent for its exercises to the nearby floodplain, and the garden was given to the inhabitants of the city. From 1804 onward, the German garden artist and court garden designer, Friedrich Ludwig von Sckell, was responsible for its design. Previously, he had gained important experiences in the homeland of the English garden and tried to give more space for usage to the middle-class individual in Munich. "In his memorandum, which combined aesthetic demands and public consumption in a rare degree, von Sckell assumes a social humanitarian point of view and draws upon some basic observations about the formal properties of garden types. A public garden in the sense of an English Garden ought to be a compromise between a park and the pomp of a baronial garden; its meaning lies in the movement and recreation of business, convivial acquaintance and access by all classes. It ought to be moral and educational, and belong to the most important art installations of a humane and sage government."[4]

On the occasion of the 200-year-festivities in 1989, 3 million visitors were counted in the English Garden in Munich during fourteen days. Why the large 370-hectare public park still counts among the most famous in Germany is obvious: with its spacious meadows, picturesquely set groves, *bosques*, lakes, and brooks alongside ample paths and staged perspectives, it represents the ideal of an open bucolic landscape that has been anchored in the viewer's mind for centuries. The public compares today's modern parks with this one and judges them by this role model. Furthermore, the unlimited use and the recreation in nature in the middle of Munich still play, according to today's visitors, an important role. But after the foundation of the English Garden, it took a period of one-and-a-half centuries and several attempts of garden reforms to allow a completely free usage of the park's lawn. "Keep off the grass" was the motto in the English Garden in Munich still at the beginning of the 1970s, and park attendants saw to its strict adherence, until students' and people's initiatives became strongly involved with the usage of the place. Jogging, games on the grass, cycling, taking the dog for a walk, having a picnic, and even skinny-dipping are not only allowed but are immensely popular in the English Garden today.

The same landscape artistic formula for success, based on the combination of ideal landscape ideas and free usability in the middle of a dense, urban space, is the basis of the nearly equal-size Central Park in New York, and this does not seem to be accidental. Andrew Jackson Downing, an American landscape architect, editor of the magazine *Horticulturist*, and prominent promoter of the park, visited the English Garden in Munich during his trip through Europe in 1848 and later wrote about the English Garden that it was a piece of practical democracy which was also appropriate for the United States of America. The bringing into being of the Central Park from 1858 onward under the artistic control of Frederick Law Olmsted marks an important change in the development of parks between the first and the second half of the nineteenth century because this was the first time that social and political concerns were the moving factors for the design of a park. The vast public popularity which the Central Park and its creative offspring all over the world enjoy today does not have to be stated, as witness Buttes Chaumont or Bois de Boulogne in Paris, the central park in Vienna or the Amsterdam Bos near Amsterdam. It is always the free usability and the harmonic, natural landscape picture of the large public parks in the middle of an urban environment that are esteemed by visitors.

By the end of the nineteenth century, the growth of public lawns could not keep pace with the fast, industrially influenced growth of many European towns. Daniel Gottlob Moritz Schreber, orthopedist and educationist from Leipzig, advocated in 1843 the installation of playgrounds for children, which his friend Ernst Hauschild began to realize. In 1864, he founded the Schreberverein zur Förderung der Jugendpflege, des Familienlebens, der Volkserziehung und Volksgesundung (Schreber Association for the Advancement of Youth Care, Family Life, Public Education and Public Health), an organization that called for the provision of space for children's playgrounds and later became a program for installing family gardens all over Germany. "Schreber gardens" promoted not only health care but also assured food in large European industrial towns. Especially during the two World Wars, the Schreber gardens, in England known as "allotments," fulfilled these two basic functions. The importance of Schreber gardens, called community garden in the United States and Canada, has decreased because of the agricultural mass production of fruits and vegetables during the last decades, and they have developed more and more into valuable private garden paradises for townspeople who want to fulfill their desire of an own garden. Because of their oftentimes rigid regulations for cultivation, conservative arrangements, and design, Schreber gardens were regarded as an expression of narrow-mindedness for a long time, but this image is changing in many places.

In public discussions about open space planning policies in Germany, aspects of its usage became prominent at the end of the nineteenth century, and a key figure in the development of functional public parks in towns between 1890 and 1925 was the garden architect Friedrich August (Fritz) Encke. He was one of those garden reformers who had a clear vision of use of public gardens: "Whenever the municipal park is a rendezvous of the wealthy inhabitants and is visited on Sundays by working class families for the sights and not for recreation, the park serves its purpose. For that larger amount of people it serves primarily as aesthetic education rather than for their health, which is [nonetheless] very important for elderly and sick people and for young children. It is hygienically clean whenever it is not over-crowded. Now look at the parks in those crowded towns that do not have wooded and picturesque surrounding! Dense masses of people move on dusty paths and look wistfully at the shady grass and groups of trees. Is it not logical to invite those people to make themselves comfortable on the grass?"[5]

The public park as a Volkspark, a people's park useable by everybody, gained many dedicated sympathizers in Germany, and led to the foundation of the German Public Park Union (Deutscher Volksparkbund) in 1913. The development of a large 180-hectare municipal park in Hamburg marks the climax of urban garden policy in Germany. This Hanseatic city, growing fast as a result of economic expansion during the industrialization at the beginning of the twentieth century, increasingly saw the urgent need of a large, open municipal park to serve public health as well as to make the laborers and citizens take pride in their factories and town. In this respect, the Central Park in New York served as a role model. In 1920, Fritz Schumacher, at that time building director for the city of Hamburg, designed a park for comfortable inhabitation which clearly corresponded to the new ideas of usage: " 'To inhabit' means 'to take possession of', for the different kinds of occupation that are related to the term 'recreation'. . . . games, sport, camping, rowing, paddling, riding, dancing, furthermore enjoying music—art—flowers, physical pleasures—those are what such a park has to offer."[6]

In contrast to scenically designed municipal parks whose aesthetic was formed by the management of free, organically rolling forms, Fritz Schumacher planned Hamburg's municipal park as a clear, architectonically designed park that keeps its scenic elements in the peripheral areas. The central axis of the park linked the main restaurant building and the 39-meter-high water tower, crossing the large central public field. Various meadows, flowers and shrubberies, sandboxes, wading pools, air and sunbaths, gymnastic fields and hammock areas as well as a symmetric water basin were the dominant elements of the municipal park. A survey made in 1974[7] shows that it is still popular, with more than 10,000 visitors coming into the park every day. Especially popular, not least with young people, is the large, open fairground for play activities, offering at the same time the feeling of a refreshing and open-minded expanse. Although the area is not scenically laid out in "natural" style, the majority of the people said that they came to seek "nature" there. For 40 percent of the surveyed persons, promenading was at the center of their activities, whereas about 30 percent spent their time in sun bathing, relaxing, sitting, reading, and lazing about. Apparently, the percentage of sporting activities is today more prominent than thirty years ago, and that imposes heavy stress on parts of the grass. But the basically high esteem of Hamburg's citizens for their municipal park remains the same.

The material distress of people after the World War I, the economic recession and the resulting drive for frugality had an effect on the principles of private garden design in Europe. Creative claims took a backseat in favor of functional criteria. The garden not only served for self-supply but also for mental recovery and health care. In Germany, Leberecht Migge, first of all, made a name for himself as an important garden reformer with his claims for the democratization of garden art.[8] He rejected the representative public gardens of the nineteenth century in favor of usable gardens that served self-supply and public health. The future garden, according to Migge, could only be a fruit and vegetable garden. His concept for the enlargement of garden culture was based on experiences gained in England, where he discovered the "hundred thousand" laborers' gardens, which contributed to the abatement of social misery.[9] Migge wrote about the use of public gardens: "People have to be drawn to it in the working week and on holidays—we do not need any Sunday gardens! The people have to throng in a people's park, otherwise it does not make any sense. It is a real people's park when its meadows are like

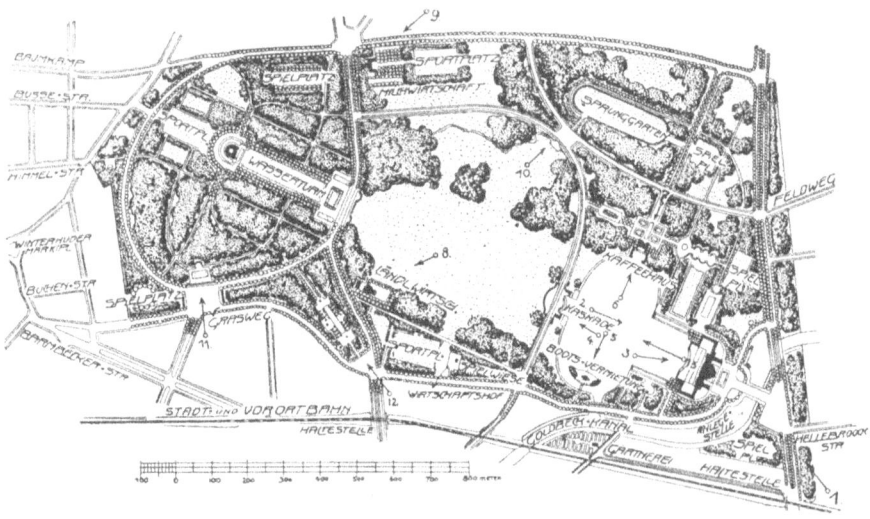

FIGURE 4.1: Fritz Schumacher, Stadtpark Hamburg, Germany: layout plan of one of the most famous Volksparks in Germany, built in the 1920s.
Source: M. L. Gothein, *Geschichte Der Gartenkunst* (Jena, Germany: E. Diederichs, 1926), 459.

green velvet and invite the people to lie down and to dance, whose waters are created for swimming, the beach for wading."[10]

In the middle of the 1920s, a return to scenically designed gardens under the name of "domestic garden style" could be noticed in private gardens, and the urge for openness and freedom prevailed more and more, not least supported by modernity's claim for the annulment of traditionally compact cities. "Free living, light, air, opening," according to Sigfried Giedion in *Befreites Wohnen*, was the new maxim in the architecture of the 1920s.[11] As with habitations, proposed by Giedion on the occasion of the Second Congrès International d'Architecture Moderne (CIAM) in 1929 in Frankfurt, gardens were also to be freed from strict architectural forms and transferred into a scenic shape. The crystalline building forms of modernity should be embedded in a garden's deliberately built pictures of nature. Furthermore, the view into the garden as an event of room enlargement, stated by Guido Harbers, municipal building director in Munich, in his influential book *Der Wohngarten* (The Domestic Garden) played a prominent role in garden design.[12] In this sense, the living space outside as an enlargement of the building was indeed separated from the landscape by open ground, but the view beyond the border of the garden was sought in order to experience and "take possession of the whole landscape."[13]

With fascism, the development of Germany's large municipal parks ended because its propaganda strategies needed clear areas for large-scale assemblies and rallies. Private gardens, on the other hand, became important shelters for many people to hide from total uniformity and were partly even hideaways from persecution. The exhibition of German Garden Culture in Hanover in 1933, the Reichsgartenschauen (National Horticultural Shows) in Dresden in 1936, in Essen in 1938, and in Stuttgart in 1939 served to consolidate fascism, its traditional-conservative design principles finding favor with the people. After the beginning of the war, landscape and garden, the so-called Wehrlandschaften (landscapes for military defence), had to fulfill new defense strategic purposes: "The open barrier towards the East has to be sealed by small *landwehrs*, if harvests and climate, human beings, people and peoples are to be preserved. The last compartment is the garden, namely the place of German people's soul."[14] Many forward-looking protagonists of the German municipal park movement who did not associate with this worldview were displaced during the years or banned from their profession. For this reason, reform tendencies were disrupted, and the traditional, romantic-naturalistic, homeland style gained popularity in horticulture, which lasted until the postwar period.

Postwar Germany was still in ruins when in 1950 the first Federal Horticultural Show was initiated to introduce improvements of horticultural and displays of garden art and, furthermore, to rebuild some of the destroyed garden and park areas, along with the reconstruction of cities. In Hanover, where large parts of the city were still in ruins, the first steps were made around the town hall, an area branded by bomb craters: "[t]he first federal garden show in 1951 resembled its predecessors by following the example of middle-class promenade parks, filled with conservative art just like a sitting room. The 'garden show model' subsequently contributed to undermining the reintroduction of people's Parks."[15] The conserved public park in Hanover that still survives, was geared to plant display and contemplation, and clearly demonstrates that the innovative idea of the democratic Volkspark (people's park) had been abandoned. Nevertheless this park is still very popular today. Neither in public nor in private gardens and parks did the modern design strategies, linked to prewar social reforms, continue; instead, it was a purely formal, casual style of traditional domestic gardens that was estimated as especially suitable in the postwar period.

In 1949, Otto Valentien, a renowned garden architect from Stuttgart, wrote in the preface to his book *Neue Gärten* (New Gardens): "[w]henever we escape from the destruction of our towns and the moral confusion of human communities to enter nature, we happily learn that not everything in life has become dark and questionable. Here, the wells of beauty and goodness flow, unreachable and unchangeable by human unrest. Let us care for the beauty in our gardens, let us feel the breath of nature during the contact with plants and renew the measures for human nature which were lost in the horrors of the past." In the domestic gardens of the early 1950s, usability was once again emphasized,[16] because during the war people had experienced how important the supply functions of gardens were. "The garden of our time will be related to the cottage garden. But the different claims of townspeople, the unchanging value of the garden as an enlargement of the home will give it a special expression," Valentien stated and recommended the creation of vegetable gardens and the planting of fruit trees as well as the installation of access and horticulture yards to optimize the efficiency of the garden.[17]

The 5th Congress of the International Federation of Landscape Architects (IFLA), which took place at the Swiss Federal Institute of Technology (ETH) in Zurich in 1956, was trend setting for the development of European garden architecture. Following the leitmotif "Die Landschaft im Leben unserer Zeit" (Landscape in the Life of Our Time), more than 250 participants and guests from twenty-five countries discussed topics like urban landscape, industrial landscape, agricultural landscape, and natural landscape. The discussion of the first two topics in particular signaled emerging changes in the postwar society, a challenge to which landscape architecture needed to respond. This became clear one year later in 1957 at the Internationale Bauausstellung (International Building Exhibition) "Interbau" held in Berlin: the rebuilding of the Hansaviertel, an urban district in the middle of Berlin, nearly completely destroyed by air raids in 1943, was seen as an extraordinary challenge, where for the first time, a modern downtown quarter could be built according to the principles of the Athens Charter. The efficacy of the new ideal of a functionally divided, open, green city had been demonstrated.

In this respect, the designed landscape played a dominant role and fulfilled several functions. On one hand, it formed large spaces in which single buildings by internationally renowned architects like Oscar Niemeyer, Alvar Aalto, Walter Gropius, Le Corbusier, and others were integrated as freestanding elements in a nearly sculptural manner. Light, air, and sun could flood the new quarters freely and provide ideal hygienic conditions for the town. Furthermore, the landscape flowed beneath and around buildings, provided backgrounds, and separated the different quarters with green areas. Leading European garden architects were responsible for the planning of the landscape, among them Walter Rossow and Herta Hammerbacher from Berlin, Wilhelm Hübotter from Hanover, Edvard Jacobsen from Karlstad, Gustav Lüttge from Hamburg, Hermann Mattern from Kassel, René Pechère from Brussels, Pietro Porcinai from Florence, Carl Theodor Sørensen from Copenhagen, Otto Valentien from Stuttgart, and Ernst Cramer form Zurich. In the construction of the Hansaviertel in Berlin, the desire to renovate the postwar society, which played an important role in the Europe of the 1950s, was very clear, yet already by the end of that decade, doubts arouse about the dogmatic functionalism that also influenced horticultural design.

G|59, the First Swiss Horticultural Show in Zurich in 1959, became a special display of new design ideas in garden architecture. This show was conceived as an "industrial show of domestic horticulture"[18] and showed a colorful variety of current garden imagery, all of which was to appeal to visitors' fancy. But the Swiss garden architect Ernst Cramer realized a very abstract contribution, the Garten des Poeten (Poet's Garden). It consisted of four grass pyramids, a grass cone, and a flat water basin with a modern steel sculpture. In his enthusiasm for abstract arts and modern architecture, the garden architect had developed during the 1950s a new design language in garden architecture that was marked by abstract geometric forms, limited plant variety, and unreserved use of concrete, the modern building material. The avant-garde Poet's Garden was furthermore evidence of a sensible intuition to use sculptural topography and modern notions of space. In contrast to the exhibitions in the rest of the horticultural show, this geometric composition did not aim at imitating nature but presented nature in a modern, abstract design language. Garden enthusiasts, annoyed by the radical experiment that openly violated all the traditions and the audience, voiced their total lack of understanding: "Is it really possible to talk about these mounds covered with sparse grass and the area of water entirely without plants as a garden?"[19] was the rhetorical question of a technical journalist in 1959, expressing what the majority of the visitors thought. Only architects and fine artists recognized in that garden the birth of a new era of garden architecture, which did more than simply obey functional demands and traditional approaches.[20]

Fast economic, technical, and social development characterized Central Europe during the 1960s. A noteworthy building boom and the rapid spread of television were some external features of that development. "The quick reconstruction of towns destroyed by the war often lacked the opportunity for thorough research and reflection, but that period was followed by the time of critical assessment," noted the mayor in Hamburg in 1963. "The physical and psychological well being of the people has to be in the centre of all considerations and measures. The result is the call for municipal green and recreation areas."[21] The demand for functionally organized open-space planning, subordinated to urban planning in respect of design, increased rapidly during the 1960s. At the same time, concern grew that the aesthetic and ecological qualities of the landscape would suffer from the uncontrolled growth of residential, recreation and commercial areas, the extension of traffic routes and the network of infrastructure as well as the pitiless exploitation of natural resources.[22] "People were not only be expelled from paradise, but even today there are forces which make life hard," the landscape architect Aloys Bernatzky wrote in 1963. "A new flood is coming, not consisting of water but of concrete, iron and plate; a deluge with toxic vapours from factories that befoul the air; with wastewater that changes rivers into cesspits; a flood of asphalt and stone."[23]

Garden designers and their audiences reacted differently to what were becoming much more complex contexts in which to work. One party developed a critical, adversary attitude toward civilization and urbanization and still saw the garden as a shelter for the more densely populated world, cut by the rapid traffic.[24] They were committed to the design of idyllic domestic gardens as spaces for recreation and leisure because human beings need "options for recreation, for a return to the sources of life, to nature from which [men and women] came [. . .]. To a nature whose last, modified remains in today's towns and settlements are their gardens. Nature and garden devotion cannot be separated!"[25] Other garden architects were inspired by the zeitgeist and developed the garden as a type of art that followed and served modernity, time, and architecture. Hermann Mattern added, "The garden as an artistic interpretation of nature-orientated, living things leads not only to practical activities. The sensibilities to colour and form as well as the abilities to observe and to combine are also activated."[26]

Outstanding avant-garde garden creations came into being in close connection with architecture and could be seen during the International Horticultural Show in Hamburg in 1963 (IGA 63) or the International Horticultural Show in Vienna in 1964 (WIG 64). Intensified international contacts and exchange, travel abroad and regular information about global developments in the subject directed attention to aesthetic, expressive Scandinavian, Brazilian, American or Japanese garden architects, to the work of Carl Theodor Sørensen, Roberto Burle Marx, James C. Rose, Akiro Sato, or Ernst Cramer. This process enriched the garden architectural design repertoire in the gardens of Europe, but did not have an impact on the common focus on the functional green in the cities.

Toward the end of the 1960s, when the limits of growth were felt all over the world, bellicose conflicts dominated the daily news and a consumer society became visibly satiated, a process of dissolution, accelerated by the vehement protests of young people, shook the environment-forming disciplines. For those garden architects who interpreted their handcraft as an individualistic practice with emphasis on the work of art (the opus), these would be hard times. The former notion of a work of art was questioned. "There was a disagreement about this concept of the work. It almost seemed as though the representatives of the older generation were still hankering after the Platonic idea of well-designed things ('education through form'), while the younger generation was asking about the rules that govern how the work comes into being." To quote Lucius Burckhardt: "We have lingered over appearance for too long. The product is like an iceberg."[27] Participatory, sociologically oriented planning permeated the profession, as human beings' needs were pushed into the centre of garden and landscape design. At the same time, the worldwide threat to the natural environment became more and more apparent for the designers and their audience.

Already in the late 1960s, in the light of global ecological disasters, a vehement paradigm shift began in landscape architecture and planning that eclipsed artificial-creative garden design and endorsed a demand for scientifically planned and determined landscape architecture. The ideological way in which the term "nature" was interpreted in the 1970s can be read in the book by the Swiss author Urs Schwarz *Der Naturgarten* (The Natural Garden), especially under the chapter heading "Die neue Einstellung" (The new attitude). This book had been a recommended trendsetter for a long time. "Above all, we change our attitude towards nature. We call foreign plants weeds, native ones leaves. And then we quietly start to make room for the leaves by removing the weeds. [. . .] We must start to judge people's attitude towards nature by the appearance of their private grounds."[28] Following the book *Design with Nature*, by Ian MacHarg, published in the United States in 1969, it was fashionable to abandon a landscape architectural aesthetic in environmental planning and garden design in favor of ecology because, anyway, nature was deemed the better designer and provided its own secure, aesthetic basis for parks and gardens. Also, Louis Le Roy became famous as the "wild gardener" who did not agree with the creative outgrowths of urban planners who, in his eyes, only made the environment more dreary, smooth, cold, and neat. Instead, he tried to build structures that were preferably multifaceted.

The paradigm shift in the 1970s brought considerable developments in landscape ecology as a multidisciplinary planning science with a necessarily stronger consideration of the problems of environmental and nature protection, and these penetrated deeply into garden design. Some of them primarily took the form of nature reservations and landscape architectural projects that identified with forceful reactions against the allegedly cold orthogonality of classic modernism. Similar reactions were apparent, too, in fashion and product design. "Living in the Green" was the slogan of the successful Federal Horticultural Show in Mannheim in 1975, and terms like local *recreation*, *inner-city greening*, and *environmental amelioration* played an important role during the planning and design period of the show in the large, 41-hectare Luisenpark in Mannheim. Interestingly, the segment originally planned at the end of the nineteenth century and rebuilt in 1975 belongs stylistically to the scenically designed municipal parks in the tradition of the English Garden in Munich, famous for their large leisure fields, playgrounds, lakes, and flowerbeds.

The display of new contents within a stylistically old, 1970s ideal garden and landscape was made excessively clear during the Second Swiss Horticultural Show, "Grün 80" (Green 80), in Basel. During this internationally acknowledged exhibition, garden architects, architects, fine artists, sociologists, ecologists, and gardeners created an Arcadian-looking, 46-hectare piece of landscape that reflected vividly the new, ideologically driven environmental thinking, with a fluid modeling of earth, nature and flower gardens, lakes and biotopes, and areas with spontaneous vegetation and vegetable patches. "In a

FIGURE 4.2: Wagenfeld, Leipacher und Boyer, Luisenpark Mannheim, Germany. This municipal park was planned at the end of the nineteenth century and rebuilt in 1975 in the popular English landscape garden style, considered "near-naturalistic" for the Federal Horticultural Show in Mannheim in 1975. Photo: Raul Lieberwirth.

time of reflection—the upheaval from quantitative to qualitative growth—the search [was on] for new values and aims."[29] The show offered a discussion panel for problems regarding human beings and nature and furthermore make a concrete contribution to the amelioration of quality of life. The fact that the nearly life-sized sculpture of an herbivorous dinosaur became the emblem of the show was symptomatic.

The effort of alerting the audience to future ecological problems almost always ended in the presentation of rather sketchy pictures of gardens and cliché images of nature. A majority of the horticultural show visitors expected bloomy attractions and, according to the statement by the management of Grün 80, did not want be reminded of lurking ecological disasters. A press report stated, "In the section 'Topic Earth', activists spread out the complete catalogue of miseries which we human beings bring to our earth in front of the feet of a dinosaur. It demonstrated what we do to our towns, mountains, lakes, streets, food, plants and animals, and how the environment is defiled, exploited and destroyed. It must be the work of a whole army of teachers, gesturing with their index fingers, otherwise the yawning boredom of this show cannot be explained."[30]

In landscape architecture new, exemplary projects in near-naturalistic design styles à la Grün 80, like the 32-hectare large park around the university Zurich Irchel built in 1986 caused yearlong debates on the correct relation between ecology and design. "In the history of garden art the garden of past centuries embodied the people's wish to differentiate those spaces from random growth and to rule and shape nature there. [. . .] Under the present circumstances it seems a logical consequence that we accept and even create 'natural wilderness' in urban areas" was how the landscape architects of the park in Zurich explained it in 1986.[31] Today, the public park in Zurich Irchel, scenically designed and built according to ecological principles, is used intensively and is experienced as a piece of authentic nature, although it is a completely artificial installation. Here, as with the earlier, famous landscape parks, an ideal image of nature is transported into the city, and this image apparently corresponds to the deep-seated ideas of nature in the mind of its observers.

FIGURE 4.3: Atelier Stern und Partner, Irchel Park Zürich, Switzerland. The Irchel Park in Zurich—here under construction—was built according to ecological principles on top of an underground parking garage and is still considered to be a "piece of nature" in the city.
Source: Direktion der öffentlichen Bauten des Kantons Zürich, *Universität Zürich-Irchel. Parkanlagen* (Zurich: Direktion der öffentlichen Bauten, Hochbauamt, 1986), 2.

Critical voices arose in the profession during the 1980s directed against the single-edged eco-design, which concentrated on an imitation of nature regardless of any real environmental conditions. Among these, the most famous voices were those of the landscape architect Dieter Kienast[32] from Zurich and the planning sociologist Lucius Burckhardt from Basel:

> The crisis of our garden art is that it loses its importance by the recurrent use of nearly every possible motive and the mixing of contradictory elements. In the end, the observer gets empty formulas. Such use of language without attending to the content is called academism. One example: during the federal horticultural show in Mannheim, an artificial pool could be seen whose banks were furnished with natural elements—low embedded sand with pebbles merged into a botanically interesting planting with small-leaf generic groups like iris, etc. In the pool there was the jetting nozzle of a strong fountain whose artificial spurt of water belied the design of the pool. This false use of markers seems symptomatic of the state of our garden art.[33]

Burckhardt cited gardens designed by the French landscape architect Bernard Lassus, Scottish artist Ian Hamilton Finlay, and the Dutch gardener Louis Le Roy as examples of design that restored horticultural art to new importance and brought more sensibility to the responses of users, but these arguments did not change the popularity of those stereotypical garden pictures spread during the horticultural shows.

Displeased with the always identical, ecologically, socially, and functionally correct but mostly aesthetically feeble efforts of horticultural planning during the 1970s, an artificial-experimental occupation of landscape and nature moved to center stage during the 1980s, and this led to a certain pluralism of style in landscape architecture that continued into the following decades. Important stimuli in respect of the release from mere ecological or functional attitudes towards landscape architecture came mainly from France, Spain, the Netherlands, and the United States. Landscape architects with an artistic background, like Bernard Lassus or the young American Martha Schwartz, developed radically artistic design concepts that took their inspiration from tendencies in pop art, minimal art, or vernacular styles. Gardens, parks, and plazas now aimed less exclusively at "saving nature" than at artistic invention, which could stimulate the living environment. One part of the public was enthused by these new tendencies, while others rejected the artistic ambitions in garden design as unnatural and un-ecological.

Fine artists, as well, discovered gardens and parks as new fields for experiment and addressed a larger audience, which liked to disappear from their dull everyday life into colorful worlds of the imagination. The Tarot Garden of the artist Niki de Saint Phalle in Italy belongs to the most famous gardens of that kind. Everyone who visits the stone pit near Garavicchio in Tuscany nowadays cannot avoid the vital expressiveness of this special location and feels the intense presence of the rebellious artist, who had been working in her paradise garden for a decade from 1979 and sporadically even lived there. Always interested in metaphysical dimensions of life, Niki de Saint Phalle chose the twenty-two pictures of the Big Arcanum, namely, the trump cards in tarot, as a leitmotif for the most famous work of her life. The twenty-two cards of destiny were transformed into extremely expressive, colorful sculptures of different dimensions and complexity, which were self-confidently placed in Macchia, the hilly *garrigue* landscape. Apart from some small interferences in the topography, the installation of intricate, interweaving paths and the creation of sight lines, horticultural design in any specific sense was not the central aim, because the artist aimed primarily at creating a colorful garden of sculptures. The spontaneous Mediterranean vegetation, the natural state, therefore, forms the more or less neutral ground on which the figurines are placed. On the lines of the free game with Tarot cards, the paths between the sculptures, edged with holly oaks, pubescent oak, olive trees, and other Mediterranean bushes, are arbitrary; the path of destiny, in a figurative sense, is therefore neither distinctly specified nor compulsively predictable. Since May 1998, the garden has been open to the public, and its mysterious colorful light reflections, glimpsed from afar, draws countless visitors every year from the coastal plain into the forested hilly landscape, a world layered with complex meaning. Those do not have to be deciphered in minute detail, according to their creator: "If our life is a card game, we are born without knowing the rules. However, we have to get along with the cards in our hands. Is Tarot only a card game or is there a philosophy behind it?"[34]

The professional audience sometimes regards these kinds of garden skeptically as the pure self-staging of popular art, ignoring the true qualities of nature, garden, and landscape. "People who confine themselves the purely aesthetic works often appear to be fighting something of a rearguard action," Dieter Kienast critically commented on the artistic tendencies in landscape architecture in 1996. "Perhaps they make it a bit too easy for themselves. [. . .] However, it's my opinion that we work in public space and what we plan shapes parts of people's everyday life. There's a difference between working in a gallery, in the Nevada desert or a private garden and working in a public park. Here we have a

FIGURE 4.4: Niki de Saint-Phallle, Tarot Garden, Garavicchio, Italy. In the Tarot garden at the centre of the Emperor—the fourth Tarot card—is a courtyard with twenty-two differently designed columns surrounding two olive trees. Photo: Udo Weilacher.

responsibility, which we can't simply avoid by references to freedom of the artist [. . .]."[35] But laypersons are fascinated by the sensible vitality and the individualistic hand of a designer in the Tarot garden and meet these sculptures with the same curiosity and astonishment that has been elicited for centuries by the Sacro Bosco in Bormazo, designed by Vicino Orsini in the later sixteenth century.

It was not only in Europe that fundamental changes in industrial production released more and more urban, often toxic wasteland that demanded new design concepts and approaches. Some of the most interesting parks, transforming industrial sites into gardens, were designed as early as 1970. One example is the famous Gas Works Park in Seattle by Richard Haag. This 9-hectare leisure site has been considered the first attempt in landscape architecture to consciously incorporate industrial relics into the design of a classic municipal park. In was installed on the area of a former, extremely environmentally damaged refinery, which was shut down in 1956. In 1969, Richard Haag became aware of the site and was greatly taken with the morbid charm, the ghostly spirit of the location. He lobbied for the preservation of the industrial ruins, at that time primarily, as he stressed, for aesthetic reasons. An open municipal park, following the classic ideal of the Central Park was to be installed on the area. "We promoted a concept of a new kind of people's park that paid homage to our rich Olmsted legacy, complementing it through contrast. [. . .] The concept of crafting a park featuring 'forgotten works' greatly appealed to the younger generation while older generations lobbied for the stereotypical image of 'park' such as English pastoralism."[36] The landscape architect was able to preserve most of the industrial ruins, and therefore, the largest part of the area was cleansed of the traces of industrial use. Today, Gas Works Park presents itself as a simply designed but very popular leisure park in a classic style within which an industrial monument is enthroned. The monument is fascinating in its aesthetic appearance but mysterious in its meaning because, for security reasons, the ruins had to be fenced off, with "no trespassing" signs, like those that once guarded the grass in the public parks at the beginning of the twentieth century.

In the 1980s, owing to structural changes in industrial society, there was considerable increase in the redevelopment of new parks on disused industrial areas. Some of the most famous examples include remodeled industrial quarters in English towns like Manchester or Sheffield, the park on the Hafeninsel (Harbour Island) in Saarbrücken designed by the German landscape architects Latz + Partner in 1982, the Parisian Parc de la Villette by Bernard Tschumi in 1983, the Parc del Clot in Barcelona by Dani Freixes and Vincente Miranda in 1985, and the Duisburg-Nord Landscape Park, also by Latz + Partner, in 1989. All of these designers, following the example of Lucius Burckhardt, aim to re-create important and generally accessible locations with an expressive design language. In doing so, Duisburg-Nord has been among the internationally renowned parks for a long time and met a positive response with the people because the newly interpreted industrial landscape not only endorses ideas of local identity but also allows free public use.[37]

Landscape architects like Peter Latz are not motivated by nostalgia, but, as the art historian Irma Noseda from Zurich once put it, as "culture followers"[38] for whom the creative integration of present industrial relicts and spontaneous vegetation is decisive. However, not only were destroyed environments to be redeveloped but users of these sites were thereby to gain fresh perspectives on industrial and landscape history. After the traces of history and layers of invisible meaning have been discovered in a site, the next step was to make them visible and imbue them with new meanings partly enriched by elements of garden art history or fine arts. New parks followed the very popular principles of people's parks (Volkspark) in the 1920s, regarding possibilities of use, and have from the beginning been open full-time and are accessible and usable by everybody. In most cases, that idea has enjoyed a resounding public success.

FIGURE 4.5: Latz + Partner, Hafeninsel Saarbrücken, Germany. The Hafeninsel park was constructed on the basis of the syntactical design, weaving together four structural Layers: the access network with linked sightlines, the public gardens, the rubble flora, and the traces of industrial use. Photo: Udo Weilacher.

During 1985 and 1986, Parc del Clot in Barcelona, for example, was installed on the former factory ground of the Spanish railway company Red Nacional de los Ferrocarriles Espanoles (Renfe), to plans by the architects Dani Freixes and Vincente Miranda. The large, 27,000-square-meter area of the national Spanish railway company had been in use until the middle of the twentieth century, situated in the suburban part of a village in the northeast of the town, which then was quickly overtaken by urban growth. Today, part of the preserved façade, similar to romantic ruins in classical landscape gardens, surrounds the northern edge of the park, and in addition, an imposing industrial chimney reminds the visitors of the former scenery with its ruins of red brick. The industrial chimney highlights the northeastern edge of the park as a clearly visible landmark. A high catwalk and a long pergola gantry lead diagonally from the opposite side of the park and the adjoining housing to the chimney stack and thereby cross the two differently handled parts of the park: the parklike northern area, the plaza-like southern part. The northern part of the area is to be read as a quotation of landscape, accentuated by a large, naturalistically shaped grass hill. The architecturally designed southern part of the park, consisting of a deep plaza surrounded by two large stairways, presents a formal contrast.

From the very beginning, the small quarter park appealed to visitors, who appreciated the multifaceted usage of the different park and plaza areas where nearly every age can find its preferred spot. The fascination of the people for "their" park is also due to the memorably composed pictures, which, especially in the park area, are connected to romantic impressions taken from English landscape gardens. Picturesque ruins embedded in an Arcadian ambiance were a preferred motif already in the eighteenth century, and their many associations with today's remnants of the industrial age, along with the successful reinterpretation and remodeling of the factory ruins, have made the park a much-cited example of landscape architecture. The hybrid character that promises both the ideal of beautiful nature as a representation of "landscape" in town and a comfortable, rich venue of urban life answers to a multiplicity of options for twenty-first-century park users.

Many traditional types of use and reception of private gardens are preserved in the twentieth century, especially for recreational and leisure functions, and these have become more and more important as a protected enclave

FIGURE 4.6: Dani Freixes and Vicente Miranda, Parc del Clot, Barcelona, Spain. Compelling axial pathways structure this popular municipal park and help people to find their bearings. Photo: Udo Weilacher.

amid the increasing density of urban housing and the acceleration of everyday life. Under the title of "Sehnsucht nach dem Paradies," Dieter Kienast wrote at the beginning of the 1990s, "[t]he garden is the last luxury of our time because it claims what has become rare and valuable in our society: time, devotion and space. It is the representative of nature in which spirit, knowledge and handicraft are used in a careful handling of a world and its microcosm, the garden. Changed social moral concepts lead to a garden renaissance."[39] Landscape architecture also interested itself in urging the observation of slow transformations that involved a creative handling of the dynamic forces of plant growth, and a search for a forward-looking concern with the heterogeneity of the non-designed. But the public at large does not immediately greet such experiments in positive terms.

An experimental postuse project whose conception begins to gain public acceptance is the Oerliker Park in Zurich, realized by Zulauf, Seippel and Schweingruber between 1999 and 2001. Benign comments characterize as demure this new, nearly 2-hectare neighborhood park surrounded by new buildings, while those who want picturesque groves on a green carpet of grass in a municipal park call it an impertinence. Approximately 1,000 small trees, planted on scarcely two hectares of mostly gravel ground, stand tightly and in strict order next to each other like trees in a tree nursery; most of them provide no shade. The first drafts of the landscape architects' design showed a different version of "living next to the park": computer-rendered pictures promised a green, shady hall of trees like those in Parisian municipal gardens or the enchanting Petersplatz in Basel. But the people using the park and those living next to it had hoped for a quicker realization of those attractive promises and saw no reason why it was not possible. Indeed, a whole branch of garden industry lives on the sale of instant-green images of nature, "instant green" with a guarantee of swift growth that becomes more and more desirable and demanded as it is purveyed by perfect computer renderings. In reality, ideal garden and landscape pictures, as far as they ever turned out the way they were planned, cannot be achieved in an accelerated fashion and later be conserved for eternity (point-and-click), for the simple reason that the only lasting characteristics of nature are its constant changing, growth and momentariness.

The Oerliker Park is a controversial "betwixt and between" in which constant process rather than finished product is at the center. Grave planning problems characterized the birth of the park, and it has had to survive on an asphalt layer that covers contaminated industrial floors, which could not be removed. Furthermore, it was not clear at the beginning of the project how quickly the new housing quarter was going to be erected to animate the area, so that what

FIGURE 4.7: Zulauf, Seippel und Schweingruber, Oerliker Park, Zurich, Switzerland. The simple lighting elements in the Oerliker Park still loom too large between the young ash trees. This imbalance will change only with time. Photo: Rita Weilacher.

might transpire would a park never surrounded by city dwellings. In the face of these imponderables, Zulauf, Seippel, and Schweingruber developed an astonishingly simple project idea: young trees, planted in patterns close to each other, were to grow over the years independent of their surroundings into a dense tree capacity which then could be used for various activities like a large green hall. To install such a tree hall quickly and immediately ready for use would have contradicted the landscape architects' process-oriented planning approach. Instead of expensive grown trees, 800 young, small ash trees, from differing tree nurseries in Switzerland and the Netherlands, Italy and Germany, were planted. In addition, 200 sweet gum trees, river birch, wild cherry, and princess trees contribute an accent of bloom. Instead of the grass that so many people hankered after, there is a water-bound surface under most of the trees. This park is a promise. "It is like giving someone a bulb or a plant-pot with a hyacinth shoot in it," the landscape architect explains. "I am not forcing anyone to do without the finished product, but I am giving them something that can grow, that they can grow with. So I'm not depriving them of the finished picture, but offering them the experience of seeing the picture emerging."[40] Zurich was convinced of the idea of a park that would grow, and residents who moved earlier than expected into the new quarter, will witness more or less patiently how a green canopy comes to stretch itself. Until 2025, the dense tree population will be thinned out bit by bit by forestry methods. Trees that die at an early stage will not be replaced. Listening to the landscape architects, the image of the grown park leaps quickly into one's mind, but "perhaps it won't happen," as Rainer Zulauf remarks, and what then? "The Oerliker Park is one of four such features, just part of a jigsaw puzzle offering a special kind of experience"[41]: an open-ended natural process that the residents only partly understand because ideal images of hundred-year-old usable municipal parks are fixed in their minds, and this new park is so alien to those visions.

Of newly designed open spaces, people expect not only a broad perception of public needs but also some unmistakable, individual character that contributes a clear identity to the new quarter and offers them sensible opportunities. If a garden or a park is to symbolize the longing for paradise, it must be able to move people. Now that landscape architecture has freed itself from the fetters of planning on a purely rational basis and insists self-confidently on its own creative role, it is allowed to arouse emotions again. And that is good, because the key point about people identifying with their environment is finding emotional access to it. Anyone who can build up positive emotional links with the built or natural environment is also more likely to take responsibility for that environment. Such links between emotion and identification with a place were neglected during the technology-driven decades, which led to the merely functional, scientifically justified landscape planning losing contact with its clients. Who wants to know if the percentage of green space in the neighborhood meets planning requirements if these open spaces do not move us and/or have any qualitative attraction?

Commitment to emotional quality goes hand in hand with a gradual acceptance of subjectivity. Emotionality and subjectivity may well not fit in with social conventions that demand scientifically based value standards, pellucid criteria of evaluation, preferring to treat people like a predictable factor that has to be held in check. Especially in designing today's living spaces, landscape architects have to accept more and more the fact of their own subjectivity and its integration into the planning process, rather than see it as merely arbitrary. The mystery of the special expressiveness that pertains to famous gardens, parks, and plazas derives, as we enter them, from our recognition in their design of something special, individual, and very subjective. Yet, for a landscape architect to express his or her own imagination in public projects is regarded as an elitist approach, and it carries risks in a society dominated by design approaches that are driven by objective justifications, scientifically established, and voted for by the majority. The high personal risk of failure—always self-evident in the fine arts—is in successful cases rewarded by its work whose edges, in a figurative sense, remain sharp and personal, not honed by the common denominator of collective option. These works are not only palpable to observers, but also substantially address them. Evidence for the quality of these "edgy" projects is in many cases the fact that they were by no means uncontroversial; emotion and subjectivity do not leave people cold.

CHAPTER FIVE

Meaning

JOHN DIXON HUNT

[I]n a garden which demands the exercise of the imagination no limits can be placed to the free play of association
—Malcolm Kelsall

All merges toward the presentation of the unspoken meanings of the earth.
—Walt Whitman

[T]he object never coincides with the meaning
—Edmund Husserl[1]

Of all the topics to be considered in a cultural history of modern gardening, none is probably so affected by its cultural contexts as is its "meaning." Although gardens, a traditional not to say atavistic medium, may continue to use the same basic materials and even deploy them in largely unchanging ways, how people respond and interpret those elements will change according to culture, time, and place. Nowadays the range of persons engaged in garden making has hugely increased, as has the spectrum of those who, while they may not create gardens themselves, nevertheless love to visit historical parks and gardens where they will be provided with interpretations and versions of original design intention; there are also those who haunt that uniquely modern institution, the garden center, and watch planting programs on television, or simply frequent public parks to engage in a full repertoire of social and recreational pursuits. Furthermore, the kind of spaces designated as gardens (beer gardens, community gardens, gardens of memory, and so on), has also been expanded, along with the increasing number of designed landscapes (parks, plazas, parkways) that eschew gardenist labels and motifs but are still considered as extended versions of the phenomenon called garden.[2] All of this increased garden activity has inevitably attracted critics and commentators, journalists and academics, who purvey their opinions and their theories. In addition, designers themselves have added their reflections, sometimes in attempts to establish landscape architecture as a cutting-edge, theoretical modern enterprise; these contributions have created a rather new genre of self-absorbed, often arcane, ruminations on professional activity.

Combined with this explosion in the number of persons involved in one fashion or another with gardens and gardening is another, frequently attested modern fact: that a corpus of shared ideas and beliefs is nowadays hard if not impossible to define, although it is familiar from earlier history or at least is claimed by historians to have existed. Neither designers of gardens nor their visitorship (there being no good word to define those who frequent and respond to gardens) can nowadays count on sharing any ideas and concepts (including earlier cultural references, legends, symbols, and myths).[3] However, this is not, if at all, a twentieth-century problem; it is simply one, inherited from at least the early nineteenth century, that is now exacerbated by the sheer quantity of gardens and gardenists inhabiting the modern world.

That it is not a late-twentieth-century issue may be gauged by reflecting briefly on eighteenth-century landscape gardens and garden taste.[4] Modern critics have sought to interpret places like Castle Howard, Stowe, Stourhead, or the Désert de Retz as being designed to articulate a series of meanings, narratives, or iconographical programs that were embraced by their original designers/owners. These commentaries have largely been predicated on what were or are supposed to have been the originators' intentions and on the articulation of meanings that if not declared or implied within the gardens themselves could readily be supported by a study of contemporary texts, paintings, and other cultural phenomena, which (it is assumed) structured and sustained both "authorial" intentions and others' receptions of them.[5] Now it is undoubtedly true that iconographical programs characterized some Renaissance gardens—Castello, Villa Lante, Villa d'Este—as well as later creations like Versailles and that these assumptions about a garden's meaning continued to hold sway into the eighteenth century,[6] but it is not certain that these inscribed or inserted meanings would have been "readable" even by their contemporary visitors. By the end of the eighteenth century, it is clear that there were wide discrepancies in how visitors responded to, understood, and interpreted designed landscapes.

During the eighteenth century, there occurred a quite radical change, engineered by a complex concatenation of events, in how all works of art came to be constructed and construed. Throughout the Renaissance and into the Enlightenment, works of art (including what we now call landscape architecture) were deemed to have content; this content was largely accessible, or assumed to be accessible, to an educated public and thus was accordingly taken to be a public content.[7] Meaning as we now understand it was not an issue, because the content was in itself unproblematic; what attracted attention and criticism was the rhetorical manner in which that content was communicated. But by the end of the eighteenth century, we witness a considerable change in how a work of art was considered (in retrospect, it was a quantum leap, though its actual process was inevitably gradual). As it concerned gardens, it was driven by a wider interest throughout the population (clearly the beginnings of our own twentieth-century situation), by the making of less and less "learned" gardens (for both economic and cultural reasons), by a growing interest in nondesigned landscapes that came to be seen as equally "visitable" and "knowable" as gardens had been, and above all by developments in psychology and notions of how the mind worked with their focus on an individual's privileged association of ideas.

All of these worked to bring into some prominence the issue of what and how a site might be said to have meaning. Authorial intentions and/or publicly shared ideas could certainly be identified in a given site, but just as crucially, any visitor's own ideas and emotions could be projected upon it. In short, the garden became the locale of a variety of possible, even contested, meanings, some of which were personal or even private responses, while others had a more general currency. As a consequence, those people interested in gardens and landscapes focused either on explaining meanings in specific sites or on trying to generalize the ways by which meanings could be understood. Some people continued to think that a public register of available, learned allusions and assumptions could still be viable.[8] Others were excited by the opportunities that gardens and landscapes offered for personal, private, even solipsist responses and associations; especially during the Romantic period, the individual's experience of a designed landscape would likely take center stage in any encounter, rather than be some studied or learned response to a meaning deemed to be inscribed in the site and perhaps available to others. And it is no accident that the examination (including the self-examination) of that personal experience has been deemed a true mark of modernity.

At the same time the arts, including the art of garden making, were being judged less for content enunciated by rhetorical or formal skills, as had been the case earlier, and more for their satisfaction of something called taste. Philosophers like the Third Earl of Shaftesbury and more journalistic writers like Joseph Addison and Richard Steele started to explain how people could cultivate their taste for different arts, but as the eighteenth century wore on, such guardians of "true taste" lost control of the process or rather they were themselves responsible for making its parameters ever more generous, not to say loose. For an increased insistence on personal values along with the diffusion of taste into different levels of society, especially merchant and trading classes, ensured that works of art came to be valued and judged in new ways. In particular, a fascination with form became paramount. We see this most strongly in the picturesque vogue and its pursuit of formal values for their own sake, without regard to content, and the judgment of forms and style was necessarily honed based on the acquisition of taste.

II

We live in that same world, now vastly augmented. It affects designers, those for whom gardens are laid out, and other "consumers" of gardens and designed landscapes. Meaning, like other aspects of cultural history reviewed in these volumes, now occupies an expanded field. So we have a considerable body of designed work that eschews meaning altogether both in its own performance and in the commentaries of its critics. What takes center stage therefore is a modernist concern with materials, with style, form, formal play, and—frequently—a concern for the programmatic frameworks within which the formal elements of a design comes into being.[9] Even when a formalist agenda is neither apparent nor the driving force of garden making, an interest in some meaning or narrative is no longer deemed essential. The considerable achievements of amateur gardeners may also be divided between those that take their lead from such professional thinking, mediated through countless magazines, newspaper columns, and garden shows, and those who insist, against the grain of popular taste, that their gardens are places where personal or even idiosyncratic imagery and meanings may be entertained. But there is also a small band of designers and critics who work hard to resuscitate different aspects of what is called meaning or narrative[10]: this is driven often by sheer boredom and frustration with the empty formalism of much modern design, but it is also the result of an increased awareness of the presence and substance of meaning and narrative in earlier gardens. The rise of garden history in the last half of the twentieth century, especially the scholarship that focused on the Italian Renaissance, French seventeenth-century, and so-called English landscape gardens, was engineered in large part by art historians and literary critics who were by training interested in meanings and their interpretation; one key effect of this garden history was to revive an interest in, demand for, and reinsertion of meaning among those who designed gardens and landscapes.

III

The design work of key figures to whom one looks for the true beginnings of modern garden art is conspicuously dedicated to form, whether or not they were exponents of a modernistic agenda: Gertrude Jekyll, William Robinson and the arts and crafts garden makers generally, such as those seen in Figures 3.1 through 3.4;[11] the modernist movement in France represented by the Exposition Internationale des Arts Décoratifs et Industriels Modernes in 1925;[12] the work of Fletcher Steele, Garrett Eckbo as shown in Figure 8.7, or Dan Kiley in the United States.[13] By form, I mean a primary concern with the shape and texture of materials, both plants and built elements. The continuing appeal of this formalism is eloquently demonstrated in many publications, like Jill Billington's *New Classic Gardens,* published by the Royal Horticultural Society of Great Britain in 2000. Many things are to be remarked about this collection of handsome photographs and design commentary; but the title's emphasis on "classic" reassures garden makers who are drawn to this book that a focus on shape, texture, and form has enjoyed a long tradition—it is indeed "classic"—but at the same time, it is not old-fashioned or fuddy-duddy—it is "new." The text never addresses anything that could be construed as meaning; its utmost stretch away from explication of formal design consists of passing references to design in other cultures (Japanese or Portuguese). Otherwise, any person drawn to this book as a resource for do-it-yourself (DIY) garden making would discover (as its dust jacket advises) all the "ingredients of modern formality" necessary to "reflect the tastes and lifestyles of gardeners in the twenty-first century."

Formal emphases may often, as there, sustain or imply some ideological agenda—a western American lifestyle, in Church's California gardens in the boom years after the World War II in Eckbo or the Englishness of Jekyll.[14] It also often sustains the celebration of locality or nationalism: a particularly conspicuous example of the invocation of formal means—plant palette and ecology above all—for political ends would be the manipulation of landscape architecture to sustain its racial agenda by the German National Socialists during the late 1920s and 1930s.[15] That particular and invidious example aside, formal concerns have often been innocent of declared ideological or even conceptual content and meanings, though they may always be shown to have implicitly harbored them, as in Jens Jensens's pleas for a scenery and formal repertoire that celebrated the American midwestern territories.

The extent of dedication to formal invention in both plan and on the ground is clear from the huge array of gardening books published during the course of modern garden, like those dedicated to the layout and maintenance of small gardens by Paul and André Vera, Fletcher Steele, Jean-Jacques Haffner, and Peter Shepheard, among others; they kept their focus strictly on the physical, not metaphysical, aspects of private gardening. So, too, in the last twenty or thirty years of the twentieth century have come many publications of both supremely sophisticated examples—a leading master in the field is Russell Page[16]—and a host of lesser talents. Books with titles like *Un jardin pour soi*, or *Reflections from a Garden*[17] address the gamut of formal layouts, sustained in most cases by a detailed and passionate horticultural enthusiasm. They explore the sensations and emotions of the gardener, but his or her involvement with the site's materials eliminates or marginalizes any concern with sustained associations and narrative. In the same way, the championing of nontraditional materials—Eckbo's aluminum garden as shown in Figure 8.7, Gabriel Guevrekian's faceted-glass globe, Robert Mallet-Stevens's concrete trees, or Steele's concrete grottoes and industrial railings at Naumkeag as shown in Figure 2.2—did not involve any sort of message beyond perhaps the promotion of modern materials.

But this formal commitment did not escape strong counterarguments, especially from professional landscape architects who attacked the dominance of design by a formal, historical vocabulary and syntax. Designers like Ian McHarg and James Corner have insisted on a series of frameworks within which design may be accomplished—sociopolitical programs and ecological constraints[18] being the most prominent—but the "lifestyle" agendas possible through design promoted by *Sunset* magazine, *Southern Living*, or *House Beautiful* can also be seen as having framed the formulation of actual sites. The exponents of such frameworks are not concerned with meaning so much as claiming some cultural relevance for their designs that might or might not be apparent in the finished product but that are essential to the production and professional justification of the work.

This professional invocation of the frameworks within which good design could be achieved has been most apparent in public parks and gardens. So it is perhaps not surprising that program has eclipsed meaning in designing public spaces throughout the twentieth century. When, in 1992, a symposium in Rotterdam debated precisely how "can designers restore lost meanings" to public parks, the result was little more than vague gestures—a call to give "meaning to what people think or what they feel about nature and the relationship between man, nature and culture"; the hope that designs would "provoke" people without recourse to "insider jokes" among architects; but in the final resort no agreement on what meanings were feasible or worthwhile, except to say that park users will "make their own interventions in space."[19] Even historical sites, like the renovated Bryant Park in New York, the Tuileries, or the Englische Garten in Munich, are largely used, one supposes, by people who make their own treaty with the space and its current significance for them. Otherwise, the competitions for new parks like Parc La Villette and Downsville Park, Toronto, were guided by an extensive set of parameters that had nothing to do with either formal stipulations or proposals of meaning. Descriptions of the ensuing designs were precisely that—descriptions of the proposed physical features and their response to various programmatic demands, as were most of the designs featured in the Museum of Modern Art exhibition and catalogue in 2005 (*Groundswell*).[20] Even a designer who cherishes the forms of abandoned industry—Rick Haag or Peter Latz—nevertheless bases his response to those "leftovers" on the new programs and functions to which they can be annexed, such as those shown in Figures 4.5 and 8.8. In none of these cases does the lack of explicit emphasis on meaning or forms result in designers actually eschewing formal vocabulary or in visitors to their sites not finding opportunities to invest them with meanings.[21]

    Whether preoccupied with forms or frameworks, many modern designers have been explicitly and implicitly concerned to register their place within the modernist movement, which is for many an obsessive dedication to professional status. Yet, gardens do not seem on the face of it to lend themselves like other arts to modernist strategies—plants, for example, have their own modus vivendi: gardens that borrowed forms from contemporary visual arts—cubist or biomorphic—had nonetheless to control plants or water into the requisite shapes through elements of the hardscape, since the morphology of the materials by themselves resisted such treatment. This concern for ensuring that garden makers were eligible for membership of the modernist arts pantheon produced some eloquent arguments about formal achievements; what it avoided was any insistence that meanings were to be inscribed and read in the built work, in part because such aspects were so clearly part of earlier designs and did not sort well with modernist ambitions. However, the professional literature of late twentieth and early twenty-first centuries has found alternative ways to ensure a conceptual freightage in designed work: this discourse (its term of choice) reflects on strategies of design, often far removed from implementation and

FIGURE 5.1: Bryant Park, New York City, as redesigned by the Olin Partnership. Courtesy of the designers.

reception of built sites, and frequently *post propter hoc* in its formulations. Yet, its theoretical pretensions seem a means of reclaiming some authority for meaning among designers.[22]

IV

So much modern garden activity takes place in the private realm that its role cannot be ignored: Peter Latz has written that "[a]mateur movements play an important role in garden culture. They formulate ideas of society in small and domestic gardens."[23] Beyond both the professional, institutionalized landscape architect and the firms that offer garden design are the thousands who visit garden centers, garden festivals, read horticultural magazines, and watch TV gardening shows. It is almost impossible to gauge the full extent and scope of this segment of contemporary society. Its cultural needs are hugely varied, as are both its economical and aesthetic resources and the opportunities available to satisfy its needs. The gamut of the sites that this swathe of the population lays out takes many forms and reveals many different intentions and meanings: even the household that covers its front yard with black plastic, with perhaps a birdbath jutting out of a hole at the center, is "saying" something about the unnecessary social obligation of maintaining a front garden. At one extreme, there is simply the anonymous front garden or backyard that can be nothing except dirt, raked gravel, or mown grass, or a collection of flowers, the simplest of materials and forms. Or the same space could be decorated with a whole range of items that either express or betray the inhabitant's fantasies, values, tastes, or practical needs: dwarfs, deer and other Hollywood dramatis personae, barbeque pit, sandbox, and climbing frame, greenhouse, tree house, lanterns, a small fountain recirculating its jet of water, a specimen tree (monkey puzzle or flowering cherry perhaps), crazy paving, and maybe even some piece of statuary from the garden centre or a "found" object from the municipal dump.[24]

Because these gardens are private and the result of individual resources and tastes, they seem generally to escape examination, and certainly, the impact of such vernacular design on professional or "posh" amateur work is minimal. Yet, there have been some remarkable creations, which reveal how gardens are an arena where people have found intense pleasure in giving expression to their imaginations, whether or not others would share their associations. Studies of African American yards have yielded some real insights into how their inhabitants express ideas and values even with limited resources, whereas more flamboyant creations like the Watts Towers in Los Angeles and the Maison Picassiette in Chartres are reminders of the potential in "gardens" for extreme forms of self-expression.[25] Bernard Lassus, a professional French designer, was an early student of what he called "paysagistes-habitants," the inhabitant-designers, who use their gardens both to tell stories and to enjoy scenarios drawn from a rich vein of popular imagery; he is a rare case of a professional who has chosen to take such traditions seriously.[26]

V

Vernacular inventions, often dismissed for flying in the face of conventional good taste, are created in many cases as responses to the ubiquity of bland

FIGURE 5.2: An image from Bernard Lassus, *Jardins Imaginaires. Les Paysagistes-Habitants* (Paris: Presses de la Conniassance, 1977).

garden layouts, whether professional or amateur, municipal park or private dwelling. But some deliberately challenge other social taboos, reasserting their own identity and condition, like the Dungerness garden of Derek Jarman.[27] But there are professional designers, too, who resist bland formalism: some by exploiting a richer formal vocabulary and syntax like Peter Walker and others by the deployment of a much more radical palette of colors, shapes, materials, and indeed cultural references, like Ken Smith. Maratha Schwartz in particular employs a deliberately startling repertoire of colors, materials, and allusions as a means of stimulating visitors to acknowledge some, not always palatable, aspects of our environment. Her task, she writes, is to imbue landscapes with "form, meaning and beauty," but in drawing on both cultural and art historical traditions she has fundamentally challenged conventional notions of gardens and offered some radical and sustainable versions for the twenty-first century by practicing a particularly modernist strategy of focusing on the medium of her own craft.[28]

Other very distinctive gardens and landscapes have confronted both the formal blandness and the empty significance of modern parkland and suburban yard. This can occur more easily within the private realm. Charles Jencks's Garden of Cosmic Speculation is an elaborate, studied attempt to use a garden to illustrate a series of scientific theories of the physical world (chaos theory, fractals, DNA, black holes); the forms themselves are often wonderfully lively and inventive, but their intended significances more likely to be available to those who have had them explained by Jencks's own book. Also in Scotland, Ian Hamilton Finlay's Little Sparta has infinitely extended the possibilities of garden meanings, through a gradually unfolding series of inventions that solicit reflections upon the relation of modern gardens to earlier traditions of political gardening and to a cluster of themes that on the face of it have nothing to do with our usually limited notions of the garden: war, the sea, the French Revolution. Finlay also extended his reach into the public domain, with similar interventions (though more restricted in scope than at Little Sparta) in urban sites, public parks, and sculpture collections.[29]

And the public domain has benefited enormously from the efforts of those landscape architects willing to tackle how deliberately constructed meanings can augment the experience of sites, in particular provoking in their visitors a more acute appreciation of the place itself. Paolo Bürgi at the Cardada site above Lugano deliberately recalls for its visitors the ancient geological activity in the nearby mountains, the *longue durée* of evolutionary time. Christophe Girot's Invalidenpark in Berlin takes a different tack, sidestepping any direct representation of the enormous cultural freightage of the site near the former Berlin Wall, but still revealing to those who are willing to meditate on its forms the integration of new open space into a once fractured and distracted city.[30]

VI

The last decade of the twentieth century saw a flurry of writings[31] that sought to address meaning in this extraordinarily diverse corpus of gardens and landscapes. The burst of commentary may be explained in part by the emergence of garden history as a (more or less) respectable academic subject that, along with the enormous popular investment in garden making, has stimulated conceptual commentary, to which cultural critics (including geographers and anthropologists) have contributed. So, too, have philosophers, who are professionally engaged with matters of cognition and what one of them calls a garden's "cognitive component."[32] Another acknowledges the "rather dumpy, amorphous" concept of meaning,[33] before partitioning it generously but so expansively that the garden itself, his declared topic, disappears under the weight of discursive phrasing.

These theoretical maneuverings around the topic of garden meaning have been nothing if not agile, suggesting the urgency and difficulty of the issue,

FIGURE 5.3: The Geological Observatory, Cardada, above Lugano, designed by Paolo Bürgi. Photo: John Dixon Hunt.

FIGURE 5.4: Invalidenpark, Berlin, designed by Christophe Girot. Photo: Udo Weilacher.

with authors trying to determine whether gardens mean and what kinds of meanings, if any, can or could exist in them or through them—that very prepositional awkwardness is perhaps crucial. Does meaning inhabit sites? Is it found, or is it put there? Do the materials of a site become the medium by which to communicate meanings that are then deemed to be inherent in that place? Can sites communicate meanings that exist elsewhere? If so, what language, vocabulary, syntax are we then talking about? Do designers insert specific triggers and prompts that will encourage visitors to take up meanings and narratives, or are visitors in effect left to their own devices?

Robert Riley argues that gardens are a "special expression" of the multitude of meanings people have discerned in the natural world.[34] But the difficulty is that it is not gardens but we ourselves who "express" what we take to be that relationship. That is the crux. There are indeed innumerable philosophical positions to be taken up about our relationship with nature, and Riley sets out some of these interestingly, but it seems wrong to declare that the garden "is an intense and particular *statement*" of them (my italics).[35] Nor is a garden really a "carrier" of meaning, for rather it is we who carry our ideas into the garden and attach them to its various physical elements that have been installed there, drawing also perhaps on what its designer or owner may have said (more statements) and on what we have discovered about a given cultural context (statements again), as well as prompted (into words) by the site itself.

Such a process by which we are encouraged and directed in our responses occurs in certain types of gardens, like cemeteries and botanical gardens, though for different reasons. Woodland Cemetery in Stockholm by virtue both of its function as crematorium and burial ground, its explicit and implicit symbolism, and its palpable references to northern cultures contains and promotes meanings, versions and elements of which pertain in other cemeteries.[36] Botanical gardens group, label, and classify their collections, generally educating their visitors to elicit certain meanings from the site—about plant characteristics, geographical provenance, cultivation history, and so on. It is we, even in these gardens, that "attempt to establish meaning" by responding to and then articulating the forms that a garden gives to nature and culture. Perhaps we relish gardens so much because they provide us with this apparently endless opportunity.

Another designer who has addressed the topic is Marc Treib, who sensibly challenges Riley as to whether it is "really possible to build into landscape architecture a semantic dimension."[37] But he still launches his own taxonomy of meanings or what he generally calls "significance" (though without explaining what difference he sees between these terms). His five miscellaneous landscape approaches, each of which is said to embody significance or meaningful concepts, are however those that "the makers or their critics" identify. What this does is shift the burden of attribution of meaning away from the garden to those who discourse about it before or after it is built (this incidentally addresses how a garden's "audience" is involved in creating meaning,[38] though Treib does not pursue this). It also recognizes implicitly the eclectic nature of possible designs and their receptions in the modern world. But Treib's heart is clearly not in the meaning business, and his writings on modern gardens elsewhere are almost wholly driven by formal analyses.[39] Too skeptical to follow Riley's path, yet unable to reject it either, he succumbs to a somewhat nervous facetiousness about the whole issue.[40] Furthermore his limitation of meaning to something that has a largely discursive (i.e., verbal) character denies him the chance to explore what he touches upon only briefly, the *pleasure* of the garden, or what I want (below) to term its "experience".

Yet, a third designer, Laurie Olin, is, by contrast, nothing if not serious and passionate: "Landscapes do have meaning."[41] He is also well versed in and has written about landscape history, and he recognizes that in the past gardens have derived social and artistic strength from "thematic content." He stigmatizes "an anti-intellectual and anti-historical bias" in modern criticism that plays down "allegorical, iconographical, symbolic, emblematic" content; and he isolates a cluster of "subject matter[s] or meanings" that "are being dealt with in the most thoughtful landscape designs today."[42] Yet, these ideas of order, of nature, of social organization ("the arrangement of cities"), and of the landscape medium and its traditions are what we extrapolate from our responsible engagement with built work; good design certainly encourages and even authorizes such reflections, but to discern these themes and meanings is the responsibility of "our imagination."[43] He usefully terms these "synthetic or 'invented' meanings." Olin has also explained some of his own designs as exemplifying a mode of representation,[44] whereby the site instigates associations, memories, and ideas: clearly, that is feasible if the site itself contains the "authorization" to do so, prompting associations for which we then take responsibility.

One aspect of these adjudications of meaning is a general reluctance to ask what tasks landscape architecture seeks to accomplish. An answer might usefully rely upon drawing an analogy between different ambitions and achievements in landscape architecture and the different registers of prose and poetry. Prose has a wide range of uses, but we value it primarily because it does the job it sets out to accomplish more or less straightforwardly. We may appreciate it not only for its own sake, its elegance, and its liveliness, but it is also primarily valued for its transparency as a medium appropriate for executing the task in hand. Similarly, there is a strong "prosaic" element to much landscape architecture, when it accepts to do a particular job. We recognize, for example, well graveled paths as meaning that proposes we walk along them; seats or benches mean one is to sit on them, and if under trees, we appreciate their shady placement; a scattering of individual chairs means a different mode of behavior; lighting and trash bins also have their readily understood function; fountains cool the atmosphere in hot urban squares and drown out adjacent noise. In all of these emphatically pragmatic moves, the garden designer may use good or bad prose, and we value and judge it for how it performs what we expect of it: badly laid or too large gravel is hard to walk on; seats that do not support the back will not do. All the while, we may certainly respond at the same time to a beautifully crafted functional item.

Poetry is always a more intense and concentrated language than prose (I am *not* talking here of verse per se). Owen Barfield called its effect a "felt change of consciousness," a "shift from an habitual sense of the world into an unfamiliar one."[45] Poetry is often invoked when the writer wishes to move beyond enunciation of the physical or positivist, to draw out significances that are not clear on the face of things, to make connections which the quotidian world has ruptured, or to explore spiritual or emotional states and experiences, in all of which metaphor and symbol can play a more integrated and resonant part. It is also used when there is no precise objective ("poetry makes nothing happen," wrote W. H. Auden).[46]

It can be argued that garden design has equally been able to seize this potential to move beyond the merely (if exemplary) practical world, even coining new forms by which to extend our consciousness. Flower gardens of exceptional skill and beauty—Robinson's own terraces and rich gestures of large plants at Gravetye Manor—or formal moves of great precision and confidence—Russell Page's Villa Silvio Pellico, outside Turin, would be cases in point. So do Tschumi's grid of bright red follies at Parc La Villette evince an energy and aplomb over and above occasional functional uses (a café, a crèche); they chart the terrain, parcel out its spaces for us to gauge them, and so extend our response to the park. Other exemplary instances can readily be adduced: Lassus's invention of a former village submerged in the flooding of a lake for the new town of L'Isle d'Abeaux, his opening up of the quarries at Crazannes,[47] and his most recent work for COLAS;[48] Rick Haag's revisioning of the abandoned gasworks infrastructure at Seattle as an industrial picturesque ruin or Peter Latz's similar but much more poetic exploitation of the remains of blast furnaces and disused bunkers at Duisburg-Nord for a whole series of athletic, horticultural, and cultural events that amaze one largely by finding them so utterly and plausibly at home in that scarred landscape;[49] Finlay's admonitions to the passerby to stop, read inscriptions, and reevaluate assumptions about nature's violence or the relevance of ships to inland gardens.[50] All these and other plausible cases involve a design language (its forms, materials, relationships) that transcends, even while in most cases conscientiously observing, what we may call its prose obligations. Sometimes a site does rely on actual words that bring its own more conventional poetry to the scene—Finlay is paradigmatic here with his many inscriptions, but so are the names on the Vietnam Memorial, that minimalist but utterly moving garden inserted like a gash in the ground of the Washington Mall, where the words have an impact beyond their documentary, prose record.

Now the poetry of gardens, rather than their prose, demands our imaginative response. As such it opens up what Malcolm Kelsall, in the motto quoted at the head of this chapter, terms the "free play of association";[51] thus, we may in certain gardens be engaged in responding imaginatively and in freely associating, and this, essentially, is where the notion of meaning comes into play. We need, therefore, a more nuanced notion of meaning, because—to start with—there are crucial, if subtle, differences between saying that something is meaningful and that there is meaning in something.

VII

Meaning has all the marks of a truly modern preoccupation, not least in its polysemic character.[52] It also, as we have seen, tends to be verbally driven. The availability and use of the term *meaning* in English (but interestingly without synonyms in other modern languages) has tended to focus upon the need to articulate meanings *in words*. The French formation that comes closest to the English—*vouloir dire*—specifies (as the English does not) the intention or willingness to speak: "il veut dire que . . . " (literally, "he wants to say that . . . ") promises a willed response or an intention as well as some clarifying speech. But it is also clear that the English meaning is not a useful, universal term for all designed sites. Nevertheless, the very fact that they are designed tends to elicit from their visitors a sense—immediate and sharply registered or subtle and barely perceptible—that these places are somehow different from others and that accordingly they seem to elicit from us a different reaction or response. Our experience of them registers them as somehow significant. Let us then posit a triad of attention to gardens and landscapes—experience, significance, and meaning (*proprement dit*).

Experience is simply, but importantly, whatever a visitor feels, notices, smells, touches, hears, and so on. Given, too, that experience has been—rightly I think—claimed as a truly modern obsession or concern,[53] and one, too, that we have some skills for accessing and even discussing, this mode of response to a garden is as crucial as it is basic. It is also thoroughly democratic. Everybody experiences something in a garden or a park, and these days more people have the opportunity to seek out such experiences. Even a negative reaction ("it's an awful or boring place") is triggered by experience. No visitor to a garden, I therefore suggest, has a *zero* experience, so when Riley argues that gardens are not a "locus of meaning . . . in modern America,"[54] he cannot be saying that people there do not have experiences in gardens; he may be right that they do not extrapolate further from their experiences. There are obviously innumerable elements that contribute to this kind of experience, but one crucial instance has to be the recognition and appreciation of the materials and forms unique to gardens in different times and places: plants, shrubs and trees along with their varied forms and composition. None of these "mean" in the larger sense, yet they are (we might say) meaningful.

Significance needs and draws upon experience, and it does so in order to make visitors aware of something that is more than just a habitual or unconscious response to their surroundings. It may be the recognition that the experience of a garden is itself significant, extraordinary, or even unique, because it is unlike other experiences or unlike experiences in other gardens. We register a splendid and clever organization of plants along a herbaceous border or their arrangement in some more tightly controlled pattern of planting. We notice something special, striking, attention catching, calming, and invigorating as we confront a statue or read the mottos on a sundial. Designers, of course, can exploit this by providing items that trigger such responses. Our primary or preliminary experience is thus acknowledged as significant and is consciously or intuitively transformed into a more acute state of mind, an awareness. Whereas it is always possible to explain the significance of one's experience in a garden, that heightened experience is important in and of itself, before and perhaps beyond words. Significance (which does have parallels in other languages) may turn out, in fact, to be a much more flexible word in connection with gardens and landscape architecture; it is also a term that bridges a crucial gap between direct experience of a place and our retrospective enunciation of its meaning.

But there will be occasions when we feel the need to spell out that heightened experience and to give it formal expression, for which it is probably necessary to retain the word, meaning. This takes the awareness of significance and certainly of experience to a different level, which (in keeping with the fullest connotations of the word *meaning* itself) implies a conscious, deliberate acknowledgement of something about the garden that needs to be articulated. So we ask, "What did that garden—or that moment in the garden—mean to me, to its creators?" The fastidiously maintained cone of sand at the Ginkakuji (Silver Pavilion) in Kyoto is experienced for itself, in contrast to the neighboring greenery, before we see its affinity with Mount Fuji and again perhaps before we register its significance as a much-revered Japanese landmark and talk about that meaning. Other, now western examples—Lawrence Halprin's abstraction of mountain cascades in the Ira Fountain, Portland Oregon, or Buontalenti's rocky giant at Pratolino in Tuscany—though they use different formal means, strike us first as physical forms, then as significant by virtue of references they make to a larger world—in Halprin's case, his own acknowledgment of inspiration from the Cascades, and at Pratolino, a reminder of the geographical locality of this Medici property. But it is also essential to realize that such meanings will be articulated in terms *other than those of the site and its components*. Elements of the site will, of course, prompt, trigger, or simply endorse our recourse to some formulated meaning, but they cannot provide the vehicle of its articulation; Mount Fuji, the Oregon mountains, and the Apennines are not in those places where they are recalled. Thus, meaning is unlikely to be coexistent in space or time with the place where it transpires. For instance, when we ask someone, "Tell me what you meant," we expect an explicit statement of some intention, but this statement is usually in words that are not coextensive with whatever action or previous speech we need to have elucidated. It is important to accept that the garden itself cannot provide the means, the medium by which to articulate what it means to us, and that it comes from outside the garden, from what we bring into it. It is also what I have elsewhere called its "afterlife," and it is a crucial element of much garden experience.[55]

Two further aspects of this triad of experience, significance and meaning, need to be acknowledged. First, they need not, indeed often are not, distinct or sequential activities, though T. S. Eliot's lament in *Four Quartets* that "[w]e had the experience but missed the meaning" points to how these responses may be disjunct. Secondly, there are a series of recognizable formats for exploring and expressing meanings, including critical assessments—verbal and visual representations of gardens (covered elsewhere in this volume). Although meaning does not invariably have to be put into words, it does require a certain deliberation or consciousness, which also marks a whole corpus of visual representations of gardens that find their own modes of discovering and declaring garden experience, significance, and even meaning.[56] So it is crucial to remember that graphic, visual, painted images can be statements or expressions of meaning. Geoffrey James's wide-angle photographs of parks and gardens allow us to see different routes, dual axes, two perspectives at once, which are an ingredient in our overall response to the place. But this level of garden experience, its afterlife when meaning is given prominence, is intended to be sharable and available for others to grasp, which is why we show our photographs or write about what gardens mean, and it may retrospectively extend our own sense of significance. But it is something *added* to the site because it is brought in to aid and augment our original experience of its phemonena.[57] And we learn to judge these meanings—liking them or leaving them: yes, that certainly says what we felt; no, that does not really articulate an adequate meaning for this place.

VIII

If one meaning does emerge strongly from many encounters with gardens and landscapes as well as in designers' proposals, it is the concept of place, which has enjoyed considerable attention for its own sake.[58] This is not surprising. Gardens are physical sites, grounded and rooted in a locality, and even if we have lost any real understanding of what the ancients termed genius loci, the fossil of that cultural idea is still with us, since we feel attachment and value in some places but not in others. Equally, soil, climate, and plants all obey and express local conditions. Different cultures still respond and use gardens in strikingly local ways. Places are spaces that have acquired significance and even meaning for those who experience them at length or in depth. Even the most globalized and globe-trotting modern designers seek to affirm something local in their projects. Others are much more dedicated to working where their knowledge of materials and culture will both guide the work, be expressed in it, and/or be visible to those with an eye and an ear for its specificity. Some gardens are even worked to remind visitors of their locality—be it ecological and geological (Yorkville Park in Toronto, laying out a miniature repertoire of local habitats) or political, such as Room 4.1.3's gardens for the National Museum of Australia shown Figure 2.6.[59]

The meaningfulness of place can be expressed or recognized in different ways, as a trio of recent gardens in Provence will reveal. Although they draw on a recognizable Provençal topography and culture, they are very different, not least in the fashion by which their creators assume responses can be triggered in visitors. They will serve finally as types of place and of the experience, significance and meanings that are discovered, inscribed or accrue in them.

Finlay's last creation before his death early in 2006, "Fleur de l'Air," presents us with a familiar conspectus of his insertions, but their placement in a much larger landscape than he has hitherto occupied and his deliberate response to locality give them a fresh resonance. If there is any overall theme, it is the celebration of the south (for which this bit of Provence stands proxy) and of earlier imaginations drawn to its resources. Moving through the site and descending its steep hillside, we encounter a field ribbed along its contours with lines of lavender, many inscriptions (a majority of which are quotations), urns, busts, a small rotunda, scattered blocks of stone, stiles set into the dry stone walls dividing the terraces of olive trees, along with plaques bearing names of French fishing boats and their port registration details, a stone *cabane*, a swimming pool, cisterns and a stone rill, a net-entwined oar cast in bronze with a reference to Homer's *Odyssey* Book XI, and a bronze post where wild boar can scratch their itchy skin beside the muddy hollow where they wallow. Some of the individual insertions will make instant sense; some will need either prior knowledge or some teasing out of their meaning; some may perhaps baffle long enough to need the help of knowledgeable interpretation.[60] The triggers and prompts are all carefully crafted, as to materials, form, placement and significance—nothing less than one would expect of Finlay and his collaborators; but it is visitors that will elicit from this site its rich matrix of meanings, sometimes aligning themselves with Finlay's known intentions, sometimes bringing into play Kelsall's "free play of association." The site is impressive in itself, its character or "genius" undoubtedly heightened by the linguistic and nonverbal encounters, from which visitors may or may not derive guidance in their interpretation of meanings. Once they have fully experienced it, exegesis will be their privilege, but it is not the garden's.[61]

Le Jardin de l'Alchimiste, created in the late 1990s by Eric Ossart and Armand Maurières near Eygalières for Alain and Marie de Larouzière, wears its constructed meanings more blatantly on its sleeve.[62] Rather than re-create a Renaissance garden beside the sixteenth-century Mas de la Brun, an itinerary was established further from the house. This is tripartite—a labyrinth in the form of the written word *Berechit* (the first word of the Hebrew Bible meaning origin or beginning), then a "Garden of Magical Plants" set out in a series of square beds, followed finally by larger squares containing red, white, and black gardens that evince a "sens spirituel" derived from the traditions of alchemy and ancient kabbalistic lore. Again, given the declared name and character of the garden, as well as the explanatory materials available on the site, the visitor is directly encouraged to find meaning here, but it is nonetheless imposed on, carried into, the site from outside. If a visitor knows or cares nothing about

FIGURE 5.5: Along the olive terraces, Fleur de l'Air, Provence. Photo: Emily T. Cooperman.

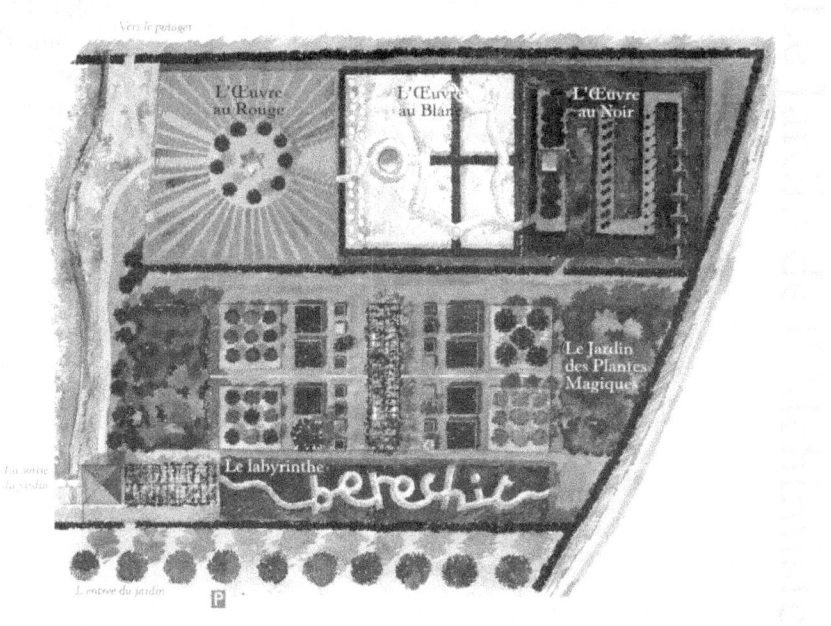

FIGURE 5.6: Plan of Le Jardin de l'Alchimiste, Eygalières, France. Courtesy of the owners.

alchemy and the Kabbala, then he or she would respond only to the performance of some carefully contrived shapes and colors within a circumscribed area of the domaine.

The same designers, Maurières and Ossart, created Le Jardin de la Noria, near St. Quentin la Poterie, for Jean and Martine Deparis. It invokes no inscriptions, no explicit allusions to a world of arcane ideas. Its name is taken from the central feature—a reconstructed *noria*, an ancient device for drawing water (we have early Arabic depictions of these machines).[63] Raised on a stone platform, the machinery extends a horizontal pole to be pushed around by a horse or a mule, the movement of which engages a chain of wooden or leather buckets to draw water up from the cistern below. The water then flows down a

FIGURE 5.7: Le Jardin de la Noria, Uzès, France. The *noria* or water-raising mechanism can be seen on the raised platform at the back; the long, Generalife-like pool lies to the right behind the planting. Photo: Harris L. Cooperman.

thin channel to other basins where it is held before flowing out of the grounds. Nearby a long, narrow pool of water, is presided over by groups of simple but clearly modern chairs, fashioned of rust-red concrete molded into a zigzag. There is also an orchard, a rosary, a prairie of fruit trees, and *kiosques*, as well as, elsewhere in the grounds of this former *mas* (or farmhouse), a potager, a grove of fir trees, and a contemporary swimming pool complex.

Le Jardin de la Noria is a wonderfully simple experience: at once austere, uncluttered, contemporary, yet richly aromatic in the hot sunshine, but also cooled by the profusion of water (this part of Provence is blessed with supplies of water). The worn wood and mechanics of the ancient *noria* are in striking contrast to the undeniably modernist lines of the water channel, the long pool, the seats, and the benches. Maybe its Arabic provenance stimulates one to see the long channel as a miniaturized feature from the Generalife in Granada, and indeed, the whole has been devised by artists fascinated by the Islamic garden culture of the Mediterranean basin, on which they have produced a very eloquent book.[64] That is certainly a significance that one may draw from the ensemble—a modernist, Mediterranean garden created in the grounds of a former farmstead for people fascinated by the local culture and the idea of southern gardens. There is, however, no meaning here. It is exactly what it is, yet significantly heightened for those who learn to see it carefully. But no alchemy, no meditations on myth, the classical past, the yearning of the north for the sun-kissed southern world, not even any representation of something old and elsewhere: nothing, in short, that we need to bring with us into the place for its understanding. The *noria* is itself, and it continues to function.

Three gardens, three experiences, three kinds of significance, some of which seem to take on an added level of meaning a sampling, that is, of the extraordinary range of things that a garden can allow its designers to lay out and its visitors to experience. But enough to suggest also that modern garden design can and must both respond to "a diverse, pluralistic culture"[65] and ensure a scale of receptions that is surely one of the major distinctive marks of modern garden-making that began in the eighteenth century and has reached a new plateau in the twentieth century. The ultimate lesson, then, consists in acknowledging the associative faculties that we take with us into these places, and they suggest how much modern garden meaning resides, after all is done and said, in the eye and mind of the beholder. The three mottos at the head of this chapter are not, then, wholly at odds: the object and its meanings may never *coincide,* yet we necessarily register their dialogue. Unspoken meanings abound, but by that very fact, they become susceptible to our speech or to our imaging, and for gardens, those meanings are necessarily rooted in how we understand "the earth" or local places. To which places, humans cannot be prevented from bringing their own imaginations, the free play of which it is the business of designers (garden makers) to promote and of critics to adjudicate the limits. Between them are the hundreds of people who go to gardens, which have perhaps become the modern open work par excellence.[66]

CHAPTER SIX

Verbal Representations

MICHAEL LESLIE

> Twice I've spoken of sadness. Is that essential to the modern view?
> —Virginia Woolf[1]

No account of the culture of the twentieth century can avoid the response to repeated cataclysms, each seemingly infinite but each exceeded by events yet more sublime in scale and terror: the carnage of World War I, the Holocaust, the threat of nuclear annihilation or ecological disaster. The garden, which one might have thought inadequate and irrelevant as humanity wrestles with destruction on a hitherto unimagined scale, paradoxically achieves a prominence in key literary works over the past century. Unsurprisingly, in a period that saw the popularization of existentialism, the reader frequently encounters the garden's antitype in landscapes of aridity and infertility, such as repeatedly in Samuel Beckett's plays, but overshadowing them all is T.S. Eliot's poem *The Waste Land* (which falls outside the scope of this volume by date). Yet, Eliot also provides in *The Four Quartets* the primary example of the power of images of the garden to articulate hope, to question, and to address the human response to chaos.

Existentialism shares with other twentieth-century intellectual movements a sense of the irrelevance, unreality, and inadequacy of traditional frames of meaning, invoking many of the great garden myths but without a sense of the numinous. There is often a powerful irony: the invocation of these myths manifests a divide, often unbridgeable, between modernity and a more naïve past.

On their own feet they came, or on shipboard,
Camel-back; horse-back, ass-back, mule-back,
Old civilisations put to the sword.
Then they and their wisdom went to rack.[2]

Jean-François Lyotard famously defined "an incredulity towards metanarratives" as a characteristic of the postmodern,[3] but it is surely present in much of modernism before that. The carved Chinamen of W. B. Yeats's "Lapis Lazuli," composed in the run-up to the World War II, are imagined to rest beneath "plum or cherry-branch" in the garden of "the little half-way house [they] climb towards."[4] Isolated from the scene on which they gaze— "on the mountain and the sky, / On all the tragic scene they stare"[5]—they enjoy mournful melodies: the artful and the orderly. In the light of chaos and destruction, the poem questions art (and artists and audiences) that achieve beauty through separation and ordering. Heartless (apparently) but not artless, how do we judge the Chinamen, ourselves, and the exceptional space of the garden?

The image of the garden figures repeatedly in twentieth-century literature in contemplations of order and disorder; the image is ambiguous and the judgment often ambivalent. It appears often as an antitype to what is feared to be desolate and dehumanizing urbanization: the "negative city" (see "The Negative City" in this chapter). The garden is insistently concerned with loss and so, necessarily, with memory, and with the ways in which gardens are—or are not—special places of preservation and redemption, signifying at best the human ability to withstand forces of chaos, at worst the human desire to escape, evade, and self-delude. There are, of course, innumerable other ways in which gardens figure in modern literature, but it is the purpose of this essay to consider some key instances that highlight and debate a cluster of themes that seem essential to modern culture.

GOODBYE TO ALL THAT: MEMORY, MYTH, AND LOSS IN THE GARDEN AFTER THE WAR TO END ALL WARS

A man knelt behind a line of headstones—evidently a gardener, for he was firming a young plant in the soft earth. She went towards him, her paper in her hand. He rose at her approach and without prelude or salutation asked: "Who are you looking for?"

"Lieutenant Michael Turrell—my nephew", said Helen slowly and word for word, as she had many thousands of times in her life.

The man lifted his eyes and looked at her with infinite compassion before he turned from the fresh-sown grass toward the naked black crosses.

"Come with me", he said, "and I will show you where your son lies."

When Helen left the Cemetery she turned for a last look. In the distance she saw the man bending over his young plants; and she went away, supposing him to be the gardener.[6]

Rudyard Kipling's story "The Gardener" (1926) reminds us that the experience of the World War I is the unavoidable context for all subsequent literature, regardless of theme, genre, mode, or figurative structure. Helen Turrell is visiting the Hagenzeele Third war cemetery, looking for the grave of the man she has brought up as the son of her ne'er-do-well brother, but in fact her own illegitimate child, a relationship never acknowledged even to the boy. Registering the pain and guilt of so many, but crucially Kipling's own following the death in 1915 of his son John at the Battle of Loos ("If any question why we died / Tell them, because our fathers lied"),[7] the story follows Helen as she leaves the orderly, stoic grief of an English village to be tossed into the chaos of the Central Authority in the battlefields and the nightmare emotions of other grieving visitors. Finally, she reaches the cemetery:

She climbed a few woodenfaced earthen steps and then met the entire crowded level of the thing in one held breath. She did not know that Hagenzeele Third counted twenty-one thousand dead already. All she saw was a merciless sea of black crosses, bearing little strips of stamped tin at all angles across their faces. She could distinguish no order or arrangement in their mass; nothing but a waist-high wilderness as of weeds stricken dead, rushing at her.[8]

The cemetery is a thing only; the graves "naked black crosses"; the individuality of the dead beneath reduced to tin stamped across their (the crosses? the slain?) faces. The impersonality appalls both Helen and the reader. Although the wooden crosses are these days replaced with solid headstones, visitors are still assaulted by the irony of those precisely arranged, seemingly unending rows of graves, their surrounding lawns immaculately tended by the unhurried, unwearied, anonymous gardeners of the War Graves Commission on which Kipling himself served: the obscene order of those garden cemeteries commemorating a convulsion of such inhuman violence that the concept of order itself seems a juvenile fantasy.

Kipling's unidentified man is an echo of Christ the Gardener, but this must be almost the latest moment at which such an allusion could be made without the protective coating of irony. Certainly, T. S. Eliot's *The Waste Land*, published four years before, had dwelt on the postwar collapse of assumed structures of belief, leaving a bleak existential landscape, a wasteland, not a garden: "That corpse you planted last year in your garden, / Has it begun to sprout? Will it bloom this year? / Or has the sudden frost disturbed its bed?"[9]

Faced with this chaos, the garden is a special space of memory and imagination; its very orderliness suggests loss, alienation, and irrecoverability. Eliot's later attempt to affirm a positive in *The Four Quartets* develops the image of the rose garden as a figure of a paradise that is real but always painfully beyond the speaker's grasp:

> Footfalls echo in the memory
> Down the passage which we did not take
> Towards the door we never opened
> Into the rose-garden . . .
> the bird called, in response to
> The unheard music hidden in the shrubbery,
> And the unseen eyebeam crossed, for the roses
> Had the look of flowers that are looked at . . .
> Go, said the bird, for the leaves were full of children,
> Hidden excitedly, containing laughter.[10]

Eliot's image has been thought to echo Frances Hodgson Burnett's evocative prewar novel *The Secret Garden* (1909), but it seems at least as likely that it is influenced by another Kipling story, "They" (1904), in which dead children become tantalizingly present to their grieving parents, heard, somehow alive, but never more than glimpsed. (Although this story is not mentioned by name, Eliot's introductory essay to *A Choice of Kipling's Verse* [1941] shows his deep appreciation of this phase of Kipling's storytelling.)

The ruminations on memory in the *The Four Quartets*'s rose garden are an authorizing point of reference for much literature concerning gardens in the twentieth century. Eliot's concern encompasses the personal and private, but extends beyond it; the same sense of the garden as a privileged territory, almost as a paradigm of the modern and modernist version of the Wordsworthian "spots of time," recurs in different languages and decades, as in a sonnet by Yves Bonnefoy in *Les Planches courbes* (2001):

> I open my eyes, it really is my native house,
> And the same very one which was and no more.
> The same little dining room of which the window
> Gives a view on to a peach tree that doesn't grow bigger.
> A man and a woman have sat themselves
> Before this window, one facing the other,
> They speak to each other, for once. The child
> From the depths of the garden sees them, watches them.
> He knows that one can be born from these words.[11]

The sonnet gathers images of the garden, parents, procreation, loss, and memory: Eden in all its emotional power and pain. Roland Barthes, in his meditations (close to prose poems) on photography *Camera Lucida* (1980), the most intimate and least Barthesian of his works, makes the inevitable connection with Proust, as he returns repeatedly to the "Winter Garden" photograph of his dead mother as a child:

> For once, photography gave me a sentiment as certain as remembrance, just as Proust experienced it one day when, leaning to take off his boots, there suddenly came to him his grandmother's true face, "whose living reality I was experiencing for the first time, in an involuntary and complete memory."[12]

The setting in the Winter Garden fixes the moment. Just so, Eliot's speaker in "La figlia che piange" arrests time and poses his subject:

> Stand on the highest pavement of the stair-
> Lean on a garden urn-
> Weave, weave the sunlight in your hair.[13]

Barthes writes that "the unknown photographer of Chennevières-sur-Marne had been a mediator of truth";[14] the verbal representation of the garden in twentieth-century literature commemorates lost innocence and tries to conjure it back into existence in the face of chaos and brutality, all the while seared by the sense of the impossibility of recovering the past.

FRUIT, TASTE, WOE, MAN: MYTHS OF THE FALL

The universal shock of the World War I was far from alone in being experienced as a definitive rupture: it was swiftly followed by the Depression, the darkening clouds of fascism and the rape of the land through squalid urbanization and industrialization. As in *The Waste Land*, literature of the interwar years frequently invokes themes, symbols, and myths of the garden with a pungent and sometimes humourless irony. Many of these themes appear in the works of the "Southern Agrarians," American writers clustered around John Crowe Ransom and Allen Tate, a group stung by the hostility of Northern writers to the culture and values of a South defeated in the American Civil War and ground down by Reconstruction. One of the most evocative works to come out of this group is Caroline Gordon's novel *The Garden of Adonis* (1937). Gordon's novel is anything but romantic or idealizing: its leading characters are scarcely amiable and they lead lives of tawdry sexual intrigue, marital and small-town dispute, depressing economic failure, and a listlessness born of emotional shallowness. That shallowness is connected with the novel's title and explained by the epigraph taken from Sir James Frazer's *The Golden Bough*, in which he describes the small pots in which plants were grown for ritual purposes:

> the plants shot up rapidly, but having no root they withered as rapidly away, and at the end of eight days were carried out with the images of the dead Adonis and flung with them into the sea or into springs. . . . [15]

Like other modernists, Gordon reaches back to the Greek myths for images of fertility and connection, but her purpose is not to celebrate but to use disparity to represent the collapse of the sense of relationship between individuals, between humans and their environment, and between modern man and the traditions and histories of earlier human societies.

In *The Garden of Adonis*, the effects of humiliating defeat and Reconstruction are compounded by the Depression. The novel's climax begins with the expected consummation of the sexual attraction between Jim Carter and Letty Allard; it will end a few pages later with the murder of Letty's father by another impoverished white sharecropper, Ote Mortimer, whose girlfriend is already pregnant and about to abandon him for a flashy bootlegger. Needing money to marry her and unable to borrow from his destitute landlord, Mortimer loses control when the landlord seeks to prevent him from harvesting their pitiful crops before maturity.

Mister Ben stood there. His incredulous eyes were fixed on Ote's face. Ote shouted at him and struck, putting all his force into the blow. Mister Ben went down upon a swathe of the new-mown hay, moved once and groaned, then was still.[16]

The murder in the field invokes Cain and Abel and the long tradition of representing original sin in the worked land to which humanity had been exiled from Eden; the reiteration of the primal crime associates the novel's catastrophe with archetypal expulsion. Its deep pain at the modern world's remorseless destruction of lives and rural perfection is summed up in the evocation of that crime, behind which stands a lost paradisial garden visible in the novel only out of the corner of one's eye, as in the fond memory of Ben Allard's dead wife Rose, who responded to flowers and gardens with a emotional warmth evinced by none of those left living.

The sense of an Edenic world survives only in its sardonic undercutting. Jim and Letty eventually have intercourse atop a Native American burial mound that had earlier been excavated:

> He came over and stood beside her. "I wish I'd been here when they opened it up . . . What did they find?"
> "Two skeletons," she said. . . .
> He nodded. "Ever find any arrowheads?"[17]

Jim finds a single arrowhead, but that's enough to act as a signpost to other classical love and garden myths. The scene parodies the great celebration of happy, healthy sexuality in the "Garden of Adonis" canto of Edmund Spenser's late-sixteenth-century poem *The Faerie Queene* (Book 3, canto 6). There, recapitulating and adapting his sources, Spenser has Venus preserve the wounded Adonis on a similar mound; from their lovemaking, all living things are created. Beneath them, the boar that gored Adonis (killing him in the original stories) is trapped forever in a cave, death not abolished but forever defeated. The surrounding garden is full of other creatures engaging in the fulfillment of similarly un-conflicted and un-condemned love and desire, including Cupid, Psyche, and their daughter Pleasure. But any sense of Cupid-inspired romance, of love provoked by an arrowhead, is almost laughed at in the joyless carnality of the scene in Gordon's novel, like Milton's Adam and Eve in postlapsarian heat:

> He put his hand out, rested it on her shoulder, then slipped it down her back, inside the thin blouse. He drew her to him. He kissed her. "For

God's sake," he said, "let's quit kidding each other. We knew all the time this was going to happen."[18]

Jim's marriage has just broken down; Lette is betraying the fiancé she is due to marry soon. This Adam and Eve fornicate as cynical, fleshed skeletons in a dead Eden, death not captive below them but casually ignored.

A similar weaving of references to classical and Biblical myths into fictions of the decline and fall of Southern culture pervades William Faulkner's *The Sound and the Fury* (1931), with the garden most clearly invoked in Caddy's climbing of a tree in order to look into the house to see the rituals of her grandmother's funeral. Knowledge of death is joined by another, sexual knowledge: her three brothers look up and see her muddied underwear. Caddy's original sins—inquisitiveness and incipient female sexuality—seem to condemn both family and culture to destruction.

Both Faulkner and Caroline Gordon draw on Judeo-Christian and classical myths of the garden in their representation of the world of the American South dying under the pressure of modernity, and they do so in a dying agrarian world. Conversely, many of the great modernist works are set in cities (*Ulysses*) or in wastelands, or both ("Unreal City, / Under the brown fog of a winter dawn, / A crowd flowed over London Bridge, so many, / I had not thought death had undone so many"),[19] and the garden when it appears is frequently an antitype. Like the shallow-set plants in the classical Gardens of Adonis, de-racination and dis-location result in physical and spiritual death.

"YOU LIKE THIS GARDEN? . . . WE EVICT THOSE WHO DESTROY!": THE GARDEN AFTER THE HOLOCAUST

One of the last great modernist novels uses many of the same techniques and myths, but applies them to the new world created by another war to end all wars. Malcolm Lowry's *Under the Volcano* is set in the late 1930s and was offered to publishers in one form in 1940; but, as its author recognized, the published version of 1947 is inevitably a meditation on the World War II and what it meant for humanity; and the image of the garden is inextricably bound up with that. Lowry wrote that the alcoholic drunkenness of his protagonist, Geoffrey Firmin, "the Consul," is "used on one plane to symbolize the universal drunkenness of mankind during the war" and that the Consul's decaying garden is a version "of the Garden of Eden, the Garden representing the whole world."[20]

The action of the novel is largely in flashback. It opens with the reminiscences of Jacques Laruelle on the Day of the Dead, 1939, remembering events on the same day exactly a year earlier, at the conclusion of which the Consul and his divorced but now returned wife Yvonne die in bizarre and dramatic circumstances. The day is immediately important in garden terms: as in many Catholic countries, November 1, All Souls Day, is celebrated in Mexico by visits to cemeteries, to decorate with flowers the graves of relatives; the locals' processions are seen and heard by M. Laruelle as he sits on the terrace of the Hotel Casino de la Selva. Its name is the first of pervasive references to Dante's *Commedia*, here to the *selva oscura* in which the Dreamer comes to himself at the beginning of the *Inferno*. Together with the epigraph (one of three) from John Bunyan, this alerts the reader to the likelihood that all references to landscape, designed and undesigned, will be symbolic in this novel.

The novel requires the reader to perceive connections to a wide range of texts, the most important being Cabbalistic literature, the *Aeneid*, the *Commedia*, *Paradise Lost*, *Pilgrim's Progress*, and—inevitably—*The Waste Land* (an ironic aridity in a novel dominated by addictive drinking). Garden myths dominate, first among them the story of the Garden of Eden filtered through other texts. When the Consul's half-brother Hugh first sees Yvonne, with whom he has had an affair, he does so with the eyes of Milton's Satan encountering Eve to tempt her: she is alone, "working in the garden, and at a distance appeared clothed entirely in sunlight."[21] This encounter with Eve will indeed end in an apocalypse and this landscape is full of snakes—just before the Consul meets his friend Dr. Vigil, he sees a cat and calls it "my-little-anguish-in-herba," a pun on a famous line in Virgil's Third Eclogue, "latet anguis in herba," a snake hiding in the grass. Hugh's falling/fallen vision contrasts with the Consul's memory of his idyllic first meeting with Yvonne: "and up, up, now they were climbing themselves, up to the Generalife Gardens, and now from the Generalife Gardens to the Moorish tomb on the extreme summit of the hill; here they plighted their troth . . ."[22] (an echo perhaps of Molly Bloom's hill, garden, and flower remembrance of her tryst with Leopold in Joyce's *Ulysses*: "the day we were lying among the rhododendrons on Howth head in the grey tweed suit and his straw hat the day I got him to propose to me yes first I gave him the bit of seedcake out of my mouth and it was leapyear like now yes 16 years ago my God after that long kiss I near lost my breath yes he said was a flower of the mountain yes so we are flowers all a womans body yes").[23] But the garden episode that dominates Lowry's novel takes place in chapter 5, when the Consul wakes from another episode of alcoholic stupor and makes his way down to the furthest extremity of his garden to find a hidden bottle of Tequila (he is supposed to be drying out). He finds himself at the conjunction of three gardens: his own, ruined; that of his neighbor, the American Mr. Quincey, both master and domain immaculate and artificially perfect; and the public garden beyond his fence. And beneath his own gardens, reminiscent of the cemetery mound of Caroline Gordon's *The Garden of Adonis* and of its source in the boar's prison cave in *The Faerie Queene*, is an iron mine; while one side is bounded by a chasm, "the frightful cleft, the eternal horror of opposites,"²⁴ an echo also of Coleridge's "deep romantic chasm" beneath Kubla Khan's stately pleasure park. The only order appears to be that of Mr. Quincey, "the green lawns of the American, at that moment being sprinkled by innumerable small whizzing hoses."²⁵ This trivial, prosaic, and manufactured perfection stands in contrast to the Consul's own disorderly garden, loved as he hopes to be "loved for [his] reckless and irresponsible appearance, or rather for the fact that, beneath that appearance, so obviously burns the fire of genius."²⁶

The encounter with his disapproving neighbor is a tour de force of pathos and farce, modeled on Adam's Biblical and Miltonic encounter with God immediately after the Fall, and the similarity is recognized by the Consul in a tipsy, garrulous speech full of humor but with an underlying seriousness:

> "Do you know, Quincey, I've often wondered whether there isn't more in the old legend of the Garden of Eden, and so on, than meets the eye. What if Adam wasn't really banished from the place at all? That is, in the sense we used to understand it [. . . .] What if his punishment really consisted," the Consul continued with warmth, "in his having to *go on living there*, alone, of course—suffering, unseen, cut off from God. . . . Or perhaps," he added, in a more cheerful vein, "perhaps Adam was the first property owner and God, the first agrarian, a kind of Cárdenas, in fact—tee hee!—kicked him out. Eh? Yes," the Consul chuckled, aware, moreover, that all this was possibly not so amusing under the existing historical circumstances, "for it's obvious to everyone these days—don't you think so, Quincey?—that the original sin was to be an owner of property. . . . "²⁷

In the middle of his playful rhapsody, *serio ludens*, God in the form of Mr. Quincey has uncovered this Adam's nakedness: the Consul's fly is open. Undeterred and claiming the indulgence owed to prophets and poets ("Licentia vatum indeed!"),²⁸ the Consul continues:

> And of course the real *reason* for that punishment—his being forced to go on living in the garden, I mean, might well have been that the poor fellow, who knows, secretly loathed the place! Simply hated it, and had done so all along. *And that the Old Man found this out—*²⁹

This funny but chilling reimagining of the Fall, its vision of alienation almost sublime in its inversions, is central to the novel's vision of the human condition.

The encounter with Mr. Quincey, or God, and the contrast between the dreary perfection of the one and the ruined Eden of the other is essential to the symbolism of the novel, but ultimately the public park has the greater resonance or, rather, the monitory but ambiguous sign at its entrance. Before this discussion of Eden, the Consul has stumbled on abandoned garden tools:

> There existed at the moment certain evidence of work left uncompleted: tools, unusual tools, a murderous machete, an oddly shaped fork, somehow nakedly impaling the mind, with its twisted tines glittering in the sunlight, were leaning against the fence, as also was something else, a sign uprooted or new, whose oblong pallid face stared through the wire at him. ¿Le gusta este jardin? It asked . . .
> ¿LE FUSTA ESTE JARDIN?
> ¿QUE ES SUYO?
> ¡EVITE QUE SUS HIJOS LO DESTRUYAN!
> The Consul stared back at the black words on the sign without moving. You like this garden? Why is it yours? We evict those who destroy! Simple words, simple and terrible words, words which one took to the very bottom of one's being, words which, perhaps a final judgement on one, were nevertheless unproductive of any emotion whatsoever, unless a kind of colourless, cold, a white agony, an agony chill as that iced mescal drunk in the Hotel Canada on the morning of Yvonne's departure.[30]

The Consul's translation, as he knows, is flawed, "but it was near enough." The correct translation, also penetrative, is "You like this garden that is yours? Don't let your children destroy it." This *lex hortorum* recurs three times, on each occasion interpreted by the Consul as a baleful expression of humanity's alienation from nature, from a benign, perhaps imagined past, from his own desired but also unwanted wife, from himself, and from any humanizing, connecting emotional response: he is judged a destroyer and banished as such from the real paradise of the common space of the park. It comes as no surprise that, when he is fatally shot, it is under the official gaze of the lean, silent, humorless Jefe de Jardineros, the chief of Gardens. (Lowry used the misreading of the sign again, in the posthumously published novel *Dark Is the Grave Wherein My Friend is Laid* (1968), where the error is made by the significantly named protagonist Sigbørn Wilderness.) Through its immensely rich garden imagery, *Under the Volcano* achieves a representation of the self-consumed in civil war, irreversibly exiled, annihilated by the weight of existence in a world seemingly without order or meaning. It is no surprise that Samuel Beckett, whose arid landscape in *En Attendant Godot*, is surely itself a woundingly ironic Eden, praised *Under the Volcano* as "a very great book."[31]

Under the Volcano was begun before the outbreak of the World War II and is set in the years of the Spanish Civil War. But Lowry himself acknowledged that, proleptically, the Consul's despair has at least as much to do with the war of 1939–45. In his dying fall into the ravine, he first imagines that he is tumbling into the volcano, but

> no, it wasn't the volcano, the world itself was bursting, bursting into black spouts of villages, catapulted into space, with himself falling through it all, through the inconceivable pandemonium of a million tanks, through the blazing of ten million burning bodies, falling—[32]

Both the madness of industrialized warfare and the acrid, sickening slaughter of the Holocaust rear up in the Consul's final vision of the world of the immediate future. No wonder he screams. The burning of human flesh has a particular immediacy for the Consul, for we were told in the first chapter that, as captain of the ironically named SS *Samaritan*, he was in some way responsible for the incineration of German officers: "They had, it was said, been kidnapped by the *Samaritan*'s stokers and burned alive in the furnaces". The Consul's cocktail-party pose of witty detachment—" 'People simply did not go round,' he said 'putting Germans in furnaces' "[33]—could only be read by 1947 through the knowledge that Germans did go round putting others in furnaces in incomprehensible numbers.

After the World War II, the secularizing communist regimes of Eastern Europe tolerated the festivities of All Souls' Day but sought to remove religious connotations. In Poland, Zaduszki became the Day of the Dead. But the customs continued and continue: one visits cemeteries, cleans family tombs and lights candles as darkness falls, and in Łodz, one looks across the valley to hillsides brilliantly lit by thousands of candles. Yet, there are sizable pockets of contrasting darkness, scarring the scene. These are the areas containing Jewish tombs. After the terrible events of the Łodz ghetto and transportation to the gas chambers, there are few family members left to participate in rites of remembrance. It is one of twentieth-century literature's pungent ironies that Kafka's sisters, gravesites unknown, met their meaningless end in Łodz.

The sense of the cemetery as a remembrance garden in which the events of the past are inscribed on the landscape—seemingly distant and concluded yet immediate, ever present in the imagination—forms the opening of Giorgio

Bassani's novel, *The Garden of the Finzi-Continis* (1962). Like *Under the Volcano*, its first chapter looks back through the experience of garden and cemetery memory to the events that form the central story: the novel's first words are "La tomba," the tomb. The unnamed narrator is driven to see a field of Etruscan tombs, at the end of a disappointing pleasure outing in 1957 in the company of a small girl. His response to the landscape and to the history he is drawn to tell is shaped by her quietly intense perception that, once we imagine their lives, the sadness of the fates of even the long dead recaptures immediacy. The grand but now empty Etruscan tombs throw him imaginatively back to the ostentatious mausoleum of the Finzi-Contini family in the Jewish cemetery in Ferrara (where, incidentally, Bassani is himself now interred), its glory undermined by the fact that only a single family member lies within it, ironically spared the annihilating Holocaust by a preemptive death from cancer.

Garden cemeteries are prominent throughout the novel: the narrator's father is responsible for the maintenance of the Jewish cemetery; Ermanno, the head of the Finzi-Contini family, claims his title of "professor" on the basis of a catalogue of the inscriptions in the Jewish cemetery on the Venice Lido; and it was there that Ermanno and his wife became betrothed. And the walled garden the Finzi-Continis have created itself has a sepulchral quality, separate from the Italian life, Jewish and Gentile, that surrounds them, preserving all who dwell there as though in an eternal present. For much of the novel, the garden suggests a haven from a darkening world, an inhabited *Wunderkammer*, filled with the rare, valuable, and unchanging. The library has works unique to its collections; the exotic trees grow to perfection, and the family recognize them all, knowing the correct Latin botanical names; even the tennis court rivals that of the club from which Jews are excluded. The family has its own private language, dubbed Finzi-Continian, and—though it is never overtly expressed—there is the assumption that retreating within its walls entails no sacrifice, no loss: the garden of the Finzi-Continis is a world in epitome. This proves an illusion: less epitome than epitaph. From one perspective a vision of happy, summer-lit, endless youth, from another the garden is a luxurious cemetery for the living dead, fated to obliteration, and betrayed by the fantasy of retreat.

Bassani's narrative takes place in the 1930s and 1940s, as Italy's fascist movement grows and anti-Semitism begins to threaten the lives of Ferrara's Jews. Knowledge of the extermination of Ferrara's Jewish community is ever present yet barely mentioned explicitly; it broods over the depiction of the narrator's obsession with Micòl Finzi-Contini, who rejects his love ("it would be like making love with a brother"),[34] and over the strange world of that family's garden. The garden's walls prove no real barrier and its timelessness a fiction.

Following the extermination of the Finzi-Continis, their dilapidated house is occupied by refugees, their beautiful, rare trees cut for firewood. It is a theme also struck in a recent poem by Benjamin Alíre Sáenz, "The Willow" (1991), set in his grandfather's garden:

> So the tree was chopped,
> stripped limb by limb until there was
> only a stump. And the stump, too
> was pulled from the ground—pulled
> so harshly that even the roots came up
> shaking the whole garden.[35]

The destruction of the willow marks the destruction of the secure, edenic world of childhood, the finality of a separation from a past now obliterated except in memory. Similarly, the cutting and burning of the trees in the Finzi-Contini garden is a symptom of the earthquake that separates the narrator forever from Arcadia supposedly achieved by their retreat from a hostile world.

It would be misleading to describe Bassani's novel as definitively political or focused only on the Holocaust: more than one earthquake destroyed that world. It has a Dickensian quality, in that the sympathetic depiction of the narrator's adolescent infatuation, not only with Micòl but with her whole family and the life within the walls enclosing their estate, encompasses the political, social, and ideological characteristics of a doomed paradise as well as those of a first (and maybe only) doomed love. Through his yearning for, experience of, and expulsion from that paradise, this Pip takes his reader into territories of woundedness that range from the intimate to the universal, and that achieve an intense immediacy through the art of writing. The representation of the garden in words, its *ekphrastic* re-creation, is essential to the novel.

Bassani's touch is light, but it is clear that he invokes many of the great garden myths. In particular, this Eden contains in Micòl its own Eve, its own Persephone. Like Lowry's Yvonne, her first description is as a being alien to the world of history and quotidian humanity. Like Yvonne, she is associated with the sun and also with the trees, "their crowns . . . swollen with the noon light like those of a tropical forest."[36] The narrator sees her watching him across the garden's high wall, as though supernaturally able to perch there (she's atop a ladder, in fact). He hesitates to act on her invitation to enter her garden using footholds she has created and so reveals a tentativeness that will doom their relationship; his search for a more official entrance expresses unbridgeable distances between them. Already, a sexual reading of the garden space is pressing on the imagination. Micòl and the garden, like Milton's Eve and the plants she tends when observed by Satan ("herself . . . fairest unsupported flower"), are figurations of each other, the garden sharing her exoticism and semidivinity, and she expressed through it almost in the manner of an early modern topographical allegory of the female body: tall trees; smooth lawns; the public space of the tennis court; the secluded paths down which she leads him to varying end points; the largely disused coach house, in which a potential sexual encounter is suddenly frustrated by a change of mood; and, finally, the gothic *Hütte*, the darkness at the centre of both garden and desired woman. Having seduced the reader with novelistic realism, Bassani ends with fantasy: the narrator, having wandered unnoticed past thirty copulating couples (despite the fact that he "grazed them with [his bicycle] wheel")[37] under the trees in the brilliant moonlight, at last scales the wall to become a trespasser in the garden, journeying by indirection always toward the *Hütte*:

> I was walking at about twenty yards from the crescent of great, dark trees of that part of the park, my face always turned to the left.[38]

That last phrase is almost a quotation. The emphasis on a spiraling, leftward approach seems to echo the narrator's voyage through the Inferno in Dante's *Commedia* (a work inevitably discussed by the novel's literate characters). But like the pilgrim's leftward journey into hell, the descent of Bassani's narrator is possibly transformed by the terrible destruction of this Eden into an emancipation from a prison of delightful and fascinating illusions. The only character who seems able to come and go freely in the garden is the gentile Malnate, a worker, a socialist, perhaps the lover of Micòl, and the object of her dying brother's desire.

If Micòl and the garden are, in a sense, one and the same, both seem trapped by beauty, by a particular perfection that would be lost should they ever change. Micòl refuses to have sex with the narrator and scorns marriage: her perfection seems to require denial of fertility. She studies Emily Dickinson and sends the narrator Dickinson's "I died for beauty," a poem about failure voiced from a tomb in a garden cemetery. Micòl collects Venetian glass ornaments, and like everything in the Finzi-Contini estate, their crystalline beauty seems to suggest that beauty requires fixity and cannot survive change. The Finzi-Continis' first child died of meningitis, and the parents see contact as the source of death; so too their garden is separate, nature subordinated, growth suspended. And the dilemma of the garden's beauty and its reliance on an ultimately unsustainable stasis figures the condition of their daughter and their whole society.

The Garden of the Finzi-Continis discreetly refuses to be explicit on these matters, perhaps because it is also contemplating itself as an analogy to the garden it describes. The narrator's story is in one sense a memorial, an entombing of people, a social order, and an innocence lost. As a result of the Holocaust, nothing remains of any of these to be given physical burial, but they can be represented in words, the novel an *ekphrasis* preserving the original: in a sense it is, as well as describes, the garden of the Finzi-Continis. That may seem a positive. But the question then seems to be whether this art also resembles the Finzi-Continis' garden in being detached, infertile, and stranded on the other side of the traumatic events it refuses to represent. And so is doomed. The remembering through words of Micòl and her family, and the endless summer of tennis games and unconsummated love, may be moving, but does the novel resemble the empty tombs of both the Etruscans and the Ferrarese Jews, empty tombs that are simply empty, signifying no resurrection?

THE NEGATIVE CITY

Alienation from the past is a frequent theme in the representation of the garden in twentieth-century literature, and that past is increasingly identified with a lost natural world. Exile from nature and the absence of a sense of belonging are deemed characteristic of the human condition as urbanization becomes the dominant manifestation of human life.

A witty but nonetheless powerful instance comes in Italo Calvino's novel of short stories, *Marcovaldo, or the Seasons in the City*, published in 1963, a year after *The Garden of the Finzi-Continis*. In "The Garden of Stubborn Cats," the penultimate story and the final one labeled Autumn, the protagonist explores a "counter-city . . . a negative city," one composed of the rapidly disappearing spaces and gaps between buildings. He follows a tabby cat, catches a fish, and then loses it to his companion, with the subsequent chase ending in a surreal vision:

> Beyond a half-rusted gate and two bits of wall buried under climbing plants, there was a little rank garden, with a small, abandoned-looking building at the far end of it. A carpet of dead leaves covered the path, and dry leaves lay everywhere under the boughs of the two plane-trees, forming actually some little mounds in the yard. A layer of leaves was yellowing in the green water of a pool. Enormous buildings rose all around, skyscrapers with thousands of windows, like so many eyes

trained disapprovingly on that little square patch with two trees, a few tiles, and all those yellow leaves, surviving right in the middle of an area of great traffic.

And in this garden, perched on the capitals and balustrades, lying on the dried leaves of the flower-beds, climbing on the trunks of the trees on the drainpipes, motionless on their forepaws, their entails making a question mark, seated to wash their faces, they were tiger cats, black cats, white cats, calico cats, tabbies, angoras, Persians, house cats and stray cats, perfumed cats and mangy cats. Marcovaldo realised he had finally reached the heart of the cats' realm, their secret island. And, in his emotion, he almost forgot his fish.[39]

The "garden of stubborn cats" is the final fragment of that which is opposed to dehumanizing urbanism; it is the epitome of the negative city. The garden and all the spaces and gaps of which it is the culmination subvert the city through misreading and misinterpretation, irresponsibly refusing to abide by codes whose inevitable endpoint would be the garden's destruction. The planned urban environment is vertical and compressed; but the cats, "prisoners of an uninhabitable city," reread and experience it as horizontal; and thus, through the pitiful garden, another possible world tenuously survives. Calvino's style is delightfully whimsical, the garden's freedom expressed in his studied inconsequentiality, but the story is nonetheless a nightmare vision of the near-total annihilation of a different relationship to nature and human nature. Beyond the humor, the effect is bleak. The garden is reduced to the scarcely recognizable form of a couple of trees, dead leaves, and a stagnant pool; the cats who had shared the city with humans in previous times now barely survive the murderous traffic and crowd into this last space, together with hundreds of birds, frogs, mice, and mosquitoes similarly exiled in the alien world constructed by man. The garden connects with a rapidly disappearing past: this final space appears to be preserved by a mysterious Marchesa, and when she dies, the oasis seems at last at the mercy of developers. However, the story ends with nature's survival fight continuing, as the stubborn cats, birds, and frogs engage in their own resistance, refusing to vacate and inhibiting the building work: "you couldn't dip up a bucket of water that wasn't full of frogs, croaking and hopping."[40] The garden expresses starkly the capacity for resistance, for the preservation of a cooperative humanity. Calvino's story has a Voltarian quality, its conclusion enigmatic in that the space being preserved scarcely merits the name of garden, yet the determination to resist obliteration offers a glimmering of hope. At the end of the tale, there is still a garden to be cultivated, just, surviving against all expectation and, like Calvino's city of swallows persisting alongside the city of rats in *Invisible Cities*, is "always about to free itself."

THE GARDEN AFTER THE AGE OF EMPIRES

Bassani's *Garden of the Finzi-Continis* equivocates about whether the subject is the garden or the memory of the garden; or even the memorial writing of the garden in the form of the novel itself. Jamaica Kincaid, from Antigua but living in the United States, is more confident in her volume *My Garden (Book)* (1999): "the garden for me is so bound up with words about the garden, with words themselves, that any set idea of the garden, any set picture, is a provocation to me."[41] On discovering that the garden she is creating in Vermont is a map of the Caribbean, Kincaid writes that "I only marvelled at the way the garden is for me an exercise in memory, . . . a way of getting to a past that is my own (the Caribbean Sea) and the past that is indirectly related to me (the conquest of Mexico and its surroundings)."[42] The essays of her volume tend and cultivate memory and cultivate knowledge of herself as a gardener, of the garden as an expression of herself and her affiliations in history, and of writing itself as a form of gardening.

Kincaid is one of a number of authors, mainly women, who engage with the garden from the position of the populations whose lives have been dominated by imperialism and its waning. Sometimes, as in Erna Brodber's *Jane and Louisa Will Soon Come Home* (1980), the image is of paradise corrupted and destroyed by the inherent brutality of the colonizing mind-set and its contemporary successor, the tourist industry:

> There is a lovely island in the Carribean Sea
> An island full of coconuts and fine banana trees
> An island where the sugar cane is waving in the breeze
> Jamaica is its name.
> We are out to build a new Jamaica.[43]

But even as the novel excoriates those whose casual assumption of power contaminates a potentially benign environment (a garden theme heard also in *Under The Volcano*, especially in the Consul's speculation on the ownership of property being the first sin, with its implied judgment on Mr. Quincey's garden and American capitalism as the latest manifestation of imperialism), Brodber, a Jamaican, gives voice to a more optimistic sense of individuals and societies emerging from colonialism to take back their environment, creating gardens in their own image:

> We are cleaning our garden. Mass Nega, wi smell you dinner but wi no want none. We are crawling around your pits and your shelter low on our bellies for we still have bellies, that organ which sheathes and protects but gives forth fruit. Crawling strengthens its muscles and dragging on the ground in time gives it its own camouflage. With luck we will grow feet and stand, then perhaps Baba could come out of the light bulb, Cock Robin could stand up and sing again and the man on the lonely donkey needn't dissipate into smoke.[44]

However, both Kincaid and Brodber are too honest to rest on superficial accusation. They recognize that their history of descent from enslavement and arbitrary migration is paired with a sense of freedom deriving from their own participation in the global village. Kincaid's witty essay "What Joseph Banks Wrought" meditates on the plant-hunting, plant-transporting, and plant-naming culture of imperialists. Again as in *Under the Volcano*, particular colonizing maneuvers of the garden—"the bougainvillea, (named for another restless European, the sea adventurer Louis de . . . Bourgainville . . ."; "I do not really like the bougainvillea"[45]—are judged, with the wider judgment that it is "character of the English people that leads them to order and shape their landscape,"[46] but the essay ends with her recognition that she is herself a transplant to Vermont, but a being transplanted of her own volition and in a new, postimperial world:

> There is no order in my garden. I live in America now. Americans are too impatient with memory, one of the things order thrives on.[47]

Playfully, with a kindly mockery of America's own myth of history-less-ness, Kincaid posits a new garden, one without memory or order, but she knows that her own horticulture denies its existence. Tellingly, postcolonialism, a modern field and mode of cultural criticism, recognizes through its use of the term *hybridity* the aptness of garden discourse to represent all of our experience in the globalized world. Kincaid's characteristic recognition and embrace of hybridity offer a future in which humanity escapes division into opposing groups. As Homi Bhabha, one of postcolonialism's leading exponents, writes, in hybridity, "we will find those words with which we can speak of Ourselves and Others. And by exploring this 'Third Space', we may elude the politics of polarity and emerge as the others of ourselves."[48] Bhabha's "third space" recalls the *tertium natura* of the early modern theorists: the garden as exceptional ground.

CODA: ARCADIA

Tom Stoppard's play *Arcadia* (1993) is not really about gardens, despite the fact that they figure prominently. Its motives are more abstract, though they have very physical manifestations: Classicism versus Romanticism ("The decline from thinking to feeling, you see"),[49] physics, entropy, and the response of all things, including humans and their loves, to forces which, while perhaps ultimately explicable and with discernible and reiterative pattern, are beyond control or understanding in the moment. But though the landscape garden setting is not at the forefront, we recognize the appropriateness of this setting for the play's twentieth-century fascinations with chaos and the hope that chaos rightly understood is order, and with memory's ability to overcome the seemingly absolute separation of the present from the past, to overcome forces entropic and irreversible. A dance to the music of time, perhaps: in the final scene, two couples, one from the early nineteenth century (Thomasina and Septimus) and one modern (Hannah and Gus), occupy the same space and hear the same waltz music from the garden:

After a moment's hesitation, [Hannah] gets up and [she and Gus] hold each other, keeping a decorous distance between them, and start to dance, rather awkwardly.

SEPTIMUS and THOMASINA continue to dance, fluently, to the piano.[50]

CHAPTER SEVEN

Visual Representations

MICHAEL JAKOB

Representation is a central aspect in the art of garden/landscape design. It is not an ancillary topic or a footnote, but an essential element inscribed in capital letters in the major text of garden history. The primordial visual component has always been linked to certain semantic qualities of gardens, or better yet, to their very meanings.

First and foremost, it must be noted that a garden by itself is at the same time presentation and representation. Throughout the centuries and across the most diverse cultures, gardens represented the idea of paradise, some transcendent and inaccessible realm beyond representation and inaccessible to human beings in their finiteness. The garden's genuine presence therefore visually evokes an invisible, mythical horizon. The garden is furthermore a model of Nature, a metonym and visual representation of a global ensemble impossible to encompass with the eye. Gardens function at the same time as representation of ideas or allegories: as the expression of their makers' ideas, the visualizations of a program, and the translation of the discourse of their time.

It is, however, in the sphere of the aesthetics of reception that the phenomenon of visual representation proves to be particularly interesting and complex. As a preliminary hypothesis, I propose the following statement: *every garden is, in the radical sense of the term, impossible to represent*. This assertion is fairly easy to defend on a subjective scale: a garden can never be grasped in one glance as a painting can be. No image or interior representation produced *in situ* is capable of containing the totality of the garden; none will be exhaustive or, as we use to say, representative. Even the most static garden conceived for a frontal reception according to the principles of an obligatory focalization is always more than its image. Exposed to the garden, the viewer finds him- or herself in a situation that is at the same time similar and very different to that of a landscape experience, the momentary contemplation of nature. Every landscape is an individual generality, an absolute, unique singularity. One never perceives the same landscape twice. When it reaches us aesthetically, the same spot takes the form of different landscapes. Although the experience of landscape occurs in our surprising meeting with Nature transformed in a framed image, the garden appears to be always already framed. The impossibility to represent the totality of a garden in a stable manner—each step in the garden leads to another new aspect—radicalizes the landscape phenomenon. Or, to put it another way, every garden is in itself an infinite world that demands an unlimited series of representations.

The discovery and interpretation of a garden, therefore, raises some very fundamental questions: What, actually, is a representation? And what is the status of an interior representation, of a *Vorstellung*, always incomplete and yet powerful enough to be committed to memory? And what is the role of the viewer, the person creating an image? Does even the most immediate representation of a garden scene not require that one draws on certain mental models (archetypes or types), that one compares the *here* with mental images or associations in our mind? The representation of a garden that originates in a single view at the same time offers too much and too little: too much considering its composite character, the fact that the imagination had already had its say; too little considering that the representation is biased by the singular, unilateral view. Hence, the necessity to go beyond the single image, beyond its imprint in a semantic framework, a narration composed of successive impressions. This state of affairs and ambiguity also characterize the intersubjective status of visual representations strictly speaking. All representations of a garden—the sketch, the canvas, the photograph, the film—are but an approximation, a unilateral vision. The image never *gives* the garden; it gives an interpretation, which necessarily implies hermeneutics, that is a critical interpretation of images.

A form of visual representation exists, however, which seems able to capture the fleeting reality of a garden: the drawing (with which the plan is also understood). This creates the illusion of representing the essence (the structure) and the origin (the starting point) of a garden. The drawing is often seen as the first and last representation of the garden, as its definitive image. But this idea presents several problems. The visibility of the drawing is quite paradoxical; in effect, it only depicts one of many strata of the garden. To reduce a garden to its drawing is to ignore its visual and aesthetic complexity. The drawing functions fairly well in the tradition of certain formal gardens, whereas all irregular gardens shy away from the idea of a drawing. The moment when space—the fundamental element for knowing the garden—enters the equation, the drawing reaches its limit.

A useful visual representation of a garden will always supply much more than a drawing. Only a complex iconic object—this is independent of the visual genre in question—is capable of capturing the spatio-temporal richness of its referent. The famous presentations by Olmsted and Vaux proposed for the Central Park competition in 1857 (*Greensward Competition Study*) are exemplary in this regard. Here the visual presentation is a subtle semiotic construction. A photographic impression captures the actual state of the site in the middle of the plate. A neutral, detached eye shows the New York wasteland, the *tabula rasa* on which the project would be triumphantly inscribed. The photographic images, however, are framed and slightly stylized; photography itself is identified as an artifice, a cultural construction. Underneath the plates, Vaux's watercolors depict the end product in full bloom. The purpose of the watercolor was not to give a personal touch to a vision of the future, but to the contrary, it served to situate and identify the project as part of a recognizable tradition: the picturesque. Finally, the future drawing of Central Park was placed above the plate more as an icon and a project logo than as a legible representation of the whole. The transposition of the drawing into metaphor deconstructed the tradition of visual representation characteristic of much proceeding in garden art. Thus, the drawings appeared as a programmatic manifesto (their creators inaugurated a mixed genre in the style of emblem art.) Moreover, they function as historic *Aufhebung* of that which precedes: not only of the watercolor and of the photographic depictions, but also of the evolution of professional representation (Repton's *Red Books* would be a historical starting point).[1] Also added to this is graphic depiction, visual signs as images of a brand.

The example of this major case in visual representation—the contemporary plates of the architectural design students have only slightly surpassed them—provides important hermeneutic and iconic knowledge. To give (a lot of) attention to visual documents related to gardens proves to be necessary for a very simple reason: gardens survive only by virtue of being (visually) represented. In China, artistic representation of gardens has often been interpreted to be more important than the gardens themselves (the real garden is always subjected to the vicissitudes of time). The poetic or pictorial trace of the garden is thus more significant than its ephemeral presence. In this way, visual representation acquires absolute dignity: it is as representation only that the garden truly exists.

II

To generalize about garden painters or garden painting is as senseless as talk about mountain or ocean paintings. The garden, an aesthetic phenomenon sui generis, once transposed to the aesthetic medium of painting, takes on varied forms and functions. In this regard, one can distinguish a realist mode of representation from an idealistic or archetypal one, which renders more the idea of the garden than its actual appearance. Paul Klee is associated with the second style. In an almost uninterrupted series of paintings, the Swiss artist unceasingly produced a neo-mythological vision of gardens. In terms of space, the garden appears both simple and complex, or better yet, as an enclosure that contains a surprising sequence of other enclosures. In the most ephemeral of artistic forms—the garden—Klee discovers the secret life of a very particular spatiality, the magic of the *locus amoenus*. The magical quality of the garden appears as a typical Gestalt effect due to an alternation between principles of repetition and of variation. Through the painter's eye, singular elements—the shrub-*simili* and tree-*simili*—are revealed equally as vegetation patterns and chromatic nuances. The semiotic metamorphosis of garden into painting, painting into garden, unveils the eminently eloquent value of gardens and the fact that everything in them can take on unusual significance. The painter's eye (Klee has long prepared his own herbarium and attempted to penetrate Nature's secrets in Goethe's footsteps)[2] distorts the usual modes of garden representation. Klee deconstructs perspective and mixes several modes of appearance of reality, inviting us to have a second look at the thing we too quickly identify as a garden. This poetic deviation confers a sense of lightness, movement, and life upon Klee's gardens in contrast to traditional, well-constructed illustrations, which, though well mastered, are cold or dead. Through this process, the painter reveals the very essence of gardens—the experience of their rhythm. The whole that is captured, or better yet, suggested in the representation that is at the same time beyond perspective and multiperspective, the play on relationships between clearly identified and nonhierarchical topical elements (trees, flowers, paths, birds, sun, etc.), and the surprising texture that the human insertion of vegetation confers upon the earth—all this represents well the musical and absolutely singular rhythm of the gardens of the world.

FIGURE 7.1: Paul Klee, *Rosengarten* (Rose Garden), 1920, Paul Klee Zentrum Bern.

If Paul Klee depicts gardens as a glow, an aesthetic epiphany and an existential territory, the realist current utilizes garden representation in order to reveal its functions. The works of Charles Mahoney, Charles Ginner, Stanley Spencer, and other British artists documented by the *Art of the Garden*[3] show are exemplary in this regard. What characterizes them is their interest in a type of garden that is neither a mythical place, nor an idyllic enclosure, nor a magical refuge. These painters' eyes are close to the survey style and render the details of utilitarian gardens with extreme minutia. Their paintings provide a catalogue of plants as much as—in a way of speaking—social usages of vegetation. They all lean toward familiar and recognizable subjects, with the effects of war being the only truly surprising element. The objective and detached approach and the social cartography that results give these representations the quality of documents. The pictorial anachronism—the realist code and mimicry—contrasts with the paradoxical charm of often-unusual motifs (monotonous, ordinary subjects etc.) Realist representation of gardens is interesting more because of its motifs—which range from the aesthetics of ugliness, banality, waste, and work, to the ironic aesthetics of vegetables—than for its technique. Internationally widespread, realist representation breaks with the major romantic and symbolic landscaped themes.

In the visual representation of gardens, Claude Monet's is the paradigmatic work of the first half of the twentieth century. Everything, almost, has been said about the famous garden developed by Monet from 1883 at Giverny. One must note, however, the truly transgressive quality of the representation process that centered on a single garden and was undertaken systematically right up to the death of the artist at the end of the 1920s. As for the visual transposition of gardens, Monet's gesture historically corresponds to the *Aufhebung* of the preceding praxis. It first appears as a continuation of a pluri-secular custom and technique. Monet produces the landscape of his garden, transforms, then radicalizes it, and in the end reinvents it. Construction, deconstruction, and invention of a new postmimicry representational form develop as a result of a long artistic process. Giverny also marks the negation of tradition; the pictorial act never culminates in a single representative painting but rather in an uninterrupted series, in an open process. Monet is the painter who breaks with

FIGURE 7.2: Charles Mahoney, Wrotham Place from the Garden. c.1938–9, Tate Gallery, London.

the timelessness of the habitual mode of representing gardens. With Monet, the garden rediscovers its life and therefore its essence: the incommensurable simultaneity and the incessant metamorphosis in such outcomes as light, wind, and an infinite number of other factors confer on it in each instant a different and transitory aspect. Monet also breaks with the impersonal side of known modes of representation. For him, the garden becomes an existential place—a microcosm physically experienced in situ. It is through his garden and in garden paintings that Monet accomplished the definitive deconstruction of western landscape painting. The absence of the horizon and of somatic indicators (above–below, left–right) as well as the resulting difficulty in orientation, attest to the transformation of the visual representation of gardens into a metaphor, and not into the simple reproduction of explored spaces. Monet's paradoxical gesture brings together the most extreme exaltation and ritual praise of gardens as well as the negation or elimination of the latter, that is, the garden's new life on the canvas. In the course of an increasingly radical approach, Monet transforms the reality he experiences in the garden into the otherness of a pictorial space in perpetual movement. He finally perfects his procedure in the transgressive space of the Tulieries Orangery that forces the viewer to move around the famous *Nymphéas* as if he were actually strolling in a garden.

Neither Klee's existentialist approach, nor Monet's epistemological one, nor the realist one (that is present in various artistic schools of thought) constitutes the characteristic twentieth-century standard of pictorial representation. During the period of technical reproducibility of the works outlined and discussed by Walter Benjamin, gardens were in effect represented in the form of a myriad of watercolor-style images. It was the increasingly popular garden journals and books, which confronted us with different technical realities by drawing upon traditional reproduction that poeticized classical frontal perspective and added a neo-impressionist touch of color and vagueness to the whole. In a period where photography was fully capable of visually translating gardens into an image, painters such as Marie Marguerite Réol (1880–1963) or Octave Victor Guillonet (1872–1967)—not to mention garden authors themselves—became indispensable as this watercolor style was prized by the public. This pictorial mode that sometimes borders on Kitsch, translates the reality of the garden from something voluntarily anachronistic into something recognizable, decorative, and cute. In this manner, visual representation functions as a means to itemize the gardens and to idealize them at the same time showing their strongest and most colorful brilliance. Yet, visual representation not only pertains to the reception of gardens but also influences their production. The watercolor style goes so

FIGURE 7.3: Paul Vera, The "modern" garden in the property of Charles de Noailles, Paris. Photo by Man Ray, from *L'Illustration*, 1932.

far as to invest in a conception of new gardens that required them in their turn to resemble the images reproduced in bulk in fashionable journals and manuals. The eclectic idiom—the Provençal, Mediterranean, neo-Roman, neo-French, neo-picturesque styles, and so on—and the luxuriance of over-abundance suggested in the artistic images mutually reinforce each other. This interplay between the garden and its pictorial representation sometimes takes on paradoxical forms. It suffices to think of the fact that avant-garde projects by André Vera or Gabriel Guevrekian,—which were influenced by avant-garde painting of the period—would be represented by their inventors in the dominant retrograde and premodern style.

III

In a radical sense, garden photography exists only rarely. It is an exception lost in the immense ocean of insignificant images that render either too much—accumulating details and forcing everything into the whole—or too little. The transition from the photography of gardens to the *art* of photographing gardens occurred during the 1920s. It was the later work of Eugène Atget that put an end to the documentary image and created a new form of photographic representation. Atget scarcely concerned himself with producing the biggest and most complete totality possible of gardens and parks in Ile-de-France, nor did he present a picturesque inventory of garden objects in the style of Charles Marville. The former actor and theater connoisseur instead constructed surprising garden scenes within which time as well as space acquired a new importance. For Atget, temporality is not limited to the single and unique absolute, the abstract moment of typical representation. In his work, time in nature and the time of the shoot are superimposed upon each other, inscribing themselves upon the negative particularly as a play of light and shadows. The often-overexposed skies and the almost unreal light spectrums (bordering on technical error) mark the irruption of creative imperfection in photography. The "subjectivity" of light–shadow effects confers an atmosphere on these garden representations that, before Atget's perspective, only literature had known how to express. As is the case with many solitary and obsessive artists,[4] Atget little by little created the possible conditions for a true encounter—a priori difficult, at odds with a conservative, epideictic, superficial hermeneutic tradition—with his subjects. This experimental aspect, the recognition of a site's physical passageways and the availability of depicting the most casual elements found there, was also evident in the spatiality of the images. Through his lenses, Atget sculpted the reality of gardens, and in translating these plastic structures into two-dimensional photography, he revealed a three-dimensional reality that the casual eye overlooks.

Before and after Atget, the garden motif appeared in several photographers' work. Josef Sudek and Jacques-Henri Lartigue, Bernard Plossu and Michael Kenna, André Kertesz, Henri Cartier-Bresson, or Lucien Hervé all captured extraordinary moments in the survival of gardens.[5] The hermeneutics of spaces that we readily imagine from an immaterial and Neoplatonic perspective of the drawing—precisely by relying on photography—or on the basis of compositions of everlasting and unreal beauty (more real than nature) should focus on the true history of gardens that is documented in this enormous and continuous work provided by many important photographers. It is, however, impossible to generalize on this basis and to draw conclusions or doctrines based on the magically graphic impressions of Kertesz or from the metaphysical compositions (in the pictorial sense) of Michael Kenna, all of whom revisit spaces once frequented by Atget.

It appears more interesting to follow the path of certain representations that are singular for their pragmatics or for their reception. The first case concerns Paul Strand. He set up a studio in Orgeval in Les Yvelines, where he photographed his garden and the surrounding area until his death in 1976. The goal of the iterative quality of the artistic act was the discovery of the garden in its most intimate details, with the result that photographic representation was inscribed in an exemplary story. In effect, Strand transposed Monet's technique to the medium of photography. The two, the painter and the photographer, reference an even more ancient, founding gesture, that of Petrarch, who chose the Vaucluse region for retirement in the middle of the fourteenth century. The poet who left us a legacy of a famous visual representation of his transalpine *locus amoenus* is also the person who conceived gardens that he unceasingly represented in his writings. Strand's obsessive attention to his garden—which became for him the world—raised photography to the rank of representative organ of thought. Petrarch, Monet, and Strand—all create a story centered in the enclosed but infinite universe of the garden.

The second example also concerns the genius loci, that is, the quality of a space as the result of aesthetic work where different strata of representation are superimposed. The case of Prospect Cottage is pertinent in several respects. This famous garden of Derek Jarman already appears as an in situ visual representation of art which precedes its composition: it cites, unconsciously or not, the ready-made collages of Schwitters's, Tinguely's machines, dry gardens, mounds and arrangements of stones from *Land Art*, and so on. The site itself then became a cinematographic setting (*War Requiem*, *The Garden*) later to be studied by photographer Howard Sooley in a series of images that unceasingly are exhibited worldwide and influence our perspective on gardens in general. In this case, more than in others, photographic representation has contributed to transforming reality into a contemporary myth. It is true that images of countless gardens of the world also transport us to the depicted sites. The image is part of a large semiotic circuit at the heart of which advertising, television, photography, and tourism work hand in hand. Our perspective comes *after*, always after awareness that we acquire by visual representation.

Photographs of the Garden of Jarman represent the negation of this cultural practice. Prospect Cottage—the anti-garden, at the same time playful and therapeutic, rational and constructed from the randomness of found-treasures—elicited a different mode of representation. The respective images are no longer those traditional, mimetic-descriptive, or sentimental-surrealistic ones, and the central perspective is also abolished. These images are, rather, metaphorical. They present themselves as an analogy of almost nothing; they are of an austere nature arranged by humankind but which—thanks to the gesture of an artist—takes on the form of almost everything or of totality rediscovered. The myth of this space and this extreme garden (not overlooking its testimonial aspect) was thus found in a prolongation of another fashion of perceiving and conceiving gardens.

IV

At the start of the nineteenth century in his novel *Elective Affinities,* Goethe gave an important boost to the critical thinking about gardens. His famous book unmasked the prize and the stakes governing large parks of the period, identifying the enclosed garden space as an impaired form of representation rendered obsolete by history.[6] One of the twentieth century's guiding works in cinema also contained a thinly veiled critique of the world of garden representation. Fritz Lang's *Metropolis* (1927) begins with a dazzling and voyeuristic incursion into the world of eternal gardens, where high society's happy few delight themselves. Such a space is at the same time the ironic synthesis or merging of all of civilization's gardens as well as their transcendence—the end of all gardens. Lang's garden is an Eden, the garden of all gardens, but it alludes to the Renaissance (grottoes and rock gardens), to the formal (symmetric layout), and to the picturesque (winding paths and streams in a hidden section of the garden) styles too. It appears to be a totally synthetic paradise, a post-Babylonian ensemble, illuminated around the clock and decorated with giant—genetically modified?—plants. Everything there is artificial and mechanical to the point that the vegetation—the only greenery to be found in the year 2026 metropolis—also seems unreal and theatrical. The fauna (the peacock and the mechanical children) and flora of this Eden-like garden all look static, immature, and out of place. "Gotho," the steward, and the mechanically erotic girls complete the overall impression of an alienated paradise that the saving appearance of a character with the predestined name of Mary will suddenly show in its true light. The radical dualism of the two worlds that characterizes Metropolis's expressionist vision confers upon the garden an important though nonetheless nefarious role: the fake plant life goes nicely with distorted social relationships, at least up to the point where the enclosure's invisible walls crumble in confrontation with reality; reality is symbolized by a young girl and the "children" that miraculously emerge from the subterranean world. The visual representation of the garden presented in *Metropolis,* cinema's first epic work of science fiction, identifies a whole series of fundamental and contemporary problems concerning gardens, such as "nature in the city," the radical modification of nature, the obsolete but all too-real power games practiced in and by gardens, the social cost, and associated ambiguities about luxury and sensuality. However, the garden also functions as the master scene of an "other" desire, as a savior that transforms the main character (Freder Fredersen) and the entire society, which the young man will eventually liberate with Marie. She is the symbolic incarnation of the oppressed subterranean world. Lang recalls this in his *Nibelungen* (Siegfried greets Kriemhild in the gardens of Worms castle.)

The *incipit* of another film, no less famous than *Metropolis*, plunges the viewer into the universe of gardens. The opening of *Citizen Kane* (1941) leads us to the window of a castle by way of an immense, almost abandoned estate. The script by Mankiewicz imagined a topography that was initially flat but that is artificially transformed into a landscape of rolling hills and valleys crowned by a fake mountain with the media magnate C. F. Kane's castle as its summit. The intensely melancholy sequence of the estate briefly reveals eclectic architectural elements close in style to Kitsch: "The castle dominates itself, an enormous pile, compounded of several genuine castles, of European origin, of varying architecture—dominates the scene, from the very peak of the mountain." Using a mixture of allegorical baroque and romantic esthetic, the sequence shows traces of an old zoological park, a golf course, a lagoon, several cottages, and an imposing bridge. Only a vast formal garden seems to have maintained its initial form. The whole estate is reflected in the sole lit window of the enormous gothic-style edifice where the main protagonist is in the process of dying. The window—a metaphor for gaze, for landscape, for pictorial and cinematographic art—and the external landscape built into the mountainside match each other. In the history of gardens, the window is a distinct place. It is from the vantage point of an exemplary window that a garden is best contemplated in its totality, be it at the Vatican (the Belvedere courtyard) or at Vaux-le-Vicomte. Gardens are themselves conceived from these spots of observation and power. Windows are also a threshold, the link between the exterior (the estate) and the interior (K's life). Thus, *Citizen Kane* begins and ends with the sign "No Trespassing." This commonplace inscription evokes the protagonist. The viewer also sees a gigantic wrought-iron *K*. It is K's estate, and he is an expression of it. To trespass it, nevertheless, in spite of the warning sign, means to read and to expose both the garden and K's life. In Welles's film, visual representation of the garden—it is a garden of all gardens, a composite catalogue of the history of gardens—is dialogic, an extremely rich intertext. Xanadu, the name of the site, brings to mind the famous Colerigerian vision of *Kubla Khan* ("And there were gardens bright with sinuous rills"). But it also evokes Fonthill, William Beckford's estate, and Edgar Allen Poe's *Domain of Arnheim*. *Citizen Kane* refers to W. R. Hearst's gigantic creation *San Simeon* (in spite of its "No Trespassing" sign, the film itself crosses, trespasses the line that separates the private and the public and the fantastical and the recognizable places) all the while aiming for a type of grandiloquent gardens in general like Biltmore in North Carolina; the *Citizen Kane* script even identifies Xanadu with Angkor Vat: "Ankor Vat, the night the last king died."

A very somber light—as bizarre as the artificial light in Fritz Lang's Eden—illuminates the space of *Citizen Kane*'s garden. These two monuments of cinematographic art cast a critical and skeptical eye on gardens. The inhumanity of the gardens in *Metropolis* and *Citizen Kane*, accentuated by their old-fashioned style, comes from the idea of enclosure and of an exclusive use of a space.

In Jacques Tati's *Mon Oncle* (1958), the viewer is confronted with a very different form of inhumanity. In Tati's first Technicolor film, there are two clearly distinct worlds: one exhibits a gaudy, flashy modernity, with exaggerated shapes and colors. The other depicts the downside of life of common folk living in working-class neighborhoods, a life of slowness and pleasant imperfection. *Mon Oncle* is the swan song of an organic and disordered world left behind by speed and technology. (In this film, Tati issues a solitary cry of alarm, much like Baudelaire had done a century earlier in condemning the death of the "vieux Paris" for the benefit of modernity's countless construction sites and their confused bric-a-brac.) Modernity—or should we already speak of postmodernity?—is symbolized by the *Villa Arpel*. The house and garden are more machines to be inhabited than places of life. Everything is cold and mechanical. The fish-shaped aluminum fountain in the middle of the garden seems like the incarnation of the false values of a bourgeoisie that adorns itself with modernity as it had previously done with other styles. In principal, this theatrical fountain is turned on only to impress important visitors; like the garden and the house, in general, it is only a showpiece. The show becomes a grotesque comedy, given that the fountain's machinery perpetually breaks down, as does that of the garage or the gate. From then on the entire garden is transformed into an impassable and inhuman space—the main path is equally absurd and antifunctional.

The villa and garden project designed for Tati by Jacques Lagrange brings to mind several well-known examples. It is impossible not to think of the Véra brothers' modernist gardens or Charles de Noailles's garden in Hyères designed by Guevrekian. To this day, these famous gardens of the 1920s and 1930s remain exceptional peculiarities without having really created a modern style. To revisit them via cinematographic representation forty years later raises fundamental questions regarding garden art idioms of the twentieth century. Tati is not antimodernist, however. His reflection rather concerns modernity's contradictions and unachieved promises. The conflict of the two poles or worlds outlined in *Mon Oncle* is also a conflict of two temporalities: that of the imprecise and full duration of time that passes in popular spaces versus the speed and saccadic rhythm characteristic of modern spaces. Only uncontrolled homeless dogs get to penetrate into the inhuman garden of the Villa Arpel from the humane time of the popular, but already lost, world.

One can pursue this voyage of garden representation in film with another major work, Alain Resnais's *Last Year at Marienbad* (1961). This disconcerting antifilm, conceived with writer Alain Robbe-Grillet, introduces anonymous people (A, a woman; M, probably her husband; X, a stranger and her lover) who participate in a vague story that is deconstructed rather than (re)constructed. The core narrative about a love triangle is diluted upon the hybrid presentation that mixes temporal and modal plans. The film is shot exclusively in a large luxury hotel of a former baroque chateau. The architecture and landscaped scenes of a formal garden seem to be more than scenery; they are separate subjects and protagonists. Alain Resnais' film presents a *mise en abyme* of art in general: it exposes the inextricable architecture of a luxury hotel, the landscape architecture, paintings, engravings, statues, antique furniture, dance, theater, music, and so on—in sum, the totality of aesthetic forms reunited in a strangely ex-territorial place apart. The boundless formal garden space that surrounds the chateau amplifies and singularizes the characters' situation. The void and the sense of extreme static confer a mechanical and uselessly ceremonial quality to the inhabitants, reinforced by being shot in black-and-white. The sterility and coldness of the formal compositions, in which every individual (tree) is but a serial element among others and therefore reproducible and replaceable, refers to the highly problematic identity of the characters who are perhaps merely reenacting a story from the "previous year." Could the lovers have met here, or elsewhere, in another chateau last year? Here, visual representation—the principal topic of the film—is imbibed with a literary element: Robbe-Grillet's *La Jalousie*, a story from Bioy Casares's *L'invention de Morel*, and an Ibsen play (*The Master Builder*) have been identified among others as possible sources for *L'année dernière à Marienbad*. Moreover, Sacha Vierny's camera evokes the atmospheres of Atget and the painter Paul Delvaux. As for the gait of the humans, it brings to mind Oskar Schlemmer's mechanical ballet. What is prominent is the sense of an enclosure that is quite *unheimlich* and freezes the characters: "There are always walls, hallways, doors, and on the other side of them, more walls, et cetera," says X. "Before reaching you, before returning to you, you have no notion of all the space that had to be crossed. And now that you are here where I have led you, you slip away again. But you are there in this garden, at arm's length, within earshot, in sight, at arm's length." Resnais shot most of the outdoor scenes in Bavaria. One of the longest sequences begins in a Parisian studio, continues in Nymphenburg castle, and ends in the Schleissheim gardens. However, this sense of movement (in filming and directing) is repeated within the film and, more precisely, in the garden. At one point in time, X. is reminiscent of a statue (a Fredrikstrasse piece); the film shows a statue on a terrace; M. later makes a remark about a painting in which this same statue appears; finally, one rediscovers the statue in the chateau's garden. The original of the statue that is always on the move—as is the identity and history of the characters—was made of papier-mâché; it is a forgery.

This uncanny aspect of the garden and the images that invoke it also characterizes the work of Michelangelo Antonioni—the filmmaker who unceasingly questioned the nature of man-made green spaces. In *I Vinti* (1952) and *La Notte* (1960), the Italian artist gave particular prominence to parks. In the latter film, at the blurry moment of daybreak a couple is seen leaving an immense villa, the site of an all-night party. The park, lit by the white light of dawn, will be the transitory place where the lovers' fate is decided and they separate. The peak of Antonioni's reflection on gardens occurs in *Blow-Up*. One can interpret this film as the story of a multifaceted fact that occurred in a park. It was inspired by a Julio Cortazar story (*Las babas del Diablo*) and received numerous interpretations from diverse perspectives.[7] The plot is simple and known: Thomas, a London-style photographer, happens on a couple in a park during an outing that momentarily removes him from his superficial world. He develops "stolen" pictures of the lovers, blows up certain perturbing shots, which throws him into a quandary. He develops a second series of photos and discovers a murder scene behind the love scene. On returning to the park (during the night and not in broad daylight), he discovers the body of a man who has disappeared by the time of the next visit. Antonioni's park seems like an uncertain, interstitial zone. The filmmaker shot the scenes in Maryon Park, Charlton, in the southeast of London. It is part of the city, but it is also detached from it, representing the *other* of urban spaces. It is the scene of a crime, a lovers' lane, and an obscure space with uncertain internal boundaries. In Antonioni's vision, the garden lost all romantic qualities for good. Disorder and danger stalked visitors instead of celebrations and relaxation. Here, nature itself seems to turn against humankind, as is evident in the unforgettable scene of the effect of the wind on the leaves of the large trees. Nature and the nature of the space seem violent—even love takes a violent form—as in the vision of Giacomo Leopardi. As is the case, too, in Goethe's *Elective Affinities*, Antonioni's park is also a place where illusions die. The illusions are particularly significant, given the fact that the park's mystery evokes the mystery of the eyes, which in turn evokes the mystery of images. Antonioni—cinematographer-painter and collector of art and photography—chooses a doubtful Thomas of a photographer as the hero of *Blow-Up* and uses film as a device for hermeneutic reflection. By beginning with "documentary" images intended to render the facts as they are, the director questions the meaning of reality itself. The construction of reality (or of necessary illusions) already characterizes the initial scene of the discovery of the couple in love. Antonioni uses forty-three different shots in order to capture and not capture the essential. The variation, repetition, and modulation that evoke body movements, the necessity to turn things around, illustrate the impossibility of an exclusive *presentation*. The photographic representation that follows shows the same difficulty. In looking at what is hidden in the park, Antonioni analyzes what hides behind the images (with the director's words, "We know that under the image revealed there is another which is truer to reality and under this image still another and yet again still another under this last one, right down to the true image or reality, absolute, mysterious, which no one will ever see or perhaps right down to the decomposition of any image, of any reality."[8]). Thomas's actions (that willingly explore the *nonplaces* of modernity, one of which is the park itself) and the cinematic narrative represent the attempt to overcome the opacity of deeds and images. The protagonist's actions and the narrative run into the effect of randomness and disappearance that risks confounding all appearance. The last part of the film presents us with several disappearances: not only that of the body and the woman in the park, but also Thomas's disappearance from the vantage point of cinematic narrator. A famous scene shows Thomas and a group of revelers miming a tennis game that ends with the disappearance of the central figure. The park in itself subsists, but only as a place of absences.

It is by more or less referring openly to *L'année dernière à Marienbad* and to *Blow-Up* that Peter Greenaway created *The Draughtman's Contract* (1982). The three films share the theme of murder, the omnipresence of the hero, and a park that Greenaway transforms into a playing field of a bittersweet story. The British filmmaker's story is about an aristocrat, Mrs. Herbert, who wants to give her absent husband a gift of a series of twelve representations of their estate. She enters into a highly uncommon contract with Mr. Neville, an artist who is very convinced of his capability, whereby she provides a sexual favor for each drawing. The film, which has been dubbed a sort of baroque *Blow-Up*, exposes the complicated relationships between exterior and interior, insider and outsider, reason and passion. The narrative thread of action leads to two murders—those of Mr. Herbert and of the artist-lover, Mr. Neville. It is also the story of the latter's loss of artistic skill in visual representation. What makes *The Draughtman's Contract* particularly interesting is the *representation of representation*—and this is independent of the eruption of the irrational and jumbled baroque that already hints at the Greenaway of the future and his sometimes-doubtful aesthetic inclinations.

First and foremost, Greenaway shows representation in action. He illustrates this by repetitively showing how to frame the landscape with the support of a grid (*reticolato* or *velo*) familiar from Alberti and Dürer. This allows the extraction of the most exact and true image. The growing distance between drawing and reality, both represented in cinematographic images, illustrates the crisis of mimesis for the profit of dangerous and murderous fiction. From a narrative standpoint, the tissue of the process of representation undermines the power and the artist's life. From a reflexive standpoint, it draws attention to the presuppositions and implications of representation (to represent is to master the world). Finally, from an auto-reflexive standpoint, the relationships between the represented subject and object are completely murky. Neville's drawings in reality are those of the director, Peter Greenaway. The film takes place in 1694. It functions as a meta-philosophical tale, or, better yet, as a postmodern exercise in semiology.

The realm of the nonself (*Nicht-Ich*), the exterior world, symbolized by the park, is the metaphor of a world where, in the last resort, everything is only representation. Whereas the park itself, the family of Herbert and the drawings remain, the artist himself disappears, just like the lord, Mr. Herbert. The park, object of a paradoxical veneration, is transformed into a place of absence and exclusion. Greenaway questions on the basis of this negativity the multiple aspects of the reception of gardens. The reception is highly ambiguous: the drawings substitute the garden (it "travels" through the world as image); at the same time, Neville wishes to sell the drawings, in order to finance the construction of a monument—another representation—of the late lord. And all this occurs in a site being already, by definition, (as a creation) a place of representation. It is impossible not to think in this context of a famous representation, Gainsborough's *Mr. and Mrs. Andrews*. Gainsborough's *conversation piece* shows a wealthy couple in their estate close to Sudbury, in Suffolk. Their highly artificial aspect and the puppetlike presence of the two figures set apart from the rural landscape reveal their nonintegration into nature, integration however wished or better, represented in the posture of the couple and that of the landscaped countryside. This idyll is in reality, just like the one invented by Greenaway or by other authors of cinemtaographic visions of gardens, only a dangerous illusion. The painting of Gainsborough brings together, just like *The Draughtman's Contract*, economy, social relations, sexuality and representation. The shotgun of Mr. Andrews expresses a doubtful virility, since the body of his wife remains empty, as if it still awaited an absent object (a child, a book, a bird hunted by the husband). The shotgun, a decisive symbol of the history of the gardens—many Renaissance gardens developed, centered in the *barco*, as hunting grounds—is replaced in Greenaway's postmodern fairy tale by the instrument of drawing, and by the talented and fatal hand of the artist.

Another cult film of the 1980s marks a final step and deconstruction in this cinematographic reflection on gardens. The famous opening of *Blue Velvet* by David Lynch (1986) destroys the post-arcadian image of the garden and dislodges the spectator definitively from this haven of peace unaffected by time and custom. The garden of Mr. Beaumont becomes the scene of a tragicomic heart seizure. It is inside the *locus amoenus* of a middle-class family in an ordinary American city (Lumberton) and a perfectly normal urban reality (expression of the good times) that the catastrophe takes place and where the glance of the camera transcends the surface of the idyll in order to descend into the violent underground realm of the insects. The garden is only an illusion that the cinematographic narration quickly cancels. The bloodred roses and yellow tulips, truer than nature; the dog; the plants; the children; the friendly firemen; and so on—the entire well-gardened and landscaped suburban paradise metamorphoses itself into its opposite. It is especially the lawn as the symbol of national identity, of freedom, and of the sociality, the American lawn that George Teyssot highlighted,[9] which *Blue Velvet* deconstructs in the gesture of the impotent hose, phallically turned around Mr. Beaumont agonizing in pain. The antithesis of the garden is the zone of the wastelands, where Jeffrey Beaumont will find a severed and decaying human ear. In *Blue Velvet*, the garden is only the waiting room for hell. Hell starts in the thick green grass, becomes terrifying in the underworld of the ugly black bugs, is again present in the grass where the severed ear is found, and takes in the end the form and extension of the whole outer world.

V

With the hindsight of history, we can observe that the phenomenon of the so-called English garden would simply have not come into being had it not been for a series of representations. Pictorial representations (ideal landscape), drawings, engravings, and especially their circulation (but also imaginative representations in the minds of travelers) created the picturesque parks that since then have become representations of these images to the second or third degree. It seems inevitable (and essential) that the representations that are today in the process of being distributed worldwide would cause a further enrichment of gardens instead of diminishing them and rendering them more uniform.

And today, more than the eighteenth century, we are in possession of many more modes or media of representation. Their different visual representations of gardens confront us with a contradictory and surprising state of affairs. The film sequences are almost always negative and critical; they identify gardens as dangerous and ambiguous places, as the precise opposite of the ideas of naturalness and nature that the images nevertheless strive to suggest. Photography and painting, contrariwise, are more likely to be celebratory, even those with melancholic, ironic, or solitary impressions. Photography praises gardens; in representing them, painting can do likewise, or at least praise the idea of gardens. Film almost never does. Representing gardens in different media consists in translating one artistic form (the garden) into another. This semiotic operation exposes itself to certain constraints: photography and painting are by definition static, while film is dynamic and discursive. The cinematic possibility of integrating gardens into a narrative context creates an interrogative and complex horizon of reflection. Yet, another aspect concerns the finality of representations. A garden photograph is at once a representation of a garden and the representation of a particular perspective. Certain films (by Lang, Resnais, and Lynch) merely use gardens, for the garden is not the object of their reflections. Other filmmakers (Tati, Antonioni, and Greenaway) seem to question, at least indirectly, the meaning and functions of the gardens or parks they show.

It is important to bring together the modes of the cinema and the many static images of artistic photography and painting. The infinite number of images (mostly photography) that circulate in journals, manuals, advertising, and books illustrate the absent original in a neutral manner. This neutrality is, however, an illusion, to which the cinematographic perspective on gardens draws our attention and in doing so touches the essence of gardens. For the vision conveyed by cinematic representations criticizes their pastness, the unilaterally historical value, the ersatz social function of them. Further, it denounces the omission of temporal implications, anachronisms, and functional absurdities. This critique of gardens in the name of gardens also pervades the best garden photography and paintings. However, a further danger lurks in the mechanical representations of the computer, for the digital visualization of gardens, thanks to certain programs (computer-aided design, or CAD) that are more and more high performance, creates the illusion of perfect representation. The virtual image seeks to presents itself as an accurate illustration not only of space but also of time. As part of this caliber of representations must be included such recent phenomena as tele-gardens[10] (gardens that Internet users upkeep, monitor, and admire from their computers) or the existence of completely virtual gardens that "exist" and "live" in the unreality of the Internet. The physical and imaginative or ideal existence of the garden increasingly seems to rely on the inexhaustible versatility of its representations.

CHAPTER EIGHT

Gardens and the Larger Landscape

DAVID LEATHERBARROW

Prato is never found on the way to Prato, but only where it is. And a person is more certain of being outside Prato when he sees it at arm's length, then he is when ten miles distant, unable to see it at all.
—Michelangelo[1]

Gardens can be distinguished from the larger landscape in a relatively simple way: the first are bounded, the second is not. Gardens have limits; the landscape extends toward the horizon. This distinction is not only intuitively clear, but is also supported etymologically: both *garden* and *yard* stem from sources that variously signify enclosure. Likewise, a Greek cognate gave rise to the Latin *hortus* and English *court*, two more instances of bounded space.[2] The reach of the landscape, by contrast, is as far as the eye can see, as in seventeenth-century Dutch paintings, prospects to which the early use of the word *landscape* seems to have referred. As with most simple distinctions, however, this one requires qualification. When one thinks a little more deeply about the distinction between the garden as a contained site and its landscape container a rather striking ambiguity presents itself: the gardens that are culturally significant establish meaningful connections to the larger landscape by means of the very elements that posit their separation. My aim in this chapter is to show how the distances that gardens open up within the landscape establish cultural continuity by virtue of separation, which is to say, create topographical identity by means of both difference and distance.

More than two-and-a-half centuries of aesthetic theory have accustomed us to the notion that cultural objects in general and works of art in particular stand apart from the spaces and settings of everyday life. A painting's frame can be taken as an instrument and sign of this separation, for it cuts the work off from both its immediate background and wider milieu. The pedestal on which a sculptural work stands accomplishes a similar sort of detachment. Likewise, acoustic isolation sustains the performance of a musical work, and darkness in the auditorium is required for theatrical production. In each of these cases, in all aesthetic situations, the world of the work begins where the world of everyday life comes to an end. When seen as cultural objects, gardens, too, would seem to require separation; each encloses itself within and against surrounding terrain. Garden walls serve this purpose, as do tree screens, hedgerows, planting beds, bodies of water, and so on. But unlike the frame that limits the painting's two-dimensional surface, the garden's living three-dimensionality can never be completely contained, for it depends on some of the same elements that animate and renew the larger landscape: waterways, sunlight, rain, and paths of pedestrian movement, to say nothing of figurative or iconographic elements, which have historical associations that far transcend those of a single work. Although the garden cannot be equated with the landscape, it cannot be separated from it either.

The larger landscape to which gardens relate includes both town and country. From this simple observation follows the single point I would like to demonstrate: the designed landscape has the task of mediating the various distances society has taken with respect to the several centers of common culture, in both the city and the country.

Distances, in this usage, can be understood in different ways, only one of which is metric. I consider four. The first is perhaps the most obvious, horizontal distance, which is to say being away from some center of cultural activity, for example, being within the ever-widening suburbs of our cities and towns. Distance in this sense spreads and divides the horizon. My second sense of the term is perhaps less immediately obvious, but no less clear, vertical distance, which opens when life's settings are removed from the level of ordinary affairs, the ground plane, and resituated above it, in a roof garden, which is not the same thing as a raised terrace, no matter how highly elevated. The horizon for this location is the sky not the street, and at a very great horizontal distance, the cloudy edge of the wider landscape. My third sense of distance is geographical. But, here, too, I am thinking of a particular kind of geography, one composed of discontinuous or displaced territories. I have in mind those landscapes in which one is removed from a given site's familiar horizon, only to find oneself in some part of a foreign terrain or country, without having traveled there, being *there* by virtue of representation. I suspect my fourth idea of distance will be the most difficult to grasp: it arises out of the technological, industrial, or postindustrial character of our time. In this case, one takes a distance from settings of any particularity because the elements of which the garden is made could be found anywhere across the globe. Comparatively, these four show gardens reaching beyond their proper limits toward greater and greater distances. Examples of mediation form the chapters of cultural history because the connections they create enable the sharing that culture assumes. The sequence of these four charts a rather simple but suggestive history of garden design. A study much longer than this one would be required to elaborate such a history. Here I limit myself to two examples for each of the four distances.

Having sketched this preliminary indication of distances within the larger landscape, let me restate this argument's principal thesis: the task of garden design is to sustain and develop common culture by mediating these four distances. Put differently, the task of design is to overcome what David Summers once called "the defect of distance,"[3] making the far appear near, without disavowing its remoteness, by providing representations, of one coherent world, not many distinct ones.

HORIZONTAL DISTANCE

The gardens designed by Roberto Burle Marx for the Museum of Modern Art in Rio de Janeiro were built on a bayside site that was previously filled with water. Land for the project was supplied by the leveling of nearby Santo Antônio hill. Both the gardens and the museum are located along the Gloria and Flamengo waterfronts, between the Guanabara Bay and Santos Dumont airport. More-distant horizons include the mountains and the city. According to a statement made by Burle Marx in 1959, seven years after the project began, his intention was to provide spaces for the "pleasure of promenade and leisure." His brief text also alluded to a need to develop the project at three scales, the garden, park, and landscape: "the gardens . . . of the Museum of Modern Art were worked out keeping in view their integration into the landscape, visualizing the area with the characteristics of a park."[4] Differentiation between these scales required the construction of spatial limitations, or the use of different instruments of enclosure in the midst of the landscape's wide expanse, at the margins of the city. The elements he selected for this purpose included tree screens (rows of royal palm), masses of planting that would create blocks of colors and texture, and strong points of contrast between gardens and sea, as well as between the garden and the city and mountains. But the differentiation of places was not only formal; Flamengo Park, he said, was also meant to contain "living spaces, terraces, gardens, patios with fountains, waterspouts, and sculpture exhibitions."[5] Obviously, they too required differentiation and boundaries of one kind or another. Finally, he also used figurative elements with local origin for purposes of garden definition: stones that were cut for but unused in the construction of the buildings were spread out or stacked up in various places to make rock gardens. Particularly striking are the upright slabs of granite set in beds of smooth and circular river rocks, an arrangement that echoes the juxtaposition of columns and water in one of the museum's courtyards.

FIGURE 8.1: Roberto Burle Marx, Gardens of the Museum of Modern Art, Flamego Park, Rio de Janeiro, 1952–1953. Photo: David Leatherbarrow.

On one scale, the park is a world unto itself, distinguished from the larger landscape of mountains, city, and sea. But on another scale, spaces within the park—the several gardens—are also distinguished from one another. Despite these separations, the gardens, park, and larger landscape form one coherent topography. The question is how?

Burle Marx asserted that the park's primary purpose was "the pleasure of promenade." This type of landscape experience was not his invention, places for promenade existed well before his park was built, in Rio to be sure, in other cities too. What's more, promenades were developed elsewhere in Rio after the museum gardens were finished. Perhaps the most famous and popular of these is the waterfront at Copacabana, also designed by Burle Marx in 1970. At Copacabana the urban edge consists of a number of elements laid out in layers or ranks: first, there are small gardens that front each of the waterfront buildings (generally hotels); then, there is an exceptionally wide terrace running the full length of each block (inscribed with abstract patterns designed by Burle Marx); the next layer consists of a heavily traveled roadway (Avenida Atlantica, divided by a wide tree-lined island, also displaying Burle Marx's designs); and then, a comparatively narrow bike path, which is edged by an exceptionally wide walkway (the promenade), which borders the beach and the seaside. The promenade is not only distinctive for its width, but also for its paving pattern. For Burle Marx, these patterns gave the walkways "rhythmic variety." This quality is particularly clear in the case of the promenade, the design of which approximates a traditional *meander* pattern. Yet, its origin was neither pedestrian nor urban, it seems to have been based on Portuguese mosaic decoration. Still, the pattern serves as an emblem of Rio's waterfront and the pleasure of meandering along its edge.

This very same pattern appears twice in the Museum's gardens, each built at a different scale with different materials: one is a stone path on the building's city side and the other is a grassy lawn facing the bay. The task of the entry walk is to mediate points of departure and arrival, which is to say, the bridge leading from the town toward the bay and the arrival space beneath the raised Museum. The paving pattern is repetitive, like that of the town's component parts, but it is also nonorthogonal, like the water's edge. Mixing these geometries mediates representations of sea and city form. Although this walk is both directional and connective, its ample width is sufficiently generous to invite use as a promenade. The side lawn also links that part to its wider horizon. In this case, however, the spaces of the Museum are joined to both the bay and the mountains beyond. A stroll across the lawn is largely nondirectional, but the line of royal palms that limits its spread suggests that it, too, is a space for "the pleasure of promenade," along the line of its meander. As at Copacabana, a walk from the city's streets to the water's edge progresses through layers or ranks, guided by variations on a single theme.

Thus, the first answer to my question about how horizontal distances are overcome is practical, for these settings, constructed at different scales, set out similar ways of accommodating a single mode of cultural practice, promenade, a practice that links discrete "gardens" to analogous places in the larger landscape.

The park also extends itself into its environmental horizons. Burle Marx is known to have spent considerable time in Brazilian forests, not only studying but also discovering new rocks and plants. Many of these were preserved and nurtured in his own greenhouses. In attempting to build ecological gardens around the museum he first established a foundation of stones and earth on the landfill, then built various "communities" of plant species that would thrive on that substrate, although the native location of many was the forest not the shore. The gardens also used plants that could resist the strong winds and salty air of the bayside location. Plants that were appropriate to one location were thus intermixed with those typical of another, canceling the distance between places near and far.

Seen together, the gardens and the park mediate local and remote conditions: on the one hand, the museum, urban edge, and seaside micro-climate, on the other, the city as a whole, the wider shore, the entire country, and—across the Atlantic—elements of Portuguese origin.

The Pedregal Gardens designed by Luis Barragán in Mexico City were part of a residential development southwest of city, outside the peripheral road, near the newly built university. What distinguished this suburban development from all the others that preceded and followed it was the land on which it was built, lava fields formed 2,500 years ago, after the eruption of several nearby volcanoes. Even today the soil is striking: very dark purple, nearly black in color, pebbles or gravel intermixed with outcroppings of rock, some shallow, some up to thirty feet deep. The spread of burned rock and black sand around the Bay of Naples has a similar appearance, but in Mexico City, there is no shore, the mountains are more distant, and the lower foothills spread out more widely. Once violent, the volcanoes that gave rise to the Pedregal site are now quiet. Since the eruptions, erosion and the slow but steady deposit of airborne particles on the site has allowed for the growth of lichen, moss, and a wide range of flowers and grasses. There is great delicacy, even fragility in some of the site's vegetation, especially when compared to its rock.

FIGURE 8.2: Luis Barragán, demonstration garden, El Pedregal, Mexico City, 1945–1950. Photo: Armando Salas Portugal.

Despite the aesthetic appeal of much of this, the development of the site in Barragán's time seemed very improbable. In the 1880s, the location was referred to as the "bad land," *mal pais*. Not only was it remote from the town, but the rock formation was also commonly taken to be unyielding: "crawling with snakes, scorpions, and criminals." Local residents referred to the site as a "primary school of witchcraft."[6] Observers from elsewhere were no more optimistic: built on a "desert of lava of the most capricious formation," the site seemed "best suited to goats." Yet, because it was marginal, the land was also inexpensive. What is more, in the 1940s, it had become a popular haunt for some of the city's leading cultural figures: painters, such as Diego Rivera; poets, such as Carlos Pellicer; and photographers, such as Armando Salas Portugal, whose images of the site are among the very best we have. And finally, the site received positive attention after archaeologists discovered traces of ancient settlements there. The digs revealed that the land had been occupied between 1200 and 400 B.C.E., thus "contemporary with the earliest Olmec cities on Mexico's Gulf Coast."[7] For individuals with nationalist leanings, this history gave it considerable importance. Barragán, for his part, had already built a garden nearby before embarking on the development. By means of this and other exploratory gardens, he felt he had discovered "possibilities" in the site, possibilities for "enhancing the beauty of the rocks, taking advantage of their texture and forms as the most decorative and impressive elements."[8]

Into this ancient, expansive, and unyielding site, Barragán cut a thirty-acre residential development. The idea of the layout was to both accentuate the original character of the landscape and provide private gardens for the houses: "one for each house, limited and enclosed with walls, trees and foliage to screen the view from the outside and from neighboring houses."[9] Barragán argued for the importance of private gardens as a form of compensation for the predominantly public character of contemporary life. This meant achieving a balance or the right proportion between open and closed gardens—the latter to provide space (and time) for mediation and creative and spiritual ideas. As for the open gardens, he proposed a number of key public spaces: an entry court, the demonstration gardens, a few other plazas, and two public parks. Sadly, very few of these public spaces survive the way he imagined them. The individual gardens, however, do remain. Privacy, Barragán thought, would not be the only point of contrast represented by the gardens: the architecture of the development had to be modern, in contrast with the architecture of the town nearby. "In order not to harm and spoil the beauty of the landscape ... architectural forms ... must be of such simplicity—abstract in quality—and primary geometric forms."[10]

Thus, although the site as a whole consisted of a number of divisions, some spatial, others practical, still others cultural, it also formed a coherent topography within the larger landscape. Consider first the distinctions that resulted from the site's natural formation. The land consists of gravel or rock that is both unyielding and fertile, the first characterizes the land's depth; the second, its surface. Below the upper crust, signs of life are entirely lacking, only rock, burned and black. Yet, by virtue of the deposit of dust through several centuries, together with the beneficent influence of a regular and even climate, a living surface has been formed that is soft, green, and productive. Barragán thought that this opposing set of conditions would sustain the development of both wet and dry gardens, each as an intensification of a local possibility, a crystallization or concentration of wider, ambient conditions and forces.

The separation and integration that is apparent in the physical aspects of the landscape are also present in its spatial order. Barragán described a tension between the spaces of the local and larger landscape: "one must not overdo the theme of circular, panoramic vistas, because a landscape that is held and framed with a proper foreground is worth double. I prefer always uneven grounds and the craziest shapes . . . blessed be the geological disturbances." Within the wide horizon—the landscape—are found and cultivated settings. The first is relatively continuous in its panoramic expanse; the second consists of spots that are invariably unique, by virtue of local irregularities and "crazy" shapes.

In practical terms, the distinction just described parallels the sharp separation between public and private settings, the demonstration gardens and public parks on one hand and the domestic enclosures on the other. The accessibility, ample compass, and shared functioning of the parks and plazas give them a public character. The residential gardens, however, have limited access (because they were sheltered behind high stone walls), are smaller in size, and accommodate domestic functions (play space for children, herb gardens, laundry lines, and so on). Despite these differences, the public and private gardens were made in the same way, out of the same materials: land was leveled, stone was stacked, and limits thus defined, as if the open and closed gardens were corresponding parts of one landscape.

The site's great antiquity allowed its designer and early occupants to understand it as an emblem of Mexican identity. As a cultural landscape, it represented ideas of nationality. Traces of ancestors were found there, vestiges of the country's early beginnings. Although the comments about the site being a school for witchcraft were disparaging, they also attest to its legacy, as a place for ancient practices that had a quasi-religious or spiritual dimension, practices that also gave rise to images and symbols that particularized the Mexican people. The site distinguished itself from its wide surrounds as a particularly intense localization of the country's specific identity. But its buildings were meant to be entirely modern, unburdened by vestiges of colonial architecture, closer in character to the works of Neutra, Wright, and Loewy, simple in form, based on the principles that guided the development of modern building, not (only) Mexican but international in character.

In sum, the Pedregal Gardens occupy a local site that is both separated from and integrated with distant forces and conditions. Many of the gardens are private, introverted, and intimate, but the closed were built with the materials and techniques of the open gardens, as if the same. The project as a whole gives visible form to ideas and aspirations for a Mexican identity, but does so with elements and geometries that can also be discovered in widely distant lands, places that had also embarked on the project of societal modernization. Distance is established by the gardens, but is overcome by their defining elements. The gardens open gaps in the wider landscape, only to indicate the continuities established by that very same topography.

VERTICAL DISTANCE

In a letter to Madame Meyer, one of his clients, Le Corbusier outlined the route he proposed from her bedroom to the roof garden: "From the boudoir one has come up on to the roof which has neither tiles nor slates, but a solarium and swimming pool with grass growing in the joints between the paving stones. The sky is above: with the walls around and no one can see us. In the evening one sees the stars and the somber outline of the trees in the Folly St. James. By means of sliding screens one can cut oneself off completely . . . rather like Robinson, or the paintings of Carpaccio . . . this garden is scarcely *à la francaise*, but a wild shrubbery."[11] About cutting oneself off from the city, but in consideration of another building, he announced that once one reaches the roof garden of the Villa Cook, "you are in Paris no longer."[12] That is only half true: while within the roof garden, you are both isolated from the city and standing at its very heart. This separation and connection were made possible by vertical distance.

The roof garden was listed as the second of Le Corbusier's famous "five points" of the new architecture.[13] In his 1926 manifesto, he offered a rather deadpan account of its origin, describing the possibilities and problems of new building materials and techniques: "reinforced concrete [of which the modern roof was to be made] demands protection against changing temperatures. Over-activity on the part of the reinforced concrete [excessive expansion and contraction following the swing of ambient temperatures] is prevented by the maintenance of a constant humidity on the roof terrace."[14] He then explained how this solution gave rise to a new type of setting: "The roof terrace satisfies both demands (a rain-dampened layer of sand covered with concrete slabs with lawns in the interstices; the earth of the flowerbeds in direct contact with the layer of sand)."[15] This meant that the newly discovered space could "display highly luxuriant vegetation." Moreover, land lost to the city thorough building could be regained above street level: "in general, roof gardens mean to a city the recovery of all the built-up area."[16] So much for his scientific account.

Le Corbusier's buildings indicate that much more was at stake in the design of roof gardens than preserving concrete structures and maximizing usable floor area. Although he never said as much, it seems rather plain that the roof gardens served as a destination for movement through his buildings, the goal of ascent. Such paths, and their destination, can be found in virtually every one of his houses from the 1920s. Yet, the ascent from street to sky was not only passage from darkness to light. The upper levels of the houses often combined settings with opposite qualities, crystal together with cavelike spaces. In the studio house he built for his painter friend Amédée Ozenfant, for example, the upper-level studio is two parts: on one side, two walls and a section of the ceiling form a half-cube of glass, reducing the body of the building to light plus geometry. Paired with this, on the other side of the same space, is an enclosure that possesses entirely contrasting qualities: at the top of a ladder is a tiny reading room and library, enclosed within thick walls and illuminated by a small puncture through the building's front façade. The studio was clearly intended to be a site of creativity. Painterly invention was thought to be possible once the artist elevated himself above the level of mundane affairs. But on one's arrival, one was greeted by contrasting images: an emblem of the earth (the library cave) and a sign of the sky (the luminous crystal).

A similar coupling of terrestrial and celestial imagery can be seen in the apartment Le Corbusier built for himself in the Porte Molitor district of Paris near the Bois de Boulogne (1931–34). The apartment has two sides, one for domestic activities (cooking, dining, and sleeping) and the other for work (the studio). I concentrate on the latter. Like the apartment as a whole, the studio couples contrasting conditions, at least as far as its material makeup is concerned. On one hand, there is the ceiling, a wide white sky that vaults across the room's entire width. It "rests" on two glass walls, one facing the building's light well and the other the expanse above the street. Both the ceiling and the glazing display the possibilities of modern construction. The wall that stands between the two glass ones, however, shows nothing of the techniques and materials of the modern world; its stone is massive, thick, unevenly finished, and rough, as if built according to traditional craft techniques, primitive and earthy. Le Corbusier often had himself photographed in front of this wall, frequently dressed as a laborer or workman. It was against this same surface that he once mounted an exhibition of "primitive art" (together with some works by his contemporaries, Léger and Laurens). The name of the exhibition is indicative of its curator's intent: "les arts primitives dans la maison d'aujourd'hui." The show, like the room itself, joined culture's archaic beginnings with its most recent and progressive accomplishments, as if the two—so distant from one another—were not essentially different.

FIGURE 8.3: Le Corbusier, roof garden, 24 Rue Nungesser et Coli, Paris, 1931–1934. Photo: Foundation Le Corbusier.

The roof garden is approached by means of a circular staircase. The fact that it turns in on itself is significant, for nowhere else in the apartment does movement diverge from the pattern of orthogonals. Once the stairway completes its twist, movement must reorient itself. I think this reorientation was meant to represent a new beginning, if not that, at least a re-presentation of the conjunction of opposites arranged in the apartment and studio below. The stair's extremely thick walls, variously hollowed to house little treasures, come to an end at the base of a lightweight framework that both corners glass screens and supports a roof that cantilevers over the paved part of the roof deck. Here again, cave and crystal are coupled. That the space of ascent was meant to be both enclosed and widely open is apparent in Le Corbusier's description: "the modest space taken up by this staircase shows that in art 'small' or 'large' dimensions do not, as such, exist."[17] I take this as an indication of his aim to establish and overcome vertical distance.

The roof garden faces west, toward and beyond the district of Boulogne. It is certainly a room, but one that is open to a very considerable degree. Le Corbusier intended it to combine domestic and Virgilian life. He admitted some uncertainty about whether to cultivate the garden or let it run wild. But the outbreak of the World War II put an end to that question: "1940 Disaster! Exodus! Paris is deserted. The garden roof . . . has been left to its own devices. Heat waves in 1940 and 42, winter, rain, and snow . . . the abandoned garden does not die but instead responds to these conditions. Wind, birds and insects fill it with seeds. Some forms of plant life respond well to this setting, others less so—the rose trees revolt against it and are transformed into huge dog rose bushes. The lawn becomes wild grass and quitch. A laburnum sprouts, as does a sycamore. Two blades of lavender suddenly flourish into bushes . . . nature has reclaimed its rights."[18] An even more explicit account was provided in his book on *Nursery Schools*: "gardening forbidden by Nazis, hence, not one snip of the shears . . . the soil acquired a tough crust . . . the flowers starved and disappeared, except for lavender . . . which returns faithfully every first of May. The winds and the birds brought seeds . . . "[19] Gifted by birds, neglected by gardeners, the isolated rooftop world concentrated the whole of the French landscape.

Once it was finished, Le Corbusier's Unité d'Habitation in Marseilles received very harsh criticism, not only from architects and art critics but also from the citizens living nearby. The architect's defense of the design is fascinating, for it indicates his sense of the importance of the building's roof garden. Before the Unité was built, he claimed, no citizen of Marseilles could see the mountains, one of the region's two most important elements, the sea being the other. The project overcame the limits of blinkered life by providing a desired view. More largely, he thought it initiated nothing less than cultural renewal by restoring contact between children, the city's future, and both sky and mountains, its foundation. Not surprisingly, the middle ground—the city of Marseilles—was omitted from this prospect, screened off by the high parapet wall.

Providing not only the project's rationale but also an assessment, Le Corbusier claimed that the design was entirely successful, for when parents and children first emerged from below, both were equally dazzled by the view. This equality gave rise to a new sense of community because all concerned were brought back into contact with culture's primitive foundation, the primary elements of the natural world. Obviously, this narrative replays the *agon* of ascent and creativity Le Corbusier choreographed in the houses, particularly those for artists. Under the clear blue Mediterranean sky, washed in bright light, directly facing the sea and the mountains, life's petty concerns receded from importance. When distant from the ground and refreshed by contact with the natural world, individuals recovered their association with one another. Quite apart from this rather generous self-assessment of the project's success,

FIGURE 8.4: Le Corbusier, roof garden, Unité d'Habitation, Marseilles, 1946–1952. Photo: David Leatherbarrow.

contemporary photographs of plays performed by nursery-school children in the rooftop theater do give one the sense that this "garden" did serve as the site for some significant experiences of community.

The roof was conceived as a substitute ground plane. On it one could find water, hills, plantings, terraces, and so on. Also, it was a space of play—playing within and being played by the wider horizon. What is more, the terrace was intended to be a site of exercise or physical culture, with the elderly in the pool, adults and teenagers in the exercise club, and younger children in an arrangement of "open-air" rooms, basically a mazelike parterre. When not in school, the children could also sun themselves on the artificial hillsides or "plant lavender" in the crevices of miniature mountains substituting those in the distance.

All of these activities, together with their spatial premises stand apart from the city that surrounds the block at ground level. Yet, while the elevated landscape keeps itself distant from the town, it maintains an unbroken dialogue with it, by reproducing or permanently recalling its salient situations (education, recreation, theater, etc.). As with Le Corbusier's other rooftop gardens, there is an absent middle ground, by virtue of the high perimeter wall—thus, enclosure and isolation. But this device also allows for a coupling of figures in the foreground and distance, the mountains, for example. Thus, again, it is a break, but one that locates itself within a continuous or extended horizon, as if the entire city and landscape were an enlarged garden or continuous topography.

GEOGRAPHICAL DISTANCE

The Wexner Center for the Visual Arts, designed by Laurie Olin and Peter Eisenman, stands at the corner of the Ohio State University campus in Columbus, Ohio. Olin began his explanatory account of the project by turning away from the particular site on which it was built, turning toward places he recalled from past experiences. His first and perhaps most significant memory was of land, specifically, the prairies of the great American Midwest and the larger structure of Jefferson's survey project. Although Ohio is, indeed, part of this frame of reference, the territory Olin recalled is much more expansive. Turing from memory to design, he explained that "the long-gone prairie is evoked, remembered—not recreated or imitated—by an exuberant series of large forms that were planted (stuffed full) with several species of grass and native flowers . . . [which were made to] rise and fall, like tectonic plates or geologic blocks."[20] Thus, from the start, a wider landscape was seen as the framework for the project, it was understood as a garden of grasses set into a grid, like the Midwest as a whole.

But the memories of even more distant territories were also influential on the project. Olin also recalled an Etruscan necropolis at Cervetri, north of Rome. In all likelihood, he was thinking of the famous *Necropoli della Banditaccia*, which dates from the seventh to the third centuries B.C.E. Many of the tombs at this site are large, circular structures, some measuring up to a hundred feet in diameter. More important than their plan size is their sectional arrangement, for they sometimes stand at ground level, and other times are partly underground, because the lower section of the enclosed space was cut directly into the lava or rock, serving as a base for masonry superstructures. Also striking is the fact that many of the roofs are covered with tall grass. As one walks alongside a row of tombs, the land seems to lie at a number of levels, below the surface on which one stands, at that level, and above it. Many of the tombs are entered along a descending path called a *dromos*, signifying not so much "running" or a "runway," as it did for the ancient Greeks, but a space for axial passage, as if it were a very deep or lengthy threshold. Key for Olin, it seems, was the fact that this type of approach descended through the several strata of planted surfaces. Passage through the forecourt at the Wexner Center also requires movement through several levels, as if the ground were alternately below, above and at the level on which one is presently standing.

FIGURE 8.5: Laurie Olin and Peter Eisenman, Wexner Center for the Visual Arts, Ohio State University, Columbus, Ohio, 1983–1989. Photo: Laurie Olin.

The shifting of levels that structures Olin's *dromos*, is apparent from the start, which is to say when one stands on the street facing the forecourt and building. The retaining wall at the front rises from knee to waist height along its full length, despite the fact that the ground on which it rests is perfectly level. Considering the prairie grid, there is no good reason for this shifting or sloping to occur. Yet, once begun, the deviations continue. The incline changes several times more as one progresses toward the building. In some places, the walls rise to a person's full height, making substructure superstructure. As the retaining walls climb well beyond their customary height the levels of the plants do as well, which means low-lying (prairie) grasses are discovered at the elevation of bushes and trees. What was viewed onto is subsequently viewed into.

Here it may be helpful to introduce yet another of Olin's recollections, also of a distant place. Once the project was completed, a surprising but vivid memory of weeds and cattails caught in the Alaskan ice and snow of his boyhood was prompted by the sound of the grasses at his shoulder, recalling a young skater's glide through a distant frozen landscape. Had the grasses not been elevated the memory would have been lost.

The rationale for upsetting the site's flat orthogonality was set out as follows: "It [the garden] heaves and lifts, imposing its humble elements—grass, earth, and stone—upon the visitor, raising them to eye level and in some cases well above one's head. It creates an experience similar to that of walking into the earth, but not."[21] This experience was outlined in Olin's preliminary sketches. They show that his aim was to organize movement from the horizontal grid of the urban plan (planned movement) to the vertical grid of the building's façade (planned appearance). The forecourt provides what the building lacks: thickness, enclosure, and substance, all of which are implied in Olin's use of the term *earth*. His argument was this: entrances are made when the ground plane is thickened and the ground is crystallized.

Yet, passage from the street to the building was not completely encaved in an earthy interior, for entry was "an experience similar to that of walking into the earth, *but not*."[22] Here, again, the project proposes a contradiction, at least the coupling of otherwise unrelated places. Let me recapitulate. First is the fact that the project's interior was defined by the characteristics of its exterior, the Center's forecourt terrace to the widely extended (Midwestern) terrain. Second, the site's flat orthogonality was opposed by the project's increasing and irregular thickness, as in the tomb landscape of Etruscan Italy. And third, the project was and was not an earthen enclosure. Olin's "but not" obviously refers to the forecourt's vertical extension, to the fact that the walks and raised beds are roofed by sky not more soil. But this negation also seems to indicate the continued relevance of the project's linearity, its profiles or geometry, made palpable by the finely finished edges of the limestone retaining walls. Entry is not walking into the earth because it is walking along the lines and angles of prairie geometry.

Despite these references, one cannot say the project is contextual, at least with respect to its immediate vicinity, for there is nothing like it nearby. Yet, it is not for that reason isolated or autonomous. Instead, it proposes links to territories that are both geographically and historically remote, the Midwest, ancient Italy, and Alaska. Put paradoxically, the forecourt garden is an enclosure that is not enclosed, a garden that defines and then transgresses its own boundaries. Distant places are brought within reach because they are understood to be necessary components of the project's fundamental purpose and idea—entry—passing from a place that is indisputably local to one that has implications for a much larger or wider landscape.

Isamu Noguchi's project for the UNESCO gardens in Paris came to him as the result of an invitation from Marcel Breuer. Breuer was among a trio of architects appointed to design the new headquarters. Their task was to be complemented by work from another group of artists, including Henry More, Alexander Calder, and Noguchi. Despite their differences, all concerned could be called modern artists. I make this point because Noguchi, no less a modernist

FIGURE 8.6: Isamu Noguchi, UNESCO Gardens, Paris, 1955–1958. Photo: David Leatherbarrow.

than any of the others, was engaged because he was thought to be capable of producing a Japanese Garden, a garden in a historical style. Most moderns would reject such an invitation on principle. Although he said yes, he also said no, admitting once it was finished that the garden was only "somewhat" Japanese.[23]

References to traditions outside the immediate framework of this project were not limited to those pointing toward Japan. In attempting to understand Noguchi's way of working with the physical materials of the project, it is important to recall his training with the Romanian sculptor Constantin Brancusi, whose work always demonstrated a dedication to the particularity of materials. Water, stone, soil, and sand have different expressive possibilities because they have different inherent properties. Also important in Noguchi's conception of the project was his earlier contact with the American dancer Martha Graham. This experience seems to have given him a strong interest in bodily movement, in its conditions, nonroutine character, and traces. Noguchi joined this concern for movement with his interest in hollow or negative space, a type of space he had observed in Japanese art, in painting, architecture, and gardens.

Noguchi's design for the UNESCO garden is exceedingly complex. Some critics think it is overly so. A key to its order, to the order of its references to larger distances and remote places, can be seen in the delegate's garden, particularly, the "stele" at its edge. The garden is *dry*, like the Zen gardens Noguchi had seen and studied in Kyoto: concrete benches, stone paving, and sculptures. Comparative material from Japan could include both traditional and modern gardens (Ryon-ji, circa 1500, and Hojo garden, Tofuju-ji, by Mirei Shigemori).[24] Stones for the garden had been sent to Paris from Japan. In fact, Noguchi had overseen the selection of stones. Laborers and experts came too. But the result was not a Japanese garden. Obviously, the scale of the site was very different from that of the examples just mentioned, as a result of the massive bulk and great height of the UNESCO building. But even more influential was the cultural context into which the garden was set—not just this site, but also the city of Paris and, more widely, the Western world. The story of the great stele makes the influence of these wider horizons clear. It stands at the edge of the delegate's terrace, just on the verge of the lower and larger garden. From the very start of the project, the stone was to be inscribed. Early on, there was a suggestion that the Japanese word for love be cut into the stone. For followers of Zen Buddhism this word was thought to be too Christian (even if it might have resonated with members of the UNESCO organization or the Parisians). Another suggestion was for the Japanese word *mu* meaning "nothingness." That, too, was rejected. Finally, there was agreement about the word for peace. But the calligraphy of the inscription was so stylized that even this was barely legible. The result was ornamental pattern—apparently Japanese, but not really.

A similar coupling of different approaches can be seen in the arrangement of views or prospects within the garden. In addition to its rather prominent stance at the edge of the delegate's terrace, the stele serves as the terminal point of an axial view from the lower garden, along the line of the stepped cascade. The exact spot from which this view is taken is precisely marked: paving slabs set into the lowest level of the cascade. The spot is made even more significant because a 90-degree turn to the right opens another axial view toward the so-called lantern sculpture, set in a paved clearing. Both prospects serve the status of the sculptural works. But in disclosing their targets so fully, these approaches contradict a basic premise of Japanese gardens: partial disclosure, or "hide and reveal" display. For Noguchi, the sculptural works had intrinsic importance, hence their freestanding position. In Japanese gardens, however, the continuity of the whole was more important than the qualities of any single piece, insofar as the whole sustained movement and renewed experience without end. This meant that in traditional gardens figures were never revealed fully, all at once, in their autonomy. Likewise, for the matter of boundaries, in Japanese gardens they are never apparent. In this one, by contrast, the surrounding walls are entirely obvious, nothing is "borrowed" from the immediate vicinity; the space closes in on itself.

These contradictions were not lost on Noguchi; he called his project a "somewhat" Japanese garden. I take this less as a failure than as evidence of his attempt to allow the garden to limit its enclosure with elements that exceeded the site's proper boundaries, making it as engaged with distant territories as it was enclosed within itself.

TECHNOLOGICAL DISTANCE

Bernard Stiegler, a historian of science and technology, wrote in *Technics and Time* that an "an industrial object [is one] that is available independently of all territorial considerations."[25] The same is true for any *system* of man-made elements: each is an integrated unity, the successful operation of which depends on the functional interdependence of parts, or what might be called an internal intentionality. More importantly, the system's self-sameness makes it indifferent to territorial considerations—portable, transferable, and widely usable. An example might be the audio system in one's house, or a building's lighting, glazing, or roofing system. Not one of these "belongs" anywhere in particular, each can be *installed* anywhere. Industrial products have global distribution. Their spread and the distances reached by their availability are in principle boundless because their parts relate to one another not some local condition. What about such a system in a garden? Can the elements of garden construction make it non-territorial, or is that a contradiction in terms?

The ALCOA Forecast Gardens designed by Garrett Eckbo between 1957 and 1959 was located in the Wonderland Park development, western Los Angeles. Built behind Eckbo's family residence, the garden was funded and publicized by the aluminum company. Although the project's spatial configuration is not particularly interesting, its use of materials is fascinating—particularly the use of materials that were new to gardens. Usage of this kind rested on a matter of principle: no material is ignoble in itself. Apart from his willingness to experiment, economic realities may have had a role in Eckbo's openness to new materials. Aluminum had widespread use during the war, especially in aviation, but in many other applications as well. In the postwar period, the question was plain: What would be the material's peacetime applications? To answer this question, two basic issues needed attention: what are the qualities of the material, and how might these be seen as part of a garden? In industrial applications, aluminum was praised because it did not rust and was noncorrosive. But these same qualities made its introduction into gardens awkward, for garden elements typically change over time, as they participate in natural cycles of growth and deterioration. This participation is one way garden elements accrue quality, and thereby both history and meaning.

Eckbo's way of overcoming the awkwardness of a metallic garden was the development of new uses for the material, uses that took advantage of the fact that garden elements include not only soil, vegetation, and water—elements of the earth—but also those of the sky, light and shade. In the ALCOA garden, aluminum was used to form sun breaks, protective screens, decorative surfaces, pavilions, and a fountain. This meant it would be used on both horizontal and vertical surfaces. Sheets of mesh, for example, were used vertically. They allowed for air circulation while enclosing private spaces. When used overhead, aluminum mesh projected a filigree of shadows on stone decks. What is more, its application for sun-shading benefited from its capacity for efficient thermal transmission, allowing heat gain to be dissipated rather than radiated. But aluminum was also used in unbroken sheets, in the fountain, for example. Here the incongruity of an aluminum flower is striking, rather like Mallet Stevens's construction of concrete trees in the Exposition of Decorative Arts garden in Paris, 1925. Yet, on a second view, properties of water that are often overlooked—its capacity to generate reflections, to increase ambient

FIGURE 8.7: Garret Eckbo, ALCOA Forecast Garden, Laurel Canyon, Los Angeles, California, 1959. Photo: Julius Shulman.

light, and the linearity of its streams—seem to be heightened or enhanced by the metal's angular and bright shine. When seen in dialogue with water and light, aluminum seems quite natural to the garden.

Yet, its ageless and "placeless" character also made it foreign to the elements that were natural to the place, which is to say, less absorptive of or adaptive to the influences of ambient forces than traditional materials. If the garden obtained coherence, it occurred in stages, first by virtue of juxtaposition, then by virtue of literal and metaphorical "absorption." In the first case, aluminum mesh and sheets found their place among stones, soil, and plants, unlikely as that place might be. In the second, something that had no specific relationship to the place (because it could be found anywhere) took on qualities of the site by virtue of its previously unforeseen capacity to modulate air, light, and views. The sun shades alternately glow with ambient light and get suffused with projected shadow. Likewise, the panels of the flower fountain are as reflective and geometric as the water it contains and sprays. No sheet of aluminum was native to this garden, but the setting's wonderful qualities would not have emerged had it not accepted into its borders something that "belongs" nowhere at all.

Peter Latz's project for the Landschaftspark, Duisberg Nord is one of many attempts to reuse old industrial areas in the Ruhr river basin (other attempts indeed have occurred throughout the Western world). Previously, the land was used as a metalworks. The site was not small: 200 hectares, or 500 acres. Although unique in size the site was not unique in function, the region had many places of this kind. What's more, similar factories used similar equipment elsewhere in Europe and in other industrialized countries. In fact, in so-called postindustrial economies, sites like this one have become very common. When the original use of this one came to an end, an important decision was made: large scale clearing and cleaning would not be undertaken; instead, reuse of the remnants would be. The impulse was not preservationist but economic; there were no funds to undertake a cleanup. This, too, is typical of other locations. Obviously, from the original designer's point of view such reuse would involve misuse. Blast furnaces, gasometers, cooling tanks, slag heaps, and so on were not intended as sites for scuba diving, lily ponds, bike paths, theaters, alpine climbing and so on. But these uses and others were established in just those places that seemed so unyielding. The most significant of the transformations on the site is perhaps the Piazza Metallica. Latz described the place as "the symbol of this entire park, [of the] metamorphosis of the existing hard and rugged industrial structure into a public park. Iron plates that were once used to cover casting moulds in the pig-iron casting work, form today the heart of the park. For the first moments of their existence, these cast iron plates have been eroded by natural physical processes. In this new place, they will continue to rust and erode."[26] As with the aluminum mesh of Eckbo's garden, this is the process of absorption, whereby the garden or park admits into its territory elements whose size, shape, and constitution were initially determined without regard for the place in which they were eventually installed.

Latz sees the process as a whole as both necessary and encouraging: "the fear of pollution and contamination has given way to a calm acknowledgement of the old structures. A fresh history and a fresh understanding of the contaminated site and of the landscape have been developing."[27] His comments point

FIGURE 8.8: Peter Latz, Duisburg-Nord Landscape Park, Duisburg, 1990–2002. Photo: David Leatherbarrow.

toward a nuanced understanding of design in postindustrial landscapes: not forgetting the industrial, but waking up from the dreams at its origin. "We cannot," he said, "discover a new continent as we did in the past. Our destiny is such that we must intervene with these sites. Politically and socially, there will be more and more of these projects. We must do this."[28] Yet, working with sites such as this means accepting the fact that the elements of which the Duisberg gardens and parks are made are by their nature those that contradict the established notion that what makes a place unique are the materials that initially define it. Yet, by virtue of design ingenuity and a series of natural processes, machinery that was designed to function in any location was absorbed into just one. Once a garden or park opens itself to the distances created by industrial culture, site specificity is not given at the outset of the project but developed over time, through agencies both within and outside the designer's control.

In consideration of these four sets of projects I have outlined a number of strategies for mediating the distances they confront: displacement, in the case of the gardens in Rio and Mexico City; substitution, in the two roof gardens by Le Corbusier; concentration of the wider geography, in the Wexner Center and UNESCO gardens; and reuse and absorption, in the ALCOA and Duisberg Nord projects. Our society gives us these distances; they form our common inheritance. These design strategies outline ways that gardens can convert them into a common culture.

NOTES

Introduction

1. Quoted in A. Lubow, "The Anti-Olmsted," *New York Times* (May 16, 2004). However, the notion that all landscape is culturally perceived has been usefully challenged by those who write about American's big national parks, where the "materiality of nature" is not to be gainsaid; see R. Grusin, *Culture, Technology and the Creation of American's National Parks* (Cambridge: Cambridge University Press, 2004), especially the introduction "Reproducing Nature."
2. Lassus has published his work in both English and French, with an emphasis on how he has explored the making of gardens and landscapes through his teaching. Schwartz has designed outside the United States, in both Europe and Asia, examples of which are shown in her book. In-text references are to B. Lassus, *The Landscape Approach* (Penn Studies in Landscape Architecture; Philadelphia: University of Pennsylvania, 1998) or to her *Vanguard Gardens and Landscapes*.
3. M. Schwartz, *The Vanguard Landscapes and Gardens of Martha Schwartz*, ed. T. Richardson (London: Thames and Hudson, 2004).
4. Schwartz, *The Vanguard Landscapes*, 10.
5. Schwartz, *The Vanguard Landscapes*, 63.
6. Schwartz, *The Vanguard Landscapes*, 108.
7. 202.
8. 108.
9. 124, 187.
10. Lassus, *The Landscape Approach*, 80.
11. Schwartz, *The Vanguard Landscapes*, 122.
12. For this, see the interview with Lassus in U. Weilacher's *Between Landscape Architecture and Land Art* (Basel: Birkhäuser, 1999).
13. 123.

14. These and other skepticisms may be found in the modern selections of J. D. Hunt, *Oxford Book of Garden Verse* (Oxford: Oxford University Press, 1993).
15. A. Pope, *Epistle to Burlington*.
16. Besides the example examined in the main text, there is a typical remark by Stan Allen that material practices like architecture and ecology nowadays "do not work exclusively with meaning and image"; *Points and Lines: Diagrams and Projects for the City* (New York: Princeton Architectural Press, 1999), 52.
17. Y. Sasaki, "The World of Dan Kiley," *Japan Landscape* 17 (1991): 92. Another implication of Sasaki's remark is that margins in a book are not for making notes but for increasing the legibility of the main text, in which case he might be implying our inability to stand back and see the design for its own sake, our craving for marginalia.
18. See Chapter 5, "Meaning," this volume.
19. W. H. Auden in the poem "Their Lonely Betters" even agrees that words have been rightly "withheld" from the birds, beasts, and insects of his garden: only he has that dubious gift; see Hunt, *Oxford Book of Garden Verse*, 249.
20. F. Steele, "Private Delight and the Communal Ideal," *Landscape Architecture* 31 (January 1941): 71.
21. D. Kienast, "Sehnsucht nach dem Paradies," *Hochparterre* 7 (1990): 50.

Chapter 1

I became interested in the issue of the arbitrary in landscape architecture while writing on Roberto Burle Marx's Parque del Este. His work was at once highly contextual and arbitrary, often introducing a series of predetermined forms into his sites. This is a complicated issue to navigate, and I have been inspired by the writings of R. Moneo on this subject, especially an unpublished lecture titled "Sobre el concepto de arbitrariedad en arquitectura," which he delivered to the Real Academia de Bellas Artes de San Fernando in 1997, and his *Theoretical Anxiety and Design Strategies in the Work of Eight Contemporary Architects* (Cambridge, MA: MIT Press, 2004). I am grateful to Elisa Silva, who lent me her copy of Moneo's manuscript while we were both fellows at the American Academy in Rome.

1. Represented in the United States by the work of, for example, Charles Platt, Warren Manning, Beatrix Jones Farrand, Ferrucio Vitale, and Innocenti & Webel.
2. "Arbitrary," *Merriam-Webster,* http://www.merriam-webster.com/dictionary/arbitrary (accessed June 27, 2007).
3. Claude Perrault's distinction between beauty that is "positive and convincing" and arbitrary beauty that is "determined by our wish to give a definite proportion, shape, or form, to things that might well have a different form without being misshapen . . ." resonates with sensibilities that favor ecological naturalism (positive beauty) over the introduction of formal configurations (arbitrary beauty) in landscape architecture. See C. Perrault, *Ordonnance for the Five Kinds of Columns after the Method of the Ancients* (1683), trans. Indra Kagis McEwen (Los Angeles: Getty Center for the History of Art and the Humanities, 1993), 51. architecture.
4. This is Eckbo's term, spelled with capital *B*, in his "Pilgrim's Progress" in *Modern Landscape Architecture: A Critical Review*, ed. M. Treib (Cambridge, MA: MIT Press, 2003), 208.

5. H. Hubbard and T. Kimball, *An Introduction to the Study of Landscape Design*, rev. ed. (New York: Macmillan, 1929).
6. Hubbard and Kimball, *An Introduction*, 33.
7. Hubbard and Kimball, *An Introduction*, 33.
8. Hubbard and Kimball, *An Introduction*, 7.
9. Hubbard and Kimball, *An Introduction*, 62.
10. G. Eckbo, *Landscape for Living* (New York: Architectural Record with Duell, Sloan, & Pearce, 1950), 165.
11. Eckbo, *Landscape for Living*, 3.
12. J. Rose, "Why Not Try Science?" *Pencil Points* 20 (December 1939): 777–79.
13. J. Rose, "Freedom in the Garden," *Pencil Points* 19 (October 1938): 640–44.
14. G. Eckbo, D. Kiley, and J. Rose, "Landscape Design in the Urban Environment," *Architectural Record* (May 1939): 70–77.
15. J. Rose, "Freedom in the Garden."
16. J. Rose, "Articulate Form in Landscape Design," *Pencil Points* 20 (February 1939): 98–100.
17. J. Rose, "Articulate Form."
18. H. Sasaki, "Thoughts on Education in Landscape Architecture: Some Comments on Today's Methodologies and Purpose," *Landscape Architecture* 40, no. 4 (1950): 158–60; K. Lynch, *Site Planning* (Cambridge, MA: MIT Press, [1962] 1969).
19. Sasaki, "Thoughts on Education in Landscape Architecture."
20. K. Lynch, *The Image of the City* (Cambridge, MA: MIT Press, 1960). See also J. O. Simonds, *Landscape Architecture: A Manual of Site Planning and Design* (New York: McGraw-Hill, 1983).
21. I. McHarg, "Ecology and Design," in *Ecological Design and Planning*, ed. George F. Thompson and Frederick R. Steiner (New York: John Wiley, 1997), 321.
22. I. McHarg, "An Ecological Method for Landscape Architecture," *Landscape Architecture* 57, no. 2 (1967): 105–7.
23. Quoted in M. Simo, *Sasaki Associates: Integrated Environments* (Washington, D.C.: Spacemaker Press, 1997), 10.
24. L. Halprin, *The RSVP Cycles* (New York: Brazillier, 1969), xx.
25. Rem Koolhass recognizes this crucial moment in design: "People use the word *arbitrary* when the set of decisions which brought the work into being are too obscure. When people cannot see those decisions, they feel the work is arbitrarily motivated. I am interested in precisely that state of mind. The point is that sometimes it is very hard to tell why something is the way it is. I am very interested in situations in which I thought I was doing one thing and then realized I was doing something very different." R. Koolhass, *S,M,L,XL* (New York: The Monacelli Press, 1998), xxiv. Also cited in R. Moneo, "Sobre el concepto de arbitrariedad en arquitectura," unpublished lecture (Real Academia de Bellas Artes de San Fernando, 1997), 28n16.
26. P. Walker, *Minimalist Gardens* (Washington, D.C.: Spacemaker Press, 1997), 19.
27. Walker's studios began with immersion on contemporary art. This included a five-day whirlwind tour to many sites, museums, and galleries from Boston to Washington, D.C., to look at contemporary sculpture, art, architecture, painting, and landscape architecture.

28. Quoted in D. Allen, "Tanner Fountain," in *Peter Walker: Experiments in Gesture, Seriality, and Flatness*, ed. L. Jewell (New York: Rizzoli, 1990), 19.
29. A. Berrizbeitia and L. Pollak, *Inside/Outside: Between Architecture and Landscape* (Gloucester, MA: Rockport Publishers, 1999), 146–51.
30. G. Hargreaves, "Postmodernism Looks beyond Itself," *Landscape Architecture* 73, no. 4 (1983): 60–65.
31. J. Beardsley, "Poet of Landscape Process," *Landscape Architecture* 85, no. 12 (1995): 46–51.
32. J. Czerniak, "Looking Back at Landscape Urbanism: Speculations on Site," in *The Landscape Urbanism Reader*, ed. C. Waldheim (New York: Princeton Architectural Press, 2006), 111.
33. Like Peter Walker, Hargreaves explored the potential of the language of landforms within the context of design studios at the Graduate School of Design (GSD) at Harvard University. In an intensive one-week landform workshop he developed in the early 1990s, students worked with 10-inch-square clay maquettes, exploring the formal qualities of natural and Euclidean landforms. The objective was, again, to stretch formal vocabularies and to develop the eye and the confidence to mix them in creative ways.
34. On recent approaches to site, see, for example, C. Girot, "Four Trace Concepts in Landscape Architecture," in *Recovering Landscape*, ed. J. Corner (New York: Princeton University Press, 1999), 59–67; S. Marot, "The Reclaiming of Sites," in *Recovering Landscape*, 45–57; and E. Meyer, "Site Citations: The Grounds of Modern Landscape Architecture," in *Site Matters*, ed. C. Burns and A. Kahn (New York: Routledge, 2005), 93–129.
35. A. Berrizbeitia, "Re-placing Process," in *Large Parks*, ed. J. Czerniak and G. Hargreaves (New York: Princeton Architectural Press; Cambridge, MA: Graduate School of Design, Harvard University, 2007), 174–97.
36. P. Fergusson, "Redefining the Campus Landscape: Alumni Valley, Wellesley College," in *Re-constructing Urban Landscapes: Complexity, Order, and Nature in the Work of Michael Van Valkenburgh Associates*, ed. A. Berrizbeitia (New Haven, CT: Yale University Press, 2009).
37. The images may come from existing aerial photography, from microscopic images of organisms, patterns of natural processes such as drainage, erosion, scouring, from abstract art, and so on. They may also come from material experiments. These are manipulations of a sensitive material, such as wax, or the combination of two materials such that they produce a reaction that is then tracked and documented through time using scanners or digital photography. They often also come from digital manipulations of geometrical figures.

Chapter 2

1. The most complete discussion of wilderness can be found in M. Oelschlaeger, *The Idea of Wilderness* (New Haven, CT: Yale University Press, 1991). The poetic and awestruck account of Thoreau's ascent of Mount Ktaadn (Katahdin) is from H. Thoreau, *The Maine Woods* (New York: Harper and Row, 1987), 93–95.

2. See the essay by D. Cosgrove, "The Idea of Landscape," in *Social Formation and Symbolic Landscape* (Madison: University of Wisconsin Press, 1984); and the collection of essays edited by W.J.T. Mitchell, *Landscape and Power* (Chicago: University of Chicago Press, 1994). Both inform our understanding of a cultural perspective of landscape and the garden.
3. For what constitutes a garden, see B. St-Denis, "Just What Is a Garden?" *Studies in the History of Gardens and Designed Landscapes* 27 (2007): 61–76; and P. Jacobs, "When Is a Garden Not a Garden?" *Landscape Architecture* 93 (2003): 133–44.
4. Two new and noteworthy academic collections have been generated: Penn Studies in Landscape Architecture, edited by J. D. Hunt, from the University of Pennsylvania Press; and the Dumbarton Oaks Contemporary Landscape Design Series, edited by M. Conan.
5. J. B. Jackson wrote an early and perceptive essay on "The Necessity for Ruins" that addresses the need to maintain a continuous and living record of the man-made environment; see *The Necessity for Ruins* (Amherst: University of Massachusetts Press, 1980).
6. In his essay, Umberto Eco suggests that one of the essential aspects of the Modern movement is to embrace the participative and open-ended nature of the creative act; see U. Eco, *L'oeuvre ouverte* (Paris: Éditions du Seuil, 1965).
7. See the survey of European (primarily German and Swiss) work in Chapter 4, "Use and Reception," this volume.
8. The three manifestos on the nature of modern landscape architecture written by Eckbo, Kiley, and Rose were comprehensive in their scope and innovative in the way that they positioned the social role of landscape. The texts were particularly avant-garde with regard to the responsibility that designers had to environment and development issues. See G. Eckbo, D. U. Kiley, and J. C. Rose, "Landscape Design in the Urban Environment," *Architectural Record* 85, no. 5 (May 1939): 70–77; "Landscape Design in the Rural Environment," *Architectural Record* 86, no. 8 (August 1939): 68–74; and "Landscape Design in the Primeval Environment," *Architectural Record* 87, no. 2 (February 1940): 74–79.
9. In addition to a proliferation of popular garden magazines and a variety of television series devoted to the garden, a number of exhibitions in major museums have contributed to the interest in, and the artistic legitimacy of, the modern garden. "Modern Gardens and the Landscape" was mounted by the Museum of Modern Art in New York City as early as 1964.
10. Dorothee Imbert's study of the modernist approach to garden design in France explores this early-twentieth-century attempt to treat the garden in the same manner as the modern art movements of the period; D. Imbert, *The Modernist Garden in France* (New Haven, CT: Yale University Press, 1993).
11. A number of insightful essays on the work of Garrett Eckbo have been collected by M. Treib and D. Imbert, eds., in *Garrett Eckbo: Modern Landscapes for Living* (Berkeley: University of California Press, 1987), which explores the relationship of social, economic, and environmental goals to Eckbo's design philosophy and practice.

12. The standard reference for this innovative and controversial approach to "garden design" can be found in B. Lassus, *Villes-paysages: couleurs en Lorraine* (Liège: Pierre Mardaga, 1989).
13. Evidence of the pervasive cultural importance of the lawn lies in the 27,400,000 entries that can be found within the heart of Google's search engines. More specifically, Georges Teyssot developed a comprehensive exhibit on the role of the lawn in the design of the contemporary environment titled *The American Lawn: Surface of Everyday Life*.
14. There is a substantial modern literature on the connection of urban quality to the provision of green spaces at all scales, from the garden to the broader landscape context. See M. Hough, *Cities and Natural Process* (London: Routledge, 1995), which explores the theoretical and practical aspects of an ecologically based approach to urban design.
15. See D. Dagenais's interesting discussion of the relationship of ecological discourse and the practice of landscape and garden design in "The Garden of Movement: Ecological Rhetoric in Support of Gardening Practice," *Studies in the History of Gardens and Designed Landscapes* 26 (2006): 313–40.
16. The context, theory, and practice of Fernando Chacel's work is developed in detail in P. Jacobs, "Echoes of Paradise," in *Contemporary Garden*, ed. M. Conan, (Washington, D.C.: Dumbarton Oaks Research Library and Collection, 2007), 121–39.
17. See the collection of essays in B. Lassus et al., *Le Jardin des Tuileries de Bernard Lassus* (London: Coracle Press, 1991).
18. See Alison Hirsch's discussion of three threatened Halprin projects in "Lawrence Halprin's Public Spaces: Design, Experience and Recover; Three Case Studies [Fort Worth Heritage Park, Denver Skyline Park, Seattle Freeway Park]," *Studies in the History of Gardens and Designed Landscapes* 26 (2006).
19. See the papers derived from the Wave Hill—National Park Service conference "Preserving Modern Landscape Architecture" and "Making Post War Landscapes Visible" in C. Birnbaum, ed., *Preserving Modern Landscape Architecture* (Washington, D.C.: Spacemaker Press, 1999); and C. Birnbaum, ed., *Making Post War Landscape Visible* (Washington, D.C.: Spacemaker Press, 2004), respectively.
20. Regarding contemporary French landscape and garden practice, see P. Jacobs, "Après Baudelaire, quoi de neuf?" *Studies in the History of Gardens and Designed Landscapes* 23 (2003): 238–39.
21. This is analyzed by A. Berrizbeitia in Chapter 1, "Design," in this volume.
22. The critical role that memory plays in our understanding of landscape and gardens is addressed in P. Shepheard, "Memory of the Western Front," in *Cultivated Wilderness* (Cambridge, MA: MIT Press, 1997), 195–230. S. Schama, *Landscape and Memory* (New York: Knopf, 1995); and by the essays in M. Mosser and P. Nys, eds., *Le Jardin, art et lieu de mémoire* (Besançon: ed. de l'Imprimeur, 1995).
23. A number of questions with respect to the use of a garden metaphor to interpret indigenous life in the Boreal forest are raised in P. Jacobs, "Unobtrusive Measures," *Landscape Architecture* 94 (2004): 28–37.
24. The narrative and symbolic values of these garden experiments have been reviewed in detail in P. Jacobs, "Folklore and Forest Fragments," *Landscape Journal* 23,

no. 2 (2004): 85–101; for a specific discussion of the "In Vitro Project," see P. Jacobs, "Seeds of Future Gardens," *Landscape Architecture* 91 (December 2001): 60–65.
25. One of the more theoretical and experimental garden competitions was initiated by Michael Van Valkenberg in 1986 titled "Transforming the American Garden" in which the invited participants were asked to imagine how they would address new challenges to the form, function, and meaning of the modern garden.

Chapter 3

1. For William Robinson, as for other gardener-writers mentioned in the text, see works listed in the volume's bibliography.
2. For Dumbarton Oaks, see works by Jane Brown, Diane Kostial McGuire, Diana Balmori and Margaret Morton, and Beatrix Jones Farrand listed in this volume's bibliography.
3. See works by Gert Groening and Joachim Wolschlke-Bulhmahn.
4. See works on Burle Marx by Anita Berrizbeitia, Sima Eliovson, Jacques Leenhardt, W. H. Adams, and Marta Iris Montero in this volume's bibliography.
5. He was a photographer who photographed his own work; see A. E. Bye, *Art into Landscape, Landscape into Art* (Mesa, AZ: PDA Publishers, 1983; 2nd ed., 1988); and M. Van Valkenberg, *Built Landscapes: Gardens in the Northeast* (Brattleboro, VT: Brattleboro Museum & Art Center, 1986), 44–49.
6. Both wrote for the popular press and for magazines, newspapers, and both wrote books that promulgated their ideas, represented and promoted landscape architecture, and generated commissions. See this volume's bibliography for works by Church and Eckbo.
7. The literal translation is not entirely happy: for commentary on Clement's work, see both Clement's writings and the article by Danielle Dagenais in this volume's bibliography.
8. See E. Hyde, *Cultivated Power* (Philadelphia: University of Pennsylvania Press, 2006).

Chapter 4

This chapter was translated by Sibylle Frers and the editor.
1. For further discussion of this historical aspect, see Vol. 5: *A Cultural History of Gardens in the Age of Empire*.
2. C. Hirschfeld, *Theorie der Gartenkunst* (Berlin: Union Verlag, 1990), 193. The translation is from the abridged American text by L. Parshall, *Theory of Garden Art* (Philadelphia: University of Pennsylvania Press, 2001).
3. See D. Hennebo, *Geschichte des Stadtgrüns I—Von der Antike bis zur Zeit des Absolutismus* (Hannover, Germany: Patzer, 1970), 99.
4. F. Hallbaum, *Der Landschaftsgarten. Sein Entstehen und seine Einführung in Deutschland durch Friedrich Ludwig von Sckell 1750–1823* (Munich: H. Schmidt, 1927), 197.
5. F. Encke, "Öffentliche Grünanlagen in der Großstadt," *Centralblatt für allgemeine Gesundheitspflege* 31 (1912): 282.

6. F. Schumacher, *Ein Volkspark* (Munich: Georg D. W. Callwey, 1928), 11.
7. R. Monard, "70 Jahre Hamburger Stadtpark. Einführung und Bedeutung," *Das Gartenamt* 29 (1980): 1.
8. See D. Haney, *When Modern Was Green: Life and Work of Landscape Architect Leberecht Migge* (New York: Routledge, 2010).
9. L. Migge, *Die Gartenkultur des 20. Jahrhunderts* (Jena, Germany: E. Diederichs, 1913), 149.
10. Migge, *Die Gartenkultur*, 25.
11. S. Giedion, *Befreites Wohnen: Licht, Luft, Öffnung* (Zürich: Orell Füssli, 1929).
12. See G. Harbers, *Der Wohngarten: Seine Raum- und Bauelemente* (Munich: Georg D. W. Callwey, 1937).
13. Harbers, *Der Wohngarten*, 13.
14. H. Wiepking-Jürgensmann, *Die Landschaftsfibel* (Berlin: Deutsche Landbuchhandlung, 1942), 30.
15. U. Poblotzki, "Gartenschauen—zwischen Kunst und Kommerz" [Garden Shows—between Art and Business], *Topos: European Landscape Magazine* 33 (December 2000): 43.
16. O. Valentien, *Neue Gärten* (Ravensburg: Otto Maier Verlag, 1949).
17. Valentien, *Neue Gärten*, 8.
18. Anon, "Was bringt die Gartenbau-Ausstellung?" *Schweizer Garten* 3 (1959): 80.
19. H. Mathys, "Der Garten des Poeten," *Schweizer Garten + Wohnkultur* 7 (1959): 154.
20. U. Weilacher, *Visionary Gardens: The Modern Landscapes by Ernst Cramer* (Basel: Birkhäuser, 2001), 102.
21. P. Nevermann, "Zum Geleit," an introduction to K.-H. Rücke, *Städtebau und Gartenkunst: Kleine Studie über ein vernachlässigtes Thema* (Hamburg, Germany: Christians, 1963), 3.
22. See E. Kühn, "Kommentar zur Grünen Charta," in *Die grüne Charta von der Mainau mit Kommentar* (Pfullingen, Germany: Deutschen Gartenbau-Gesellschaft, 1963), 7–13.
23. A. Bernatzky, *Gärten für uns: Ihre Anlage und Gestaltung* (Gütersloh, Germany: Bertelsmann, 1963), 10.
24. H. Mathys, "Bedeutung und Aufgabe des Gartens in unserer Zeit," *Schweizer Garten + Wohnkultur,* 2 (1962): 21–22.
25. H. Mattern, *Gärten und Gartenlandschaften: Geplant und gebaut von Hermann Mattern, besprochen und beschrieben mit Beate Mattern* (Stuttgart: Hatje, 1960), 32. For the following remark, see A. Hernandes, "Randnotizen zur Tagung," *SWB Kommentaire 14, February 1970* (Basel: Schweizerischer Werkbund, 1970), 123.
26. Mattern, *Gärten und Gartenlandschaften*, 32.
27. L. Burckhardt, quoted in Hernandes, "Randnotizen zur Tahung," 123.
28. U. Schwarz, *Der Naturgarten* (Frankfurt: Verlag Wolfgang Krüger GmbH, 1980), 89.
29. Anon, "Präambel der Grün, 80"; cf. *Grün 80. 2. Schweizerische Ausstellung für Garten- und Landschaftsbau 1980, Basel. 12. April–12. Oktober 1980. Schlussbericht der Direktion* (Basel: Direktion Grün 80, 1980).
30. K. Kocher, "Grün 80. Eine verpasste Chance"; cf. *Grün 80*, 14.
31. Direktion der öffentlichen Bauten des Kantons Zürich, ed., *Universität Zürich-Irchel Parkanlagen* (Zürich: Direktion der öffentlichen Bauten, Hochbauamt, 1986): 10.
32. D. Kienast, "Vom Gestaltungsdiktat zum Naturdiktat—oder: Gärten gegen Menschen?" *Landschaft + Stadt* 3 (1981): 120–28.

33. L. Burckhardt, "Gartenkunst wohin?" in *Grün in der Stadt*, ed. M Andritzky and K Spizer (Reinbek, Germany: Rowohlt, 1981); cf. M. Andritzky and K. Spitzer, eds., *Grün in der Stadt*, 258.
34. Text from the cover blurb of N. Saint-Phalle, *Der Tarot-Garten* (Wabern-Bern, Germany: Bentelli, 2000).
35. D. Kienast; cf. U. Weilacher, *Between Landscape Architecture and Land Art* (Basel: Birkhäuser, 1999), 154.
36. R. Haag, quoted R. Pirzio-Biroli, "Adaptive Re-Use, Layering of Meaning on Sites of Industrial Ruin," *Arcade Journal*, 23 (2004): 109.
37. See U. Weilacher, *Syntax of Landscape: The Landscape Architecture of Peter Latz and Partners* (Basel: Birkhäuser, 2007).
38. I. Noseda, "Die Lektion der Kulturfolger," in *Gute Gärten—Gestaltete Freiräume in der Region Zürich*, ed. BSLA Regionalgruppe Zürich (Zürich: BSLA, Regionalgruppe Zürich, 1995).
39. D. Kienast, "Sehnsucht nach dem Paradies," *Hochparterre* 7 (1990): 50.
40. R. Zulauf, interview with the author in February 2002.
41. See U. Weilacher, "Versprechen statt fertiger Antworten," in *Schweingruber Zulauf*, ed. H. Wirz (Lucerne: Quart, 2006), 21.

Chapter 5

1. M. Kelsall, "The Iconography of Stourhead," *Journal of the Warburg and Courtauld Institutes* 46 (1983): 138; W. Whitman, "A Song of the Rolling Earth"; and E. Husserl, *Logical Investigations*, tr. J.N. Finlay (New York: Routledge Kegan Paul, 1970), 267.
2. See J. Hunt, *Greater Perfections: The Practice of Garden Theory*, Penn Studies in Landscape Architecture (Philadelphia: University of Pennsylvania, 2000), specifically 219–23.
3. The British poet Philip Larkin referred rather dismissively to this cultural baggage as a "common myth kitty"; see P. Larkin, *Required Writing: Miscellaneous Pieces 1955–1982* (London: Publisher, 1983), 79.
4. It is after all in the late eighteenth century that we may locate what Yve-Alain Bois has called the "rupture of modernity"; see A. Bois, "A Picturesque Stroll around Clara-Clara," *October* 29 (1984): 61.
5. For an examination of this reception of one particular site, see J. Hunt, "Stourhead Revisited and the Pursuit of Meaning in Gardens," *Studies in the History of Gardens and Designed Landscapes* 26 (2006): 328–41.
6. Readers are also referred to the relevant chapters on meaning in the earlier volumes of the Cultural History of Gardens series.
7. Instructive here is the argument of John Barrell's study of the loss of public meanings and responsibilities in the arts; see J. Barrell, *The Political Theory of Painting from Reynolds to Hazlitt: The Body of the Public* (New Haven, CT: Yale University Press, 1986).
8. That this was the case is shown clearly by the publication of Joseph Spence's *Polymetis* (1747), which its author argued was needed to help people recall the names, attributes, and actions of all classical deities; interestingly, he choose to construct

this pedagogical memory theatre in the form of a landscape dotted with temples in each of which specific gods and goddesses were presented through compendia of images and texts.
9. See Chapter 1 of this volume by Anita Berrizbeitia.
10. On the issue of designing stories or narrative, see M. Potteiger and J. Purinton, *Landscape Narratives: Design Practices for Telling Stories* (New York: John Wiley & Sons, 1998); for one particular case study of the creation and reception of meaning, see J. Hunt, *Nature over Again: The Garden Art of Ian Hamilton Finlay* (London: Reaktion Books, 2008).
11. See works by D. Ottewill and J. Tankard listed in this volume's bibliography.
12. See D. Imbert, *The Modernist Garden in France* (New Haven, CT: Yale University Press, 1993).
13. For a study of Steele, see R. Karson, *Fletcher Steele, Landscape Architect, and Account of the Gardenmaker's Life, 1885–1971* (New York: Harry N. Abrams/Saga Press, 1989); of Church, see M. Treib, ed., *Thomas Church Landscape Architect: Designing a Modern California Landscape* (San Francisco: William Stout, 2003); and of Eckbo, see M. Treib and D. Imbert, *Garrett Eckbo: Modern Landscapes for Living* (Berkeley: University of California Press, 1997).
14. For discussions of national identity in English gardening, see M.-L. Egbert, *Garten und Englishness in der englischen Literatur* (Heidelberg: Winter, 2006); A. Helmreich, *The English Garden and National Identity: The Competing Styles of Garden Design 1870–1914* (Cambridge: Cambridge University Press, 2002); and D. Matless, *Landscape and Englishness* (London: Reaktion Books, 1998).
15. On this depressing episode, see the essays in J. Wolschke-Bulmahn, ed., *Nature and Ideology: Natural Garden Design in the Twentieth Century*, Dumbarton Oaks Colloquium on the History of Landscape Architecture 18 (Washington, D.C.: Dumbarton Oaks, 1997), in particular those by Wolschke-Bulmahn and Gert Groening.
16. On Russell Page, see M. Schinz and G. van Zuylen, *The Gardens of Russell Page* (New York: Stewart, Tabori & Chang, 1991). Also see Chapter 3, by McGlade and Olin, in this volume.
17. See works in the bibliography by Anne Cauquelin, Ruth Shaw Ernst, Susan Hill and Rory Stuart, Laroze and de Virieu, Jim Nollman, Jean-Pierre Otte, Michael Pollan, and Peter Timms for a small sampling of a vigorous and flourishing genre.
18. The ecological literature is extensive, but see works by Ian McHarg; F. Herbert Bormann, Diana Balmori, and Gordon T. Geballe; and George F. Thompson and Frederick R. Steiner listed in the volume's bibliography; and Wolschke-Bulmahn, *Nature and Ideology*.
19. See M. Knuijt et al., *Modern Park Design: Recent Trends* (Bussum, the Netherlands: Thoth Uitgeverij, 1993), specifically 86–89.
20. P. Reed, ed., *Groundswell: Constructing the Contemporary Landscape* (New York: Museum of Modern Art, 2005).
21. A prime example would be David Leatherbarrow's analysis of Latz's work in Chapter 8 of this volume.
22. This seems a wholly different arena of meaning than the others explored here, being often no more than designers talking to a few other designers. See work by

Julia Czerniak, including her remarks in J. Czerniak, C. Davidson, L. Olin, and P. Eisenman, *Fertilizers: Olin/Eisenman* (Philadelphia: Institute of Contemporary Art, 2006).

23. P. Latz, "The Idea of Making Time Visible," *Topos* 33 (December 2000): 95.
24. The impulse to fill one's garden with a host of ingredients was nicely satirized in drawings by Stephen Dowling in R. J. Yeatman and W. C. Sellar, *Garden Rubbish* (London: Methuan, 1936), reproduced in S. Wrede and W. Howard Adams, eds., *Denatured Visions: Landscape and Culture in the 20th Century* (New York: The Museum of Modern Art, 1991), 30–31. See also the modern chapters of A. Scott-James and O. Lancaster, *The Pleasure Garden* (Ipswitch, MA: Gambit, 1977). Relevant here, too, is the ironic view of meaning-obsessed gardens in the novel *The Decadent Gardener*, by A. Martin and J. Fletcher (Sawtry, UK: Dedalus, 1996).
25. For African American gardens, see R. Westmacott, "The Gardens of African-Americans," in *The Vernacular Garden*, ed. J. Hunt and J. Wolschke-Bulmahn, Dumbarton Oaks Colloquium on the History of Landscape Architecture 14 (Washington, D.C.: Dumbarton Oaks, 1993), 77–106; and G. Gundaker and J. McWillie, *No Space Hidden: The Spirit of African American Yard Work* (Knoxville: University of Tennessee Press, 2005). For Watts Towers, see B. Goldstone, *The Los Angeles Watts Towers* (Los Angeles: Getty Publications, 1997); and L. Whiteson, *The Watts Towers* (Oaksville, ON: Mosaic Press, 1998). For Picassiette, see E. Franzosini, *Raymond Isidore e la sua cattedrale* (Milan: Adelphi, 1995); and M. Ragon, *Picassiette: suivi de De Gaudi á Isidore* (Paris: Hoebeke, 2001).
26. See B. Lassus, *Jardins Imaginaires: Les Paysagistes-Habitants* (Paris: Presses de la Conniassance, 1977); and B. Lassus, *The Landscape Approach*, Penn Studies in Landscape Architecture (Philadelphia: University of Pennsylvania Press, 1998), especially 1 and 79–80.
27. See D. Jarman, *Derek Jarman's Garden* (Woodstock, NY: Overlook Press, 1996); and Chapter 6 in this volume.
28. T. Richardson, ed., *The Vanguard Landscapes and Gardens of Martha Schwartz* (New York: Thames and Hudson, 2004), in particular 121ff. The work of Ken Smith in the United States is also extremely agile in manipulating conventional design to provoke visitors to reconsider what gardens and places could be.
29. See works by Y. Abrioux, S. Bann, H. Gilonis, J. D. Hunt, and J. Sheeler, among others, listed in the bibliography to this volume.
30. See the collection of sketches and writings on this site in C. Girot, ed., *Zeitgeist Berlin Invalidenpark* (Zurich: GTA Verlag, 2006); also, see Reed, *Groundswell*, 52–57.
31. Here are the major items in that bibliography, in chronological order: M. Miller, M. Treib, R. Riley, S. Ross, L. Olin (1988), J. Gillette, and D. Cooper (see bibliography in this volume).
32. The term is Ross's from S. Ross, *What Gardens Mean* (Chicago: University of Chicago Press, 1998), 163. Such a notion of meaning is particularly demanding, depending on our ability to express our understanding of something in words, namely, that the idea or concept that we have thought about (cogitated) is translatable into words.

33. D. Cooper, *A Philosophy of Gardens* (Oxford: Oxford University Press, 2006), 109. The difficulty with philosophers writing about garden meanings is their greater proficiency at *using* gardens for their own philosophical discriminations than their intimate knowledge of gardens and garden literature in the first place.
34. R. Riley, "From Sacred Grove to Disney World: The Search for Garden Meaning," *Landscape Journal* 7, no. 2 (1988): 235–46.
35. Riley, "From Sacred Grove to Disney World."
36. On this site and its meanings, see C. Constant, *The Woodland Cemetery: Towards a Spiritual Landscape* (Stockholm: Byggforlaget, 1994); and M. Treib, "Woodland Cemetery: A Dialogue of Design and Meaning," *Landscape Architecture* 76 (1986): 42–49.
37. Treib, M. "Must Landscapes Mean? Approaches to Significance in Recent Landscape Architecture," *Landscape Journal* 14 (1995): 47–62.
38. This concern for what Ernst Gombrich has termed "the beholder's share" is a significant concern of late romanticism and acutely so of modernism.
39. See Treib's skepticism of "the power of water at [a] cosmological level," in M. Treib, "Design Vocabulary II: WATER," *Landscape Architecture* 77, no. 1 (1987): 72; or his analysis of Noguchi's UNESCO garden in M. Treib, *Noguchi in Paris: The UNESCO Garden* (San Francisco: William Stout Publishers, 2003).
40. Or in his two articles on the Woodland Cemetery in Stockholm, he wavers between acknowledging the "theme" of resurrection and its "alternation of perceptions and associations" in constructing its significance (M. Treib, "Constructing Significance," *Landscape Australia* 16 [1994]: 56) and plays down that same theme in an earlier piece (M. Treib, "Woodland Cemetery").
41. W. Byrd, Jr., ed., *The Work of Garrett Eckbo, Proceedings of a Symposium* (Charlottesville: University of Virginia School of Architecture, 1987), 33. He qualifies this remark with "meaning and content of a certain kind, not conventional in a literary sense" (33). Otherwise, L. Olin's essay "Form, Meaning, and Expression in Landscape," *Landscape Architecture* 7 (1988): 149–68, is what is discussed here.
42. Olin, "Form, Meaning, and Expression."
43. Olin, "Form, Meaning, and Expression."
44. See L. Olin, "What I Do When I Can Do It: Representation in Recent Works," *Studies in the History of Gardens and Designed Landscapes* 19 (1999): 102–21.
45. O. Barfield, *Poetic Diction: A Study in Meaning* (London: Faber and Gwyer, 1928), 48. This study of literary language offers some very suggestive analogies for the analysis of what gardens and landscapes undertake. The following quotation is by Stephen Metcalf in his discussion of Barfield's work, *T.L.S.*, January 12, 2007.
46. W. H. Auden, "In Memory of W. B. Yeats," in *Collected Poems* (London: Faber, 1959), 65.
47. See Lassus, *The Landscape Approach*, 110–15, 176–81; and M. Conan, *The Crazannes Quarries by Bernard Lassus: An Essay Analyzing the Creation of a Landscape*, Dumbarton Oaks Contemporary Landscape Design Series 1 (Washington, D.C.: Spacemaker Press, 2004).
48. See B. Lassus et al., *Les Jardins Suspendus de Colas* (Paris: privately printed for Colas S.A., 2007).

49. This site is much discussed, but economically presented in Reed, *Groundswell*, 124–31.
50. I have explored the role of meaning in Finlay's garden art in *Nature over Again*.
51. Kelsall's remark occurs in his article on Stourhead that rebukes its commentators for a variety of what a less-strict critic might term the free play of associative imaginations; this raises the issue of how such "absurd" commentaries might still contribute to the meaning of a site; see M. Kelsall, "The Iconography of Stourhead," *Journal of the Warburg & Courtauld Institutes* 465 (1983): 133–43.
52. Paul Ricoeur has convincingly argued that all words are "polysemic," that they have more than one meaning and that by extension all human activities are polysemic too; see P. Ricoeur, *The Rule of Metaphor: Multidisciplinary Studies in the Creation of Meaning in Language* (Toronto: University of Toronto Press, 1977).
53. See H.-G. Gadamer, *Truth and Method*, ed. and trans. G. Barden and J. Cumming (New York, 1975), chap. 2, sec. b, part ii. Also L. Parshall, introduction to L. Hirschfeld, *Theory of Garden Art* (Philadelphia: University of Pennsylvania, 2001), 13.
54. Riley, "From Sacred Grove to Disney World."
55. The role of interpretation in the afterlife of a garden, see J. Desranleau and P. Jacobs, "From Conception to Reception: Transforming the Japanese Garden in the Montreal Botanical Garden," *Studies in the History of Gardens and Designed Landscapes* 29 (2009): 200–216; and for commentary on the distortions of interpretation, F. Choay, *L'allégorie du patrimone* (Paris: Seuil, 1992).
56. See, to start, Chapter 6 in this volume; also a group of studies of garden representations by R. Strong, *The Artist and the Garden* (New Haven, CT: Paul Mellon Centre for Studies in British Art, Yale University Press, 2000); E. de Jong and Dominicus-Van Soest, *Aardse Paradijen: De Tuin in De Nederlandse Kunst*, 2 vols. (Gent: Snoeck-Ducaju & Zoon, 1992). L. Impelluso, *Gardens in Art* (Los Angeles: J. Paul Getty Museum, 2007); N. Alfrey, S. Daniels, and M. Postie, eds., *The Art of the Garden: The Garden in British Art, 1800 to the Present Day* (London: The Tate Gallery, 2005); and Hunt, *Greater Perfections*, chap. 6 (with further bibliography).
57. This maybe explains the otherwise somewhat curious claim by James Corner (see the introduction to *Recovering Landscape* [New York: Princeton University Press, 1999]) that the term *landscape* refers not so much to a physical place or environment as it is an "idea" or "cultural way of seeing," which we bring to the site.
58. The bibliography on place is considerable, but see works by Marc Augé, Gaston Bachelard, Augustin Berque, Edward S. Casey, J. Nicholas Entrikin, Dolores Hayden, Tony Hiss, Yi-Fu Tuan, and James Duncan and David Ley.
59. For Yorkville, see A. Tate, *Great City Parks* (New York: Spon Press, 2001); and E. Meyer, "The Post-Earth Day Conundrum," in *Environmentalism in Landscape Architecture*, ed. M. Conan (Washington, D.C.: Dumbarton Oaks, 2000), 238–42; for Canberra, see the presentation of the work of Room 4.1.3 in R. Weller, *4.1.3: Innovations in Landscape Architecture*, Penn Studies in Landscape Architecture (Philadelphia: University of Pennsylvania, 2005).
60. Finlay's Wild Hawthorne Press published a book on the garden, and Harry Gilonis has written an essay that expounds much of this richly associative place. One also imagines that the owner will also expound the garden's more arcane allusions as he accompanied guests (it is not open to the public).

61. In this respect, consider Arthur Danto's insistence that art works required interpretation; to be interpreted is their essence; A. Danto, *The Transfiguration of the Commonplace* (Cambridge, MA: Harvard University Press, 1981), 125.
62. And in an explanatory booklet, *Promenade au Jardin de l'Alchimiste*, purchasable on-site; the garden is open to the public.
63. See T. Schioler, *Roman and Islamic Water-Lifting Wheels*, tr. P. Katborg (Odense, Denmark: Odense University Press, 1973).
64. A. Maurierers and E. Ossart, *Jardiniers de Paradis* (Paris: Editions du Chene, 2000).
65. Riley, "From Sacred Grove to Disney World," 145.
66. My reference is to Umberto Eco's claim for an open aesthetic that resists any single interpretation in his *The Open Work* (Cambridge, MA: MIT Press, 1989). He calls such productions "works in movement," an intriguing parallel to Gilles Clément's "garden of movement" in the Parisian Parc André Citroen that defies and then redefines ideas of what a garden might be today; see B. St-Denis, "What Is a Garden?" *Studies in the History of Gardens and Designed Landscapes* 27 (2007): 61–76; and D. Dagenais, "The Garden of Movement: Ecological Rhetoric in Support of Gardening Practice," *Studies in the History of Gardens and Designed Landscapes* 26 (2006): 313–40.

Chapter 6

1. V. Woolf, *The Diary of Virginia Woolf*, vol. 2, ed. A. O. Bell (London: Hogarth Press, 1978), 56.
2. W. B. Yeats, "Lapis Lazuli," *Collected Poems*, 2nd ed. (London: Macmillan, [1933] 1950), 338–39, lines 25–28.
3. J.-F. Lyotard, *The Postmodern Condition: A Report on Knowledge*, tr. G. Bennington and B. Massumi (Minneapolis: University of Minnesota Press, 1984), xxiv.
4. Yeats, "Lapis Lazuli," 339, lines 47–48.
5. Yeats, "Lapis Lazuli," 339, lines 51–52.
6. R. Kipling, "The Gardener," in *Debits and Credits* (London: Macmillan, 1926), 399–414.
7. R. Kipling, "Epitaphs of the War," *The Definitive Edition of Rudyard Kipling's Verse* (London: Hodder & Stoughton, 1989), 390.
8. Kipling, "The Gardener," 414.
9. T. S. Eliot, "The Waste Land," *Complete Poems and Plays of T.S. Eliot* (London: Faber & Faber, 1969), 63.
10. T. S. Eliot, "The Four Quartets," *Complete Poems and Plays of T.S. Eliot* (London: Faber & Faber, 1969), 171–72.
11. Translation is my own.
12. R. Barthes, *La Chambre claire* (Paris: Gallimard, Seuil, 1980; tr. R. Howard, *Camera Lucida: Reflections on Photography* [New York: Hill and Wang], 1981), 70. This and subsequent page numbers refer to the translated edition.

13. T. S. Eliot, "La figlia che piange," *Complete Poems and Plays of T.S. Eliot* (London: Faber & Faber, 1969), 34.
14. Barthes, *Camera Lucida*, 70.
15. Quoted in C. Gordon, *The Garden of Adonis* (New York: Scribner, 1937).
16. Gordon, *The Garden of Adonis*, 299.
17. Gordon, *The Garden of Adonis*, 236.
18. Gordon, *The Garden of Adonis*, 242.
19. Eliot, "The Waste Land."
20. M. Lowry, *Selected Letters of Malcolm Lowry*, eds. H. Breit and M. Bonner Lowry (London: Jonathan Cape, 1967), 68.
21. Lowry, *Under the Volcano* (New York: Reynal & Hitchcock, 1947), 95.
22. Lowry, *Under the Volcano*, 292.
23. J. Joyce, *Ulysses*, ed. J. Johnson (Oxford: Oxford University Press, 1993), 731, episode 18.
24. Lowry, *Under the Volcano*, 130.
25. Lowry, *Under the Volcano*, 131.
26. Lowry, *Under the Volcano*, 129–30.
27. Lowry, *Under the Volcano*, 133.
28. Lowry, *Under the Volcano*, 134.
29. Lowry, *Under the Volcano*, 134.
30. Lowry, *Under the Volcano*, 128–29.
31. Quoted in A. Cronin, *Samuel Becket: The Last Modernist* (New York: HarperCollins, 1997), 479.
32. Lowry, *Under the Volcano*, 375.
33. Lowry, *Under the Volcano*, 33.
34. G. Bassani, *The Garden of the Finzi-Continis*, tr. W. Weaver (New York: Knopf, 2005), 184.
35. B. Sáenz, "The Willow," in *Calendar of Dust* (Seattle: Broken Moon Press, 1991), 46.
36. Bassani, *The Finzi-Continis*, 38.
37. Bassani, *The Finzi-Continis*, 240.
38. Bassani, *The Finzi-Continis*, 240.
39. I. Calvino, "The Garden of Stubborn Cats," in *Marcovaldo; or, the Seasons of the Ctiy*, tr. W. Weaver (New York: Harcourt Brace Jovanovich, 1983), 105–6.
40. Calvino, "Stubborn Cats," 111.
41. J. Kincaid, *My Garden (Book)* (New York: Farrar, Straus Giroux, 1999), 7.
42. Kincaid, *My Garden (Book)*, 8.
43. E. Brodber, *Jane and Louisa Will Soon Come Home* (London: New Beacon Books, 1980), 9.
44. Brodber, *Jane and Louisa*, 147.
45. J. Kincaid, "What Joseph Banks Wrought," in *My Garden (Book)* (New York: Farrar, Straus Giroux, 1999), 135, 141.
46. Kincaid, "Joseph Banks," 132.
47. Kincaid, "Joseph Banks," 142.
48. B. Homi, "Cultural Diversity and Cultural Differences," in *The Post-Colonial Studies Reader*, ed. B. Ashcroft, G. Griffiths, and H. Tiffin (London: Routledge, 1995), 209.

49. T. Stoppard, *Arcadia* (London: Samuel French, 1993), 27.
50. Stoppard, *Arcadia*, 97.

Chapter 7

1. A. Rogger, *Landscapes of Taste: The Art of Humphrey Repton's Red Books* (London: Routledge, 2007).
2. P. Klee, "Unendliche Naturgeschichte. Prinzipielle Ordnung der bildnerischen Mittel, verbunden mit Naturstudium, und konstruktive Kompositionswege," in *Form- und Gestaltungslehre*, vol. 2, ed. J. Spiller (Basel: Schwabe, 2007).
3. N. Alfrey, S. Daniels, and M. Postie, eds. *The Art of the Garden: The Garden in British Art, 1800 to the Present Day* (London: The Tate Gallery, 2005); and the more recent S. Schulze, ed., *Garten-Ordnung, Inspiration und Gluck* (Frankfurt am Main: Stadel Museum, 2006).
4. See G. Kubler, *The Shape of Time: Remarks on the History of Things* (New Haven, CT: Yale University Press, 1962).
5. See J. Hunt, *The Afterlife of Gardens* (London: Reaktion Books, 2004).
6. Goethe's famous novel has been "translated" into film several times. See *Die Wahlverwandtschaften*, dir. S. Kühn (1974); *Le affinità elettive*, dir. G. Amico (1977); *Les affinités électives*, dir. C. Chabrol (1981); and *Le affinità elettive*, dir. V. Taviani (1996).
7. C. T. Samuels, "Michelangelo Antonioni," in *Encountering Directors* (New York: Capricorn Books, 1972), 23.
8. Samuels, "Michelangelo Antonioni," 23.
9. See G. Teyssot, *The American Lawn: Surface of Everyday Life* (New York: Princeton Architectural Press, 1999).
10. The Telegarden, Ars Electronica Museum, Linz, Austria (1996–97).

Chapter 8

1. *I Ricordi di Michelangelo*, ed. C. Bardeschi and P. Barocchi (Florence: Sansoni, 1970), 368.
2. John Dixon Hunt has provided a full summary of this etymology in *Greater Perfections: The Practice of Garden Theory*, Penn Studies in Landscape Architecture (Philadelphia: University of Pennsylvania Press, 2000), 14–20.
3. D. Summers, "Real Metaphor," in *Visual Theory*, ed. N. Bryson and K. Moxey (London: Polity, 1991), 246.
4. R. Marx, "The Gardens at the Museum of Modern Art," in *Affonso Eduardo Reidy*, ed. N. Bonduki (Lisbon: Editorial Blau Instituto Lina Bo e P. M. Bardi, 2000), 180.
5. Marx, "The Gardens at the Museum of Modern Art," 180.
6. F. Fernández del Castillo, *Apuntes Para la Historia de San angel y sus Alrededoes: Tradiciones, Historia, Leyendas*, 2nd ed. (Mexico City: Editorial Porrua, 1987), 149; cited in K. Eggener, "Postwar Modernism in Mexico," *Journal of the Society of Architectural Historians* 58, no. 2 (June 1999): 126.

7. K. Eggener, *Luis Barragán's Gardens of El Pedregal* (New York: Princeton Architectural Press, 2001), 107.
8. L. Barragán, "Gardens for Environment," *Journal of the American Institute of Architects* 17 (April 1952): 168. This is from an address he gave to the California Council of Architects and the Sierra Nevada Conference, Coronado, California, October 6, 1951.
9. Barragán, "Gardens for Environment," 168
10. Barragán, "Gardens for Environment," 171.
11. Le Corbusier and P. Jenneret, *Oeuvre Compléte 1910–1929* (Zurich: Les Editions d'Architecture Erlenback, 1929), 89.
12. Le Corbusier, *Oeuvre Compléte*, 89.
13. Le Corbusier, *Oeuvre Compléte*, 128.
14. Le Corbusier, *Oeuvre Compléte*, 128.
15. Le Corbusier, *Oeuvre Compléte*, 128.
16. Le Corbusier, *Oeuvre Compléte*, 128.
17. Quoted, but not referenced in J. Sbriglio, *Immeuble 24 N.C. et Appartement Le Corbusier* (Basel: Birkhäuser, 1996), 60.
18. Le Corbusier, "Reportage sur un toit-jardin," in *Le Corbusier Oeuvre Complète 1938–1946* (Zurich: Girsberger, 1946), 140.
19. Le Corbusier, *Nursery Schools* (New York: Orion, 1968), 57.
20. L. Olin, "Memory not Nostalgia," (unpublished essay), 5–6, kindly loaned to me by the author. A shorter version of this essay was published under the same title in *Memory, Expression, Representation*, ed. W. Smith (Austin: University of Texas, 2002), 8–17.
21. Olin, "Memory not Nostalgia."
22. Olin, "Memory not Nostalgia," 6.
23. I. Noguchi, *Isamu Noguchi: The Sculpture of Space* (New York: Whitney Museum of American Art, 1980), 108.
24. These comparisons have been made by Marc Treib. See M. Treib, *Noguchi in Paris: The UNESCO Garden* (New York: United Nations Educational, Scientific, and Cultural Organization [UNESCO], 2003), 31–38, 107–17.
25. B. Stiegler, *Technics and Time, 1: The Fault of Epimetheus* (Stanford, CA: Stanford University Press, 1998), 70.
26. P. Latz, "Metamorphosis," http://www.latzundpartner.de/L3/eng/e-4-du.htm (accessed July 5, 2007).
27. Latz, "Metamorphosis."
28. Latz, "Metamorphosis."

BIBLIOGRAPHY

Abrioux, Y. *Ian Hamilton Finlay: A Visual Primer*. London: Reaktion, 1983; rev. and expanded ed., 1992.
Adams, W. *Grounds for Change: Major Gardens of the Twentieth Century*. Boston: Little, Brown, 1993.
Adams, W. *Roberto Burle Marx, the Unnatural Art of the Garden*. New York: Museum of Modern Art, 1991.
Aitken, R., and M. Looker. *The Oxford Companion to Australian Gardens*. New York: Oxford University Press, 2002.
Alfrey, N., S. Daniels, and M. Postie, eds. *The Art of the Garden: The Garden in British Art, 1800 to the Present Day*. London: The Tate Gallery, 2005.
Allen, D. "Tanner Fountain." In *Peter Walker: Experiments in Gesture, Seriality, and Flatness*, ed. L. Jewell, 14–19. New York: Rizzoli, 1990.
Allen, M. *William Robinson, 1838–1935: Father of the English Flower Garden*. London: Faber & Faber, 1982.
Allen, S. *Point and Lines: Diagrams and Projects for the City*. New York: Princeton Architectural Press, 1999.
The Amelia Island, Florida: A Report on the Master Planning Process for a New Recreational Community. Report for Sea Pines Company. Philadelphia: Wallace McHarg Roberts & Todd, 1971.
Amidon, J. *Ten Landscapes: Stephen Stimson Associates*. Gloucester, MA: Rockport Publishers, 2002.
Amidon, J., and K. Gustafson. *Radical Landscapes: Reinventing Outdoor Space*. London: Thames and Hudson, 2004.
Andritzky, M., and K. Spitzer, eds. *Grün in der Stadt*. Reinbek, Germany: Rowohlt, 1981.
Anon. "Was bringt die Gartenbau-Ausstellung?" *Schweizer Garten* 3 (1959): 80ff.
Appleton, J., ed. *The Aesthetics of Landscape*. Oxon, UK: The Rural Planning Services, 1980.

Aronson, S. *Making Peace with the Land: Designing Israel's Landscape.* Washington, D.C.: Peacemaker Press, 1998.
Augé, M. *Non-places: Introduction to an Anthropology of Supermodernity.* London: Verso, 1995.
Auricoste, I., and H. Tonka. *Parc-Ville Villette: Vaisseau de Pierres 2.* Champ Vallon, France: Seyssel, 1987.
Bach, P. *New Land Marks: Public Art Community, and the Meaning of Place.* Washington, D.C.: Editions ARIEL, Grayson Publishing, 2001.
Bachelard, G. *The Poetics of Space.* Paris: Presses Universitaires de France, 1958; Boston: Beacon Press, 1969.
Baeyer, E., von, and P. Crawford, eds. *Garden Voices: Two Centuries of Canadian Garden Writing.* Toronto: Random House, 1995.
Balmori, D., D. Kostial McGuire, and E. McPeck. *Beatrix Farrand's American Landscapes: Her Gardens and Campuses.* Sagaponack, NY: Sagapress, 1985.
Balmori, D., and M. Morton. *Transitory Gardens: Uprooted Lives.* New Haven, CT: Yale University Press, 1993.
Bann, S. "A Description of Stonypath." *Journal of the History of Gardens* 1 (1981): 113–44.
Bann, S. "A Luton Arcadia: Ian Hamilton Finlay's Contribution to the English Neo-Classical Tradition." *Studies in the History of Gardens and Designed Landscapes* 13 (1993): 104–24.
Barfield, O. *Poetic Diction: A Study in Meaning.* London: Faber and Gwyer, 1928.
Baridon, M. *Les Jardins: Paysagistes, Jardiniers, Poètes.* Paris: Editions Robert Laffont, 1999.
Barone, S., and F. Oehmichen. *Les Graminées: au jardin et dans la maison.* Montreal: Les Éditions de l'homme, 2001.
Barragán, L. "Gardens for Environment." *Journal of the American Institute of Architects* 17 (April 1952): 167–72.
Barrell, J. *The Political Theory of Painting from Reynolds to Hazlitt: The Body of the Public.* New Haven, CT: Yale University Press, 1986.
Barthes, R. *La Chambre claire.* Paris: Gallimard, Seuil, 1980; tr. R. Howard, *Camera Lucida: Reflections on Photography.* New York: Hill and Wang, 1981.
Beardsley, J. *Art and Landscape: In Charleston and the Low Country, a Project of Spoleto Festival USA.* Washington, D.C.: Spacemaker Press, 1988.
Beardsley, J. *Earthworks and Beyond: Contemporary Art in the Landscape.* New York: Abbeville Press Publishers, 1984.
Beardsley, J. *A Landscape for Modern Sculpture: Storm King Art Center.* New York: Abbeville Press Publishers, 1985.
Beardsley, J. *Ten Landscapes: Mario Schjetnan.* Gloucester, MA: Rockport Press, 2002.
Beazley, E. *Design and Detail of the Space between Buildings.* London: The Architectural Press, 1968.
Beeler, R, ed. *The Princeton Journal: Thematic Studies in Architecture.* Vol. 2, *Landscape.* Princeton, NJ: Princeton Architectural Press, 1986.
Beringer, H. *Chambres vertes, Festival International des Jardins/Jardins de Métis.* Grand-Métis, Quebec: Musée d'art contemporaine de Montréal, 2001.

Berjman, S. *La Plaza Espanola en Buenos Aires: 1580/1880*. Buenos Aires: Kliczkowski Publishers, 2001.

Bernatzky, A. *Gärten für uns: Ihre Anlage und Gestaltung*. Gütersloh, Germany: Bertelsmann, 1963.

Berque, A. *Médiance: de milieux en paysages*. Montpellier: Reclus, 1990.

Berque, A., et al. *Cinq Propositions pour une Théorie du Paysage*. Seyssel, France: Editions Champ Vallon, 1994.

Berrizbeitia, A., ed. *Michael Van Valkenburgh Associates. Re-Constructing Urban Landscapes*. New Haven, CT: Yale University Press, 2008.

Berrizbeitia, A. "Re-placing Process." In *Large Parks*, ed. J. Czerniak and G. Hargreaves. New York: Princeton Architectural Press; Cambridge, MA: Graduate School of Design, Harvard University, 2007.

Berrizbeitia, A. *Roberto Burle Marx in Caracas, Parque del Este, 1956–1961*. Penn Studies in Landscape Architecture. Philadelphia: University of Pennsylvania Press, 2005.

Berrizbeitia, A., and L. Pollak. *Inside/Outside: Between Architecture and Landscape*. Gloucester, MA: Rockport Publishers, 1999.

Bhabha, H. "Cultural Diversity and Cultural Differences." In *The Post-Colonial Studies Reader*, ed. B. Ashcroft, G. Griffiths, and H. Tiffin, 206–9. London: Routledge, 1995.

Billington, J. *New Classic Gardens: Formality Redefined for Today's Gardener*. London: The Royal Horticultural Society, 2000.

Birnbaum, C., ed. *Making Post War Landscape Visible*. Washington, D.C.: Spacemaker Press, 2004.

Birnbaum, C., ed. *Preserving Modern Landscape Architecture*. Washington, D.C.: Spacemaker Press, 1999.

Birnbaum, C., J. Brown Gillette, and N. Slade. *Preserving Modern Landscape Architecture: Making Postwar Landscapes Visible*. Washington, D.C.: Spacemaker Press, 2004.

Birnbaum, C., and R. Karson, eds. *Pioneers of American Landscape Design*. New York: McGraw-Hill, 2000.

Bliss, R. Woods, ed. *Beatrix Jones and Her Gardens*. Washington, D.C.: Judd and Detweiler, 1960.

Bois, Y.-A. "A Picturesque Stroll around Clara-Clara." *October* 29 (1984): 33–62.

Bormann, F. H., D. Balmori, and G. Geballe. *Redesigning the American Lawn: A Search for Environmental Harmony*. New Haven, CT: Yale University Press, 1993.

Bourassa, S. *The Aesthetics of Landscape*. London: Belhaven Press, 1991.

Bourg, D., ed. *Les Sentiments de la Nature*. Paris: Editions la Découverte, 1993.

A Breath of Fresh Air: Chicago's Neighbourhood Parks of the Progressive Reform Era, 1900–1925. Chicago: Grand Army of the Republic Museum, 1989.

Brett, L. *Landscapes in Distress*. London: The Architectural Press, 1965.

Brown, B., T. Harkness, and D. Johnston, eds. "Eco-Revelatory Design: Nature Constructed/Nature Revealed." Special issue, *Landscape Journal* 17, no. 1 (1998).

Brown, C., and W. Morrish. *The Fourth Coast: An Expedition on the Mississippi River*. Cambridge, MA: MIT Press, 1991.

Brown, J. *Beatrix, the Gardening Life of Beatrix Jones Farrand, 1872–1959.* New York: Viking, 1995.

Brown, J. *Eminent Gardeners: Some People of Influence and their Gardens 1880–1980.* New York: Viking, 1990.

Brown, J. *Gardens of a Golden Afternoon: The Story of a Partnership; Edwin Lutyens & Gertrude Jekyll.* London: Penguin Books, 1994.

Brown, J. *Lanning Roper and His Gardens.* New York: Rizzoli, 1987.

Brown, J. *The Modern Garden.* London: Thames and Hudson, 2000.

Built Landscapes: Gardens in the Northeast. Brattleboro, VT: Brattleboro Museum & Arts Center, 1984.

Bull, C. *New Conversations with Old Landscape: Landscape Architecture in Contemporary Australia.* Victoria: Images Publishing, 2002.

Burckhardt, L. "Gartenkunst wohin?" In *Grün in der Stadt*, ed. M. Andritzky and K. Spizer. Reinbek. Germany: Rowohlt, 1981.

Burton, P., and M. Botnick. *Private Landscapes: Modernist Gardens in Southern California.* New York: Princeton Architectural Press, 2002.

Bye, A. E. *Art into Landscape, Landscape into Art.* Mesa, AZ: PDA Publishers, 1983; 2nd ed., 1988.

Bye, A. E. *Moods in the Landscape.* Washington, D.C.: Spacemaker Press, 1999.

Byrd, W., Jr., ed. *The Work of Garrett Eckbo, Proceedings of a Symposium.* Charlottesville: University of Virginia School of Architecture, 1987.

Cahiers du CCI. *Paysage, parcs urbains et suburbains.* Paris: Editions du Centre Pompidou, 1988.

Caldenby, C., and O. Hultin. *Asplund.* Stockholm: Arkitektur Förlag, 1985.

Campbell, C. *Water in Landscape Architecture.* New York: Van Nostrand Reinhold, 1978.

Carver, H. *Compassionate Landscape: People and Places in a Man's Life.* Toronto: University of Toronto Press, 1976.

Casey, E. *The Fate of Place: A Philosophical History.* Berkeley: University of California Press, 1997.

Cauquelin, A. *Le site et le paysage.* Paris: Quadrige/Presses Universitaires de France, 2002.

Cauquelin, A. *L'invention du Paysage.* Paris: Quadrige/Presses Universitaires de France, 2000.

Cauquelin, A. *Petit Traitè du Jardin Ordinaire.* Paris: Manuels Payot, 2003.

Cautley, M. *Garden Design: The Principles of Abstract Design as Applied to Landscape Composition.* New York: Dodd, Mead, 1935.

Cerver, F. *Urban Spaces I (Streets and Squares): World of Environmental Design.* Barcelona: Arco Editorial Board, 1994.

Chacel, F. *Paisagismo e ecogénese.* Rio de Janeiro: Fraiha, 2001.

Chadwick, G. *The Park and the Town.* London: The Architectural Press, 1966.

Chambers, D. *Imagining Nature.* Victoria: Deakin University Press, 1984.

Chambers, D. *Stonyground: The Making of a Canadian Garden.* Toronto: Alfred A. Knopf, 1996.

Champ, O., ed. *Composer le Paysage: Construction et crises de l'espace (1789–1992).* Seyssel, France: Vallon, 1989.

Childs, H. C. *Gardens and Graveyards of the Southeastern Seaboard: A Photographic Journey*. Washington, CT: Painter Ridge Publishers, 1994.
Choay, F. *L'allégorie du patrimone*. Paris: Seuil, 1992.
Church, T. *Gardens Are for People*. New York: Reinhold Publishing, 1955.
Church, T. *Your Private World, a Study of Intimate Gardens*. San Francisco: Chronicle Books, 1969.
Clay, G. *Close-Up: How to Read the American City*. Chicago: University of Chicago Press, 1980.
Clay, G. *Right before Your Eyes: Penetrating the Urban Environment*. Washington, D.C.: Planners Press, 1987.
Clément, G. *Une école buissonnière*. Paris: Fondation Électricité de France, 1977.
Clément, G., and C. Eveno. *Le Jardin Planétaire: le colloque*. Paris: Éditions de l'aube, 1999.
Conan, M., ed. *Contemporary Garden Aesthetics, Creations and Interpretations*. Washington, D.C.: Dumbarton Oaks, 2007.
Conan, M. *The Crazannes Quarries by Bernard Lassus: An Essay Analyzing the Creation of a Landscape*. Dumbarton Oaks Contemporary Landscape Design Series 1. Washington, D.C.: Spacemaker Press, 2004.
Conan, M., ed. *Environmentalism in Landscape Architecture*. Washington, D.C.: Dumbarton Oaks, 2000.
Conan, M., ed. *Performance and Appropriation: Profane Rituals in Gardens and Landscapes*. Washington, D.C.: Dumbarton Oaks, 2007.
Condon, P. *Sustainable Urban Landscapes: The Surrey Design Charrette*. Vancouver: University of British Columbia, 1996.
Condon, P., and J. Proft. *Sustainable Urban Landscapes: The Brentwood Design Charrette*. Vancouver: University of British Columbia, 1999.
Constant, C. *The Woodland Cemetery: Towards a Spiritual Landscape*. Stockholm: Byggforlaget, 1994.
Contemporary Landscapes in the World. Tokyo: Process Architecture, 1988.
Cooper, D. *A Philosophy of Gardens*. Oxford: Oxford University Press, 2006.
Corner, J., ed. *Recovering Landscape*. New York: Princeton University Press, 1999.
Corner, J., and A. MacLean. *Taking Measures across the American Landscape*. New Haven, CT: Yale University Press, 1996.
Corny, I. *Jardins du Maroc*. Paris: Le Temps Apprivoisé, 1991.
Cosgrove, D. *Social Formation and Symbolic Landscape: With a New Introduction*. Madison: University of Wisconsin Press, 1984.
Cranz, G. *The Politics of Park Design: A History of Urban Parks in America*. Cambridge, MA: MIT Press, 1982.
Critiques of Built Works of Landscapes Architecture. Baton Rouge: Louisiana State University School of Landscape Architecture, yearly volumes from 1994.
Crowe, S. *Garden Design*. London: Country Life, 1958.
Crowe, S. *Garden Design, Line Drawings by Carol Moller*. New York: Hearthside Press, 1959.
Crowe, S. *The Landscape of Power*. London: The Architectural Press, 1958.

Crowe, S. *Tomorrow's Landscape*. London, The Architectural Press, 1963.
Czerniak, J. *CASE: Downsview Park, Toronto*. Munich: Harvard University Graduate School of Design, 2001.
Czerniak, J. *Downsview Park Toronto*. Harvard Graduate School of Design. New York: Prestel, 2001.
Czerniak, J. "Looking Back at Landscape Urbanism: Speculations on Site." In *The Landscape Urbanism Reader*, ed. C. Waldheim, 105–24. New York: Princeton Architectural Press, 2006.
Czerniak, J., C. Davidson, L. Olin, and P. Eisenman. *Fertilizers: Olin/Eisenman*. Philadelphia: Institute of Contemporary Art, 2006.
Dagenais, D. "The Garden of Movement: Ecological Rhetoric in Support of Gardening Practice." *Studies in the History of Gardens and Designed Landscapes* 26 (2006): 313–40.
Dagognet, F., ed. *Mort du Paysage? Philosophie et esthétique du paysage*. Seyssel, France: Champ Vallon, 1982.
Danto, A. *The Transfiguration of the Commonplace*. Cambridge, MA: Harvard University Press, 1981.
De Chiara, J., and L. Koppelman. *Site Planning and Standards*. New York: McGraw-Hill, 1978.
Descombes, G. *Il Territorio Transitivo: Shifting Sites*, ed. Giordano Tironi. Rome: Gangemi, 1988
Design with the Land: Landscape Architecture of Michael Van Valkenburgh. New York: Princeton Architectural Press, 1994.
Designed Landscape Forum 1. Washington, D.C.: Spacemaker Press, 1998.
Desranleau, J., and P. P. Jacobs. "From Conception to Reception: Transforming the Japanese Garden in the Montreal Botanical Garden," *Studies in the History of Gardens and Designed Landscapes* 29 (2009): 200–216.
Devolder, A.-M., ed. *The Public Garden: The Enclosure and Disclosure of the Public Garden*. Rotterdam: Architecture International, 2002.
Dillon, D. *The FDR Memorial: Designed by Lawrence Halprin*. Washington, D.C.: Spacemaker Press, 1998.
Direktion der öffentlichen Bauten des Kantons Zürich, ed. *Universität Zürich-Irchel Parkanlagen*. Zürich: Direktion der öffentlichen Bauten, Hochbauamt, 1986.
Downsview: Genesis of an Urban National Park. Toronto: Canadian Landscape Collaborative, 2000.
Drabelle, D. *The Art of Landscape Architecture*. Washington, D.C.: Partners for Liveable Places, 1990.
Drake, R. *The American Woodland Garden*. Portland, OR: Timber Press, 2002.
Dramstad, W., J. Olson, and R. Forman. *Landscape Ecology Principles in Landscape Architecture and Land-Use Planning*. Cambridge, MA: Harvard University, Island Press and ASLA, 1996.
Druse, K. *The Natural Garden*. New York: Clarkson, Potter, 1989.
Druse, K. *The Natural Shade Garden*. New York: Clarkson, Potter, 1992.
Duncan, J., and D. Ley, eds. *Place/Culture/Representation*. London: Routledge, 1993.
Eade, J.C., ed. *Projecting the Landscape*. Canberra, Australia: Humanities Research Center, 1987.

Eckbo, G. *The Art of Home Landscaping*. New York: F. W. Dodge, 1956.
Eckbo, G. *Garrett Eckbo, Philosophy of Landscape*. Tokyo: Process Architecture, 1990.
Eckbo, G. *Landscape for Living*. New York: Architectural Record with Duell, Sloan, & Pearce, 1950.
Eckbo, G. "Pilgrim's Progress." In *Modern Landscape Architecture: A Critical Review*, ed. M. Treib, 206–19. Cambridge, MA: MIT Press, 2003.
Eckbo, G. *Urban Landscape Design*. New York: McGraw-Hill, 1964.
Eckbo, G., D. U. Kiley, and J. C. Rose. "Landscape Design in the Urban Environment," *Architectural Record* 85, no. 5 (May 1939): 70–77.
Eckbo, G., D. U. Kiley, and J. C. Rose. "Landscape Design in the Rural Environment," *Architectural Record* 86, no. 8 (August 1939): 68–74.
Eckbo, G., D. U. Kiley, and J. C. Rose. "Landscape Design in the Primeval Environment," *Architectural Record* 87, no. 2 (February 1940): 74–79.
Eco, U. *L'oeuver ouverte*. Paris: Éditions du Seuil, 1965.
Eco, U. *The Open Work*. Cambridge, MA: MIT Press, 1989.
Egbert, M.-L. *Garten und Englishness in der englischen Literatur*. Heidelberg: Winter, 2006.
Eggener, K. *Luis Barragán's Gardens of El Pedregal*. New York: Princeton Architectural Press, 2001.
Eggener, K. "Postwar Modernism in Mexico." *Journal of the Society of Architectural Historians* 58, no. 2 (June 1999): 122–45.
Eliot, C. *Charles Eliot: Landscape Architect*. Cambridge, MA: Harvard University Press, 1924.
Eliovson, S. *The Gardens of Roberto Burle Marx*. New York: Harry N. Abrams/Saga Press, 1991.
Elkins, J. "Conceptual Analysis of Gardens." *Journal of Garden History* 13 (1993): 189–98.
Encke, F. "Öffentliche Grünanlagen in der Großstadt." *Centralblatt für allgemeine Gesundgeitsplege* 31 (1912): 282ff.
Engel, D. *Japanese Gardens for Today*. Rutland, VT: Charles E. Tuttle, 1959.
Entrikin, J. *The Betweenness of Place: Towards a Geography of Modernity*. Baltimore: Johns Hopkins University Press, 1991.
Ernst, R. *The Naturalist's Garden*. Old Saybrook, CT: Globe Pequot Press, 1987.
Fairbrother, N. *Men and Gardens*. London: The Hogarth Press, 1956.
Fairbrother, N. *The Nature of Landscape Design*. London: The Architectural Press, 1974.
Fergusson, P. "Redefining the Campus Landscape: Alumni Valley, Wellesley College." In *Re-constructing Urban Landscapes: Complexity, Order, and Nature in the Work of Michael Van Valkenburgh Associates*, ed. A. Berrizbeitia. New Haven, CT: Yale University Press, 2009.
Fernández del Castillo, F. *Apuntes Para la Historia de San angel y sus Alrededoes: Tradiciones, Historia, Leyendas*. 2nd ed. Mexico City: Editorial Porrua, 1987.
Ferry, L. *Homo Aestheticus: The Invention of Taste in the Democratic Age*. Chicago: University of Chicago Press, 1993.
Festing, S. *Gertrude Jekyll*. London: Penguin Books, 1993.

Fifty Years of Landscape Architecture: The Canadian Society of Landscape Architects, 1934–1984. The Canadian Society of Landscape Architecture. Guelph, ON: University of Guelph, 1998.

Finlay, I. *Works in Europe 1972–1995*. Ostfildern, Germany: Cantz Verlag, 1995.

Fleming, N. *Money, Manure, & Maintenance: Ingredients for Successful Gardens of Marian Coffin Pioneer Landscape Architect 1876–1957*. Weston, MA: Country Place Books, 1995.

"*Fleur de l'Air*": *A Garden in Provence by Ian Hamilton Finlay*. Photographs by V. Herre, notes on the photographs by H. Gilonis, and introduction by J. Hunt. Little Sparta, Scotland: Wild Hawthorne Press, 2004.

Forestier, J. *Gardens: A Notebook of Plans and Sketches*. Translated by H. Morgenthau Fox. New York: Scribner's, 1924.

Forestier, J.C.N. *Jardines: Cuaderno de dibujos y planos*. Barcelona: Editorial Stylos, 1985.

Forum: Het Landschap, "Lectura Architectonica," vol. 19, no. 4. Hilversum: G. van Saane, 1965.

Franzosini, E. *Raymond Isidore e la sua cattedrale*. Milan: Adelphi, 1995.

French, J. *Urban Green: City Parks of the Western World*. Dubuque, IA: Kendall/Hunt, 1973.

Gadamer, H.-G. *Truth and Method*. Edited and translated by Garrett Barden and John Cumming. New York: Seabury Press, 1975.

Gardenkunst: Bilder und Texte von Garten und Parks. Catalogue of exhibition at the State Historical Museum. Vienna: State Historical Museum, n.d.

Gillette, J. "Can Gardens Mean?" *Landscape Journal* 24 (2006): 85–97.

Gilonis, H. "Where Time Becomes Space—Ian Hamilton Finlay's Garden in Provence." *Word & Image* 21, no. 4 (2005): 308–22.

Girling, C., and K. Helphand. *Yard, Street, Park: The Design of Suburban Open Space*. New York: John Wiley & Sons, 1994.

Girot, C. "Four Trace Concepts in Landscape Architecture." In *Recovering Landscape*, ed. James Corner, 59–68. New York: Princeton University Press, 1999.

Girot, C., ed. *Zeitgeist Berlin Invalidenpark*. Zurich: GTA Verlag, 2006.

Goheen, E. *Wrapped Walk Ways*. New York: Abrams, 1978.

Goldstone, B. *The Los Angeles Watts Towers*. Los Angeles: Getty Publications, 1997.

Goldsworthy, A. *Touching North*. London: Carlsson Murray, 1989.

Gothein, M. *Geschichte der Gartenkunst*. Jena, Germany: E. Diederichs, 1926.

The Greening of Boston: An Action Agenda. Boston: The Boston Foundation/Carol R. Goldberg Seminar, 1987.

Greenways, Public Ways. Vancouver: Urban Landscape Task Force, 1992.

Grese, R. *Maker of Natural Parks and Gardens: Jens Jenson*. Baltimore: Johns Hopkins University Press, 1992.

Groening, G., and J. Wolschke-Bulman. "Some Notes on the Mania for Native Plants in Germany." *Landscape Journal* 11, no. 2 (Fall 1992): 116–26.

Groth, P., and T. Bressi, eds. *Understanding Ordinary Landscapes*. New Haven, CT: Yale University Press, 1997.

Grün 80. 2. Schweizerische Ausstellung für Garten- und Landschaftsbau 1980, Basel. 12. April–12. Oktober 1980. Schlussbericht der Direktion. Basel: Direktion Grün 80, 1980.

Grusin, R. *Culture, Technology and the Creation of American's National Parks.* Cambridge: Cambridge University Press, 2004.

Gundaker, G., and J. McWillie. *No Space Hidden: The Spirit of African American Yard Work.* Knoxville: University of Tennessee Press, 2005.

Haffner, J.-J. *Compositions de Jardins.* Paris: Vincent Freal et Cie, 1931.

Hallbaum, F. *Der Landscaftsgarten. Sein Entstehen und seine Einführung in Deutschland durch Friedrich Ludwig von Sckell, 1750–1823.* Munich: H. Schmidt, 1927.

Halprin, L. *The Franklin Delano Roosevelt Memorial.* San Francisco: Chronicle Books, 1997.

Halprin, L. *Notebooks: 1959–1971.* Cambridge, MA: MIT Press, 1972.

Halprin, L. *The RSVP Cycles: Creative Processes in the Human Environment.* New York: Brazillier, 1969.

Haney, D. *When Modern Was Green: Life and Work of Landscape Architect Leberecht Migge.* New York: Routledge, 2010.

Harbers, G. *Der Wohngarten: Seine Raum- und Bauelemente.* Munich: Callwey, 1937.

Harbison, R. *The Built, the Unbuilt and the Unbuildable: In Pursuit of Architectural Meaning.* Cambridge, MA: MIT Press, 1992.

Harbison, R. "The Life of Ideas in Architecture." *Harvard Design Magazine* (Summer 1997): 68–70.

Hargreaves, G. "Postmodernism Looks beyond Itself." *Landscape Architecture* 73, no. 4 (1983): 60–65.

Hayden, D. *The Power of Place: Urban Landscapes as Public History.* Cambridge, MA: MIT Press, 1995.

Helmreich, A. *The English Garden and National Identity: The Competing Styles of Garden Design 1870–1914.* Cambridge: Cambridge University Press, 2002.

Helphand, K. *Colorado: Visions of an America Landscape.* Niwot, CO: Roberts Rinehart Publishers, 1991.

Helphand, K. *Defiant Gardens: Making Gardens in Wartime.* San Antonio, TX: Trinity University Press, 2006.

Helphand, K. *Dreaming Gardens: Landscape Architecture and the Making of Modern Israel.* Harrisonburg: University of Virginia Press, 2002.

Hennebo, D. *Geschichte des Stadtgrüns I—Von der Antike bis zur Zeit des Absolutismus.* Hannover, Germany: Patzer, 1970.

Hernandes, A. "Randnotizen zur Tagung," *SWB Kommentaire 14, February 1970.* Basel: Schweizerischer Werkbund, 1970.

Higuchi, T. *The Visual and Spatial Structure of Landscapes.* Translated by C. Terry. Cambridge, MA: MIT Press, 1988.

Hilderbrand, G. *The Miller Garden: Icon of Modernism.* Washington, D.C.: Spacemaker Press, 1999.

Hill, S., and R. Stuart. *Reflections from a Garden.* London: Pavilion, 1995.

Hills, G. A. *The Ecological Basis for Land-Use Planning.* Research Report No. 46. Ottawa: Ontario Department of Lands and Forests Research Branch, 1966 (originally published 1961).
Hirsch, A. "Lawrence Halprin: The Choreography of Private Gardens." *Studies in the History of Gardens and Designed Landscapes* 27, no. 4 (2007): 258–361.
Hirsch, A. "Lawrence Halprin's Public Spaces: Design, Experience and Recovery; Three Case Studies [Fort Worth Heritage Park, Denver Skyline Park, Seattle Freeway Park]." *Studies in the History of Gardens and Designed Landscapes* 26, no. 1 (2006): 1–98.
Hirsch, J. *Seeing the Getty Gardens.* Los Angeles: The Getty Museum, 1998.
Hirschfeld, C. *Theorie der Gartenkunst.* Berlin: Union Verlag, 1990; tr. L. Parshall, *Theory of Garden Art.* Philadelphia: University of Pennsylvania, 2001.
Hiss, T. *The Experience of Place.* New York: Knopf, 1990.
Hobhouse, P. *A Book of Gardening.* London: National Trust, 1986.
Hobhouse, P. *Color in Your Garden.* Boston: Little, Brown, 1985.
Hobhouse, P. *The Country Gardener.* Boston: Little, Brown, 1989.
Hobhouse, P. *Penelope Hobhouse on Gardening.* New York: Macmillan, 1984.
Hoskins, W. G. *English Landscapes: How to Read the Man-Made Scenery of England.* London: British Broadcasting Corp., 1974.
Hough, M. *Cities and Natural Process: A Basis for Sustainability.* London: Routledge, 1995.
Hough, M. *City Form and Natural Process: Towards a New Urban Vernacular.* London: Routledge, 1989.
Hough, M. *Out of Place: Restoring Identity to the Regional Landscape.* New Haven, CT: Yale University Press, 1990.
Hough, M., and S. Barrett. *People and City Landscapes: A Study of People and Open Space in Metropolitan Areas of Ontario.* Toronto: Conservation Council of Ontario, 1987.
Hough, M., et al. *The Urban Landscape: A Study of Open Space in Urban Metropolitan Areas.* Toronto: Conservation Council of Ontario, 1971.
Howett, C. *Abstracting the Landscape: The Artistry of Landscape Architect A. E. Bye.* University Park: Pennsylvania State University, Department of Landscape Architecture, 1990.
Hubbard, H., and T. Kimball. *An Introduction to the Study of Landscape Design.* Rev. ed. New York: Macmillan, 1929.
Hunt, J. D. *The Afterlife of Gardens.* London: Reaktion Books, 2004.
Hunt, J. D. "Bernard Lassus in Eden." *Eden* 3 (1996): 67–77.
Hunt, J. D., ed. *Garden History: Issues, Approaches, Methods.* Washington, D.C.: Dumbarton Oaks Research Library and Collection, 1992.
Hunt, J. D. *Greater Perfections: The Practice of Garden Theory.* Penn Studies in Landscape Architecture. Philadelphia: University of Pennsylvania Press, 2000.
Hunt, J. D. *Nature over Again: The Garden Art of Ian Hamilton Finlay.* London: Reaktion Books, 2008.
Hunt, J. D. *Oxford Book of Garden Verse.* Oxford: Oxford University Press, 1993.
Hunt, J. D. "Stourhead Revisited and the Pursuit of Meaning in Gardens." *Studies in the History of Gardens and Designed Landscapes* 26 (2006): 328–41.

Hunt, J. D., and J. Wolschke-Bulmahn, eds. *The Vernacular Garden*. Dumbarton Oaks Colloquium on the History of Landscape Architecture 14. Washington, D.C.: Dumbarton Oaks, 1993.

Husserl, E. *Logical Investigations*. Translated by J. N. Finlay. New York: Publisher, 1970.

Hyde, E. *Cultivated Power*. Philadelphia: University of Pennsylvania Press, 2006.

Imbert, D. *The Modernist Garden in France*. New Haven, CT: Yale University Press, 1993.

Impelluso, L. *Gardens in Art*. Los Angeles: J. Paul Getty Museum, 2007.

Ito, T. *The Gardens of Japan*. Tokyo: Kodansha International; New York: Harper and Row, 1984.

Ito, T. *The Japanese Garden: An Approach to Nature*. New Haven, CT: Yale University Press, 1972.

Ito, T. *Nature and Thought in Japanese Design*. Tokyo: Secretaliat, 1960.

Ito, T. *Space and Illusion in the Japanese Garden*. New York: Weatherhill, 1973.

Jackson, J. *Discovering the Vernacular Landscape*. New Haven, CT: Yale University Press, 1984.

Jackson, J. *Landscapes*. Cambridge: University of Massachusetts Press, 1970.

Jackson, J. *The Necessity for Ruins: And Other Topics*. Amherst: University of Massachusetts Press, 1980.

Jackson, J. *A Sense of Place, a Sense of Time*. New Haven, CT: Yale University Press, 1994.

Jacobs, P. "Après Baudelaire, quoi de neuf?" *Studies in the History of Gardens and Designed Landscapes* 23 (2003): 328–39.

Jacobs, P. "Echoes of Paradise." In *Contemporary Garden*, ed. M. Conan. Washington, D.C.: Dumbarton Oaks Research Library and Collection, 2007.

Jacobs, P. "Folklore and Forest Fragments." *Landscape Journal* 23, no. 2 (2004): 85–101.

Jacobs, P. "Seeds of Future Gardens." *Landscape Architecture* 91 (December 2001): 60–65.

Jacobs, P. "Unobtrusive Measures." *Landscape Architecture* 94 (2004): 28–37.

Jacobs, P. "When Is a Garden Not a Garden?" *Landscape Architecture* 93 (October 2003): 133–44.

James, G. *Genius Loci*. Ottawa: Canadian Museum of Contemporary Photography, 1986.

James, G. *The Italian Garden*. New York: Abrams, 1991.

James, G. *Morbid Symptoms*. Princeton, NJ: Princeton Architectural Press, 1986.

Jarman, D. *Derek Jarman's Garden*. Woodstock, NY: Overlook Press, 1996.

Jekyll, G. *Colour Schemes for the Flower Garden*. London: Country Life, 1908.

Jekyll, G. *A Gardener's Testament*. London: Country Life, 1937.

Jekyll, G. *Home and Garden*. London: Longmans, Green, 1900.

Jekyll, G. *Home and Garden: Notes and Thoughts, Practical and Critical, of a Worker in Both*. London: Longmans, Green, 1901.

Jekyll, G. *Wall, Water and Woodland Gardens, including the Rock Garden and the Heath Garden*. London: Country Life, 1933.

Jekyll, G. *Wood and Garden*. London: Longmans, Green, 1899.

Jekyll, G., and L. Weaver. *Gardens for Small Country Houses*. London: Country Life, 1913.
Jellicoe, G. *The Landscape of Civilisation: As Experienced in the Moody Historical Gardens*. East Sussex, UK: Garden Art Press, 1989.
Jellicoe, G. *Studies in Landscape Design*. Vol. 1. London: Oxford University Press, 1960.
Jellicoe, G. *Studies in Landscape Design*. Vol. 2. London: Oxford University Press, 1970.
Jellicoe, G., S. Jellicoe, P. Goode, and M. Lancaster, eds. *The Oxford Companion to Gardens*. Oxford, UK: Oxford University Press, 1986.
Jencks, C. *The Garden of Cosmic Speculation*. London: Frances Lincoln, 2003.
Jensen, J. *Siftings*. Chicago: Ralph Fletcher Seymour, 1939.
Jewell, L., ed. *Peter Walker: Experiments in Gesture, Seriality and Flatness*. New York: Rizzoli, 1990.
Johnson, J. *Modern Landscape Architecture: Redefining the Garden*. New York: Abbeville Press Publishers, 1991.
Jong, E., de, and Dominicus-Van Soest. *Aardse Paradijen: De Tuin in De Nederlandse Kunst*. 2 vols. Gent: Snoeck-Ducaju & Zoon, 1992.
Karavan, D. *Hommage to Walter Benjamin*. Tel Aviv: Tel Aviv Museum of Art, 1997.
Karson, R. *Fletcher Steele, Landscape Architect, an Account of the Gardenmaker's Life, 1885–1971*. New York: Harry N. Abrams/Saga Press, 1989.
Karson, R. *The Muses of Gwinn: Art and Nature in a Garden Designed by Warren H. Manning, Charles Platt, & Ellen Biddle Shipman*. Sagaponack, NY: Saga Press, Sagaponic, 1995.
Kassler, E. *Modern Gardens and the Landscape*. New York: Museum of Modern Art, 1964; rev. ed., 1984.
Kelsall, M. "The Iconography of Stourhead." *Journal of the Warburg & Courtauld Institutes* 46 (1983): 133–43.
Kemp, E. *How to Lay Out a Garden: Intended as a General Guide in Choosing, Forming, or Improving an Estate (from a Quarter of an Acre to a Hundred Acres in Extent, with Reference to Both Design and Execution)*. New York: Wiley & Halsted, 1858.
Keswick, M., J. Oberlander, and J. Wai. *In a Chinese Garden: The Art & Architecture of the Dr. Sun Yat-Sen Classical Chinese Garden*. Vancouver: The Dr. Sun Yat-Sen Garden Society of Vancouver, 1990.
Kienast, D. "Sehnsucht nach dem Paradies." *Hochparterre* 7 (1990): 46–50.
Kienast, D. "Vom Gestaltungsdiktat zum Naturdiktat—oder: Gärten gegen Menschen?" *Landschaft + Stadt* 3 (1981): 120–28.
Kiley, D., and J. Amidon. *Dan Kiley: The Complete Works of America's Master Landscape Architecture*. Boston: Bullfinch, 1999.
Klee, P. "Unendliche Naturgeschichte. Prinzipielle Ordnung der bildnerischen Mittel, verbunden mit Naturstudium, und konstruktive Kompositionswege." In *Form- und Gestaltungslehre*, vol. 2, ed. Jürg Spiller. Basel: Schwabe, 2007.
Kliass, R. *Parques Urbanos de São Paulo*. São Paulo: Pini Editora, 1993.
Knuijt, M., et al. *Modern Park Design: Recent Trends*. Bussum, the Netherlands: Thoth Uitgeverij, 1993.
Koolhass, R. *S,M,L,XL*. New York: Monacelli Press, 1998.

Kostial, D., ed. *American Garden Design: An Anthology of Ideas that Shaped Our Landscape*. New York: Macmillan, 1994.

Kreisman, L. *The Bloedel Reserve: Gardens in the Forest*. Bainbridge Island, WA: The Arbor Fund, 1988.

Krieger, A., and L. Green. *Past Futures: Two Centuries of Imagining Boston*. Cambridge, MA: Harvard University Graduate School of Design, 1985.

Kubler, G. *The Shape of Time: Remarks on the History of Things*. New Haven, CT: Yale University Press, 1962,

Kühn, E. "Kommentar zur Grünen Charta." In *Die grüne Charta von der Mainau mit Kommentar*. Pfullingen, Germany: Deutschen Gartenbau-Gesellschaft, 1963.

Lady Allen of Hurtwood. *Planning for Play*. London: Thames and Hudson, 1968.

Lady Allen of Hurtwood and S. Jellicoe. *The New Small Garden*. London: Architectural Press, 1956.

Lady Allen of Hurtwood and S. Jellicoe. *The Things We See: Gardens*. London: Penguin Books 1953.

Landeker, H. *Martha Schwartz: Transfiguration of the Commonplace*. Washington, D.C.: Spacemaker Press, 1997.

Land Forum [journal]. Washington, D.C.: Spacemaker Press, 1997–c. 2002.

Landscape Architecture in Conservation: A Conference of the Australian Institute of Landscape Architects Held in Association with the Australian Conservation Foundation. Adelaide: Australian Institute of Landscape Architects and the Australian Conservation Foundation, 1971.

Larkin, P. *Required Writing: Miscellaneous Pieces 1955–1982*. London: Faber and Faber, 1983.

Laroze, C., and C. de Virieu. *Un jardin pour soi*. Arles, France: Actes Sud, 1996.

Lassus, B. *Couleur, Lumière ... Paysage: Instants d'un Pédagogie*. Centre des Monuments nationaux. Paris: Monum, Éditions du patrimoine, 2004.

Lassus, B., ed. *Hypothèses pour une Troisième Nature*. Paris: Cercle Charles-Rivière Dufresny; London: Coracle, 1992.

Lassus, B. *Jardins Imaginaires: Les Paysagistes-Habitants*. Paris: Presses de la Conniassance, 1977.

Lassus, B. *Jeux Images à re-regarder*. Paris: Editions Galilée, 1977.

Lassus, B. *The Landscape Approach*. Penn Studies in Landscape Architecture. Philadelphia: University of Pennsylvania Press, 1998.

Lassus, B. *Villes-paysages: couleurs en Lorraine*. Liege: Pierre Mardaga, 1989.

Lassus, B., et al. *Le Jardin des Tuileries de Bernard Lassus*. London: Coracle Press, 1991.

Lassus, B., et al. *Les Jardins Suspendus de Colas*. Paris: privately printed for Colas S.A., 2007.

Latz, P. "The Idea of Making Time Visible." *Topos* 33 (December 2000): 94–99.

Latz, P. "Landscape Architecture as an Intercultural Principle." *Topos* 50 (March 2005): 6–12.

Laurie, M. *An Introduction to Landscape Architecture*. New York: American Elsevier Publishing, 1976.

Lawrence Halprin & Associates. *Take Part: A Report on New Ways in Which People Can Participate in Planning Their Own Environments*. San Francisco: Lawrence Halprin & Associates, 1972.

Le Corbusier. *Nursery Schools*. New York: Orion, 1968.
Le Corbusier. "Reportage sur un toit-jardin." In *Le Corbusier Oeuvre Complète 1938–1946*, 140–41. Zurich: Girsberger, 1946.
Le Corbusier and P. Jeanneret. "Les 5 points d'une architecture nouvelle" (1926). In *Oeuvre Compléte 1910–1929*. Zurich: Les Editions d'Architecture Erlenback, 1929.
Leatherbarrow, D. *Topographical Stories: Studies in Landscape and Architecture*. Penn Studies in Landscape Architecture. Philadelphia: University of Pennsylvania Press, 2004.
Leccese, M. *Robert Murase: Stone and Water*. Washington, D.C.: Spacemaker Press, 1997.
Leclerc, B. *Jean Claude Nicolas Forestier 1861–1930: Du jardin au paysage urbain*. Paris: Ed Picard, 2000.
Leenhardt, J., ed. *Dans les jardins de Roberto Burle Marx*. Arles, France: Crestet Centre D'art/Actes Sud, 1994.
Leopold, A. *A Sand County Almanac: With Other Essays on Conservation from Round River*. New York: Oxford University Press, 1966.
Le Temps des Jardins. Catalogue of exhibition at Fontainebleau. Melun, France: Seine et Marne Conseil Général, 1992.
Levy, L. *Kathryn Gustafson: Sculpting the Land*. Washington, D.C.: Spacemaker Press, 1998.
Levy, L., ed. *Walter Hood: Urban Diaries*. Washington, D.C.: Spacemaker Press, 1997.
Leyrit, C., and B. Lassus, eds. *Autoroute et Paysages*. Paris: Les Editions du Demi-Cercle, 1994.
Lloyd, C. *The Adventurous Gardener*. New York: Random House, 1983.
Lyall, S. *Designing the New Landscape*. London: Thames and Hudson, 1991.
Lyle, J. *Design for Human Ecosystems: Landscape, Land Use, and Natural Resources*. New York: Van Nostrand Reinhold, 1985.
Lyotard, J.-F. *The Postmodern Condition: A Report on Knowledge*. Translated by G. Bennington and B. Massumi. Minneapolis: University of Minnesota Press, 1984.
Lynch, K. *The Image of the City*. Cambridge, MA: MIT Press, 1960.
Lynch, K. *Managing the Sense of a Region*. Cambridge, MA: MIT Press, 1976.
Lynch, K. *Site Planning*. Cambridge, MA: MIT Press, [1962] 1969.
Macy, C., and S. Bonnemaison. *Architecture and Nature: Creating the American Landscape*. London: Routledge, 2003.
Making Better Civic Places: Urban Design at the University of Calgary. Calgary: Faculty of Environmental Design, University of Calgary, 2003.
Mann, R. *Rivers in the City*. New York: Praeger Publishers, 1973.
Mann, W. *Landscape Architecture: An Illustrated History in Timelines, Site Plans, and Biography*. New York: John Wiley & Sons, 1993.
Marot, S. "The Reclaiming of Sites." In *Recovering Landscape*, ed. J. Corner, 45–57. New York: Princeton University Press, 1999.
Marsh, W. *Landscape Planning: Environmental Applications*. Reading, MA: Addison-Wesley Publishing, 1983.
Marshall, L., ed. *Landscape Architecture into the 21st Century*. Washington, D.C.: American Society of Landscape Architects, 1981.

Martin, A., and J. Fletcher. *The Decadent Gardener*. Sawtry, UK: Dedalus, 1996.

Martin, R., ed. *The New Urban Landscape*. New York: Olympia and York Companies, 1990.

Marx, L. *The Machine in the Garden: Technology and the Pastoral Ideal in America*. Oxford: Oxford University Press, 1979.

Marx, R. "The Gardens at the Museum of Modern Art." In *Affonso Eduardo Reidy*, ed. N. Bonduki. Lisbon: Editorial Blau Instituto Lina Bo e P. M. Bardi, 2000.

Massingham, B. *Miss Jekyll: Portrait of a Great Gardener*. 4th imp. North Pomfret, VT: David & Charles, 1984.

Mathur, A., and D. da Cunha. *Mississippi Floods: Designing a Shifting Landscape*. New Haven, CT: Yale University Press, 2001.

Mathys, H. "Bedeutung und Aufgabe des Gartens in unserer Zeit." *Schweizer Garten + Wohnkultur* 2 (1962): 21–22.

Mathys, H. "Der Garten des Poeten." *Schwiezer Garten + Wohnkulter* 7 (1959): 154ff.

Matless, D. *Landscape and Englishness*. London: Reaktion Books, 1998.

Mattern, H. *Gärten und Gartenlandschaften: Geplant und gebaut von Hermann Mattern, besprochen und beschrieben mit Beate Mattern*. Stuttgart: Hatje, 1960.

Maurierers, A., and E. Ossart. *Jardiniers de Paradis*. Paris: Editions du Chene, 2000.

Mawson, T. *The Art & Craft of Garden Making*. London: B. T. Batsford, 1900.

Mawson, T. *The Life and Work of an English Landscape Architect*. London: The Richards Press, 1927.

McGuire, D. *Beatrix Farrand's Plant Book for Dumbarton Oaks*. Washington, D.C.: Dumbarton Oaks, 1980.

McHarg, I. *Design with Nature*. New York: Doubleday/Natural History Press, 1969.

McHarg, I. "An Ecological Method for Landscape Architecture," *Landscape Architecture* 57, no. 2 (1967): 105–7.

McHarg, I. "Ecology and Design." In *Ecological Design and Planning*, ed. G. Thompson and F. Steiner. New York: John Wiley, 1997.

McHarg, I., ed. *The Potomac: The Report of the Potomac Planning Task Force*. Washington, D.C.: United States Government Printing Office, 1967.

Mee, M. *Bromelias Brasileiras: Aquearelas de Margaret Mee*. Sao Paulo, Brasil: Instituto de Botâica de Sao Paulo, 1992.

Meining, D. W. *The Interpretation of Ordinary Landscapes: Geographical Essays*. New York: Oxford University Press, 1979.

Meyer, E. "The Post-Earth Day Conundrum." In *Environmentalism in Landscape Architecture*, ed. M. Conan. Washington, D.C.: Dumbarton Oaks, 2000.

Meyer, E. "Site Citations: The Grounds of Modern Landscape Architecture." In *Site Matters*, ed. C. Burns and A. Kahn, 93–129. New York: Routledge, 2005.

Migge, L. *Die Gartenkultur des 20. Jahrhunderts*. Jena, Germany: E. Diederichs, 1913.

Miller, M. *The Garden as an Art*. Albany: State University of New York, 1993.

Miller, P., and L. Diamond, eds. *The Frontier Landscape: Selected Proceedings, IFLA Congress, 1981*. Vancouver: University of British Columbia, 1982.

Mitchell, W. *E-Topia: Urban life, Jim—But Not as We Know It*. Cambridge, MA: MIT Press, 1999.

Mitchell, W.J.T., ed. *Landscape and Power*. Chicago: University of Chicago Press, 1994.

Monard, R. "70 Jare Hamburger Statpark. Einführung und Bedeutung." *Das Gartenamt* 29 (1980): 1ff.

Moneo, R. *Theoretical Anxiety and Design Strategies in the Work of Eight Contemporary Architects*. Cambridge, MA: MIT Press, 2004.

Montero, M. *Roberto Burle Marx, the Lyrical Landscape*. Berkeley: University of California Press, 2001.

Moore, C., W. Mitchell, and W. Turnbull, Jr. *The Poetics of Gardens*. Cambridge, MA: MIT Press, 1988.

Morgan, K. *Shaping an American Landscape: The Art and Architecture of Charles A. Platt, Hood Museum of Art*. Hanover, NH: Dartmouth College, 1995.

Morrow, B. *A Dictionary of Landscape Architecture*. Albuquerque: University of New Mexico Press, 1988.

Mosser, M., and P. Nys, eds. *Le Jardin, art et lieu de mémoire*. Besançon, France: Editions de l'Imprimeur, 1995.

Murck, A., and W. Fong. *A Chinese Garden Court: The Astor Court at the Metropolitan Museum of Art*. New York: The Metropolitan Museum of Art, 1981.

Muschamp, H., et al. *The Once and Future Park*. New York: Princeton Architectural Press, 1993.

Nairn, I. "Outrage." Special issue, *Architectural Review* 117, no. 702 (June 1955): 365–456.

Nassauer, J. *Caring for the Countryside: A Guide to Seeing and Maintaining Rural Landscape Quality*. St. Paul: University of Minnesota Agricultural Experiment Station, 1986.

Nature Conservation outside Protected Areas. Ljubljana, Slovenia: Ministry of Environment, Office for Physical Planning Ministry of Environment and Physical Planning, 1996.

Nevermann, P. "Zum Geleit." Introduction to K.-H. Rücke, *Städtebau und Gartenkunst: Kleini Studie über ein vernachlässigtes Thema*. Hamburg, Germany: Christians, 1963.

Newton, N. *An Approach to Design*. Cambridge, MA: Addison-Wesley Press, 1951.

Newton, N. *Design on the Land: The Development of Landscape Architecture*. Cambridge, MA: The Belknap Press of Harvard University Press, 1973.

Noguchi, I. *Isamu Noguchi: The Sculpture of Space*. New York: Whitney Museum of American Art, 1980.

Nollman, J. *Why We Garden*. New York: Holt, 1994.

Noseda, I. "Die Lektion der Kulturfolger." In *Gute Gärten—Gestalete Freiräume in der Region Zürich*, ed. BSLA Regionalgruppe Zürich. Zürich: BSLA, Regionalgruppe Zürich, 1995.

Oelschlaeger, M. *The Idea of Wilderness*. New Haven, CT: Yale University Press, 1991.

Ogrin, D. *The World Heritage of Gardens*. London: Thames and Hudson, 1993.

Oldham, J., and R. Oldham. *Gardens in Time*. Sydney: Lansdowne Press, 1980.

Olin, L. *Across the Open Field: Essays Drawn from English Landscapes*. Philadelphia: University of Pennsylvania Press, 2000.

Olin, L. "Form, Meaning, and Expression in Landscape Architecture." *Landscape Architecture* 7 (1988): 149–68.

Olin, L. "What I Do When I Can Do It: Representation in Recent Works." *Studies in the History of Gardens and Designed Landscapes* 19 (1999): 102–21.
100 Years of Landscape Architecture at the National Capital Commission: Submission for 50th Annual ASLA 1999 Professional Awards. Ottawa: National Capital Commission, 1999.
Origo, B., M. Livingston, L. Olin, and J. Hunt. *La Foce*. Penn Studies in Landscape Architecture. Philadelphia: University of Pennsylvania Press, 2001.
Otte, J.-P. *L'Amour au Jardin*. Paris: Phébus, 1995.
Ottewill, D. *The Edwardian Garden*. New Haven, CT: Yale University Press, 1989.
Oudolf, P., and H. Gerritsen. *Planting the Natural Garden*. Portland, OR: Timber Press, 2003.
Oudolf, P., with N. Kingsbury. *Designing with Plants*. Portland, OR: Timber Press, 1999.
Padilla, V. *Southern California Gardens, an Illustrated History*. Berkeley: University of California Press, 1961.
Page, R. *The Education of a Gardener*. London: William Collins Sons, 1962.
Page, R. *Ritratti di Giardini Italiani*. Milan: Electa, 1998.
Paine, C. *Fifty Years of Landscape Architecture: The Canadian Society of Landscape Architects 1934–1984, Proceedings of the 1984 50th Jubilee Congress*. Guelph, ON: Canadian Society of Landscape Architects, 1998.
Parc de Loisirs: Espaces libres pour les loisirs en région urbaine, parcs de loisirs en région parisienne. Institut d'Aménagement et d'Urbanisme de la Region Parisienne. Paris: Cahiers de l'I.A.U.R.P., 1968.
Parsons, S. *The Art of Landscape Architecture: Its Development and Its Application to Modern Landscape Gardening*. New York: G.P. Putnam's Son's, 1915.
Parsons, S. *Landscape Gardening Studies*. New York: John Lane, 1910.
Parsons, S., Jr. *How to Plan the Home Grounds*. New York: Doubleday & McClure, 1899.
Parsons, S., Jr., et al. *Homes in City and Country*. New York: Charles Scribner's Sons, 1893.
Pioneers of American Landscape Design II: An Annotated Bibliography. Washington, D.C.: National Parks Service, U.S. Department of the Interior, Cultural Resources, Heritage Preservation Services, 1995.
Pirzio-Biroli, R. "Adaptive Re-Use, Layering of Meaning on Sites of Industrial Ruin." *Arcade Journal* 23 (2004): 28–31.
Platt, C. *Italian Gardens*. New York: Harper & Brothers, 1894.
Plumptre, G. *The Garden Makers: The Great Tradition of Garden Design from 1600 to the Present Day*. New York: Random House, 1993.
Plumptre, G. *Great Gardens, Great Designers*. London: Ward Lock, 1996.
Poblotzki, U. "Garenshauen—zwishen Kunst und Kommerz" [Garden Shows—Between Art and Business]. *Topos: European Landscape* 33 (December 2000): 43ff.
Pollan, M. *Second Nature: A Gardener's Education*. New York: Dell, 1991.
Potteiger, M., and J. Purinton. *Landscape Narratives: Design Practices for Telling Stories*. New York: John Wiley & Sons, 1998.
Poullaouec-Gouidec, P., M. Gariepy, and B. Lassus. *Le Paysage: Territoire d'intentions*. Montreal: Harmattan, 1999.

Poullaouec-Gonidec, P., and D. Lemieux. *"Garden Rooms": Festival International de Jardins*. Montreal: Éditions Les 400 coups, 2002.

Poullaouec-Gonidec, P., S. Paquette, and G. Damon, eds. *Le Temps du Paysage*. Montreal: Presses de l'Université de Montréal, 2003.

Profiles in Landscape Architecture. Washington, D.C.: American Society of Landscape Architects 1992.

Pugh, S. *Garden Nature Language*. Manchester: Manchester University Press, 1988.

Racine, M. *Créateurs de Jardins et de paysages en France du XIXe siècle au XXIe siècle*. Arles, France: Actes Sud, 2002.

Ragon, M. *Picassiette: suivi de De Gaudi à Isidore*. Paris: Hoebeke, 2001.

Reed, P., ed. *Groundswell: Constructing the Contemporary Landscape*. New York: Museum of Modern Art, 2005.

Richardson, T. *Avant Gardeners. Fifty Visionaries of the Contemporary Landscape*. London: Thames and Hudson, 2008.

Richardson, T., ed. *The Vanguard Landscapes and Gardens of Martha Schwartz*. New York: Thames and Hudson, 2004.

Richardson, T., and N. Kingsbury, eds. *Vista: The Culture and Politics of Gardens*. London: Thames and Hudson, 2005.

Ricoeur, P. *The Rule of Metaphor: Multidisciplinary Studies in the Creation of Meaning in Language*. Toronto: University of Toronto Press, 1977.

Riley, R. "From Sacred Grove to Disney World: The Search for Garden Meaning." *Landscape Journal* 7, no. 2 (1988): 235–46.

Rivero, E. *Turismo ecológico: Red de Espacios Naturales de Castilla y León*. Valladolid: Junta de Castilla y León.

Robinson, C. *The Improvement of Towns and Cities; or, The Practical Basis of Civic Aesthetics*. New York: G. P. Putnam's Sons, c. 1913.

Robinson, W. *The English Flower Garden*. London: John Murray, 1883.

Robinson, W. *Garden Design and Architect's Gardens*. London: John Murray, 1892.

Robinson, W. *The Wild Garden*. London: John Murray, 1894.

Roger, A. *Court Traité du Paysage*. Mayenne, France: Editions Gallimard, 1997.

Rogers, E. *Landscape Design, a Cultural and Architectural History*. New York: Harry N. Abrams, 2001.

Rogers, E. *Rebuilding Central Park: A Management and Restoration Plan*. Cambridge, MA: MIT Press, 1987.

Rogger, A. *Landscapes of Taste: The Art of Humphry Repton's Red Books*. London: Routledge, 2007.

Rose, B. *Beverly Pepper: Three Site-Specific Sculptures*. Washington, D.C.: Spacemaker Press, 1998.

Rose, J. "Articulate Form in Landscape Design." *Pencil Points* 20 (February 1939): 98–100.

Rose, J. *Creative Gardens*. New York: Reinhold Publishing, 1958.

Rose, J. "Freedom in the Garden." *Pencil Points* 19 (October 1938): 640–44.

Rose, J. *Gardens Make Me Laugh: A New Edition*. Baltimore: Johns Hopkins University Press, 1990.

Rose, J. *The Heavenly Environment: A Landscape Drama in Three Acts with a Backstage Interlude*. Hong Kong: New City Cultural Service, 1987.

Rose, J. "Why Not Try Science?" *Pencil Points* 20 (December 1939): 777–79.
Ross, S. *What Gardens Mean.* Chicago: University of Chicago Press, 1998.
Rowe, P. *Making a Middle Landscape.* Cambridge, MA: MIT Press, 1991.
Rudofsky, B. *Streets for People: A Primer for Americans.* Garden City, NY: Anchor Press/Doubleday, 1969.
Saint-Phalle, N. *Der Tarot-Garten.* Wabern-Bern, Germany: Bentelli, 2000.
Samuels, C. "Michelangelo Antonioni." In *Encountering Directors*, 15–32. New York: Capricorn Books, 1972.
San Martin, I., ed. *Luis Barragán: The Pheonix Papers.* Tempe, AZ: Center for Latin American Studies Press, 1997.
Sasaki, H. "Thoughts on Education in Landscape Architecture: Some Comments on Today's Methodologies and Purpose." *Landscape Architecture* 40, no. 4 (1950): 158–60.
Saunders, W., ed. *Richard Haag: Bloedel Reserve and Gas Works Park.* New York: Princeton Architectural Press, 1998.
Sbriglio, J. *Immeuble 24 N.C. et Appartement Le Corbusier.* Basel: Birkhäuser, 1996.
Schama, S. *Landscape and Memory.* New York: Knopf, 1995.
Schinz, M., and G. van Zuylen. *The Gardens of Russell Page.* New York: Stewart, Tabori & Chang, 1991.
Schioler, T. *Roman and Islamic Water-Lifting Wheels.* Translated by Pauline M. Katborg. Odense, Denmark: Odense University Press, 1973.
Schjetnan, M. *Ten Landscapes.* Gloucester, MA: Rockport Publishers, 2002.
Schulze, S., ed. *Gärten: Ordnung, Inspiration, Glück.* Frankfurt am Main: Städel Museum, 2006.
Schumacher, F. *Ein Volkspark.* Munich: Georg D. W. Callwey, 1928.
Schwarz, U. *Der Naturgarten.* Frankfurt: Verlag Wolfgang Krüger GmbH, 1980.
Scott-James, A., and O. Lancaster. *The Pleasure Garden.* Ipswich, MA: Gambit, 1977.
Scully, V. *Architecture: The Natural and the Manmade.* New York: St. Martin's Press, 1991.
Seddon, G. *Land Prints: Reflections on Place and Landscape.* Cambridge: Cambridge University Press, 1997.
Shaping Tomorrow's Landscape, IFLA, 2 vols. Amsterdam: Djambartan, 1964.
Sheeler, J. *Little Sparta: The Garden of Ian Hamilton Finlay.* London: Francis Lincoln, 2003.
Shepard, P. *Man in the Landscape: A Historic View of the Esthetics of Nature.* 2nd ed. College Station: Texas A&M University Press, 1991.
Shepheard, P. *The Cultivated Wilderness; or, What Is Landscape?* Cambridge, MA: MIT Press, 1997.
Shepheard, P. *Gardens.* London: Macdonald in association with the Council of Industrial Design, 1969.
Shepheard, P. *Modern Gardens.* London: The Architectural Press, 1953.
Shepheard, P. *What Is Architecture? An Essay on Landscapes, Buildings, and Machines.* Cambridge, MA: MIT Press, 1994.
Shepherd, J. C., and G. A. Jellicoe. *Gardens & Design.* London: Ernest Benn, 1927.
Shlomo Aronson & Associates. *Shlomo Aronson & Associates: Architects, Landscape Architects, Townplanners, Ltd.* Jerusalem: Shlomo Aronson & Associates, 1991.

Shore, S. *The Gardens of Giverny: A View of Monet's World*. Millerton, NY: Aperture, Silver Mountain Foundation, 1983.
Simo, M. *Forest and Garden: Traces of Wildness in a Modernizing Land, 1897–1949*. Charlottesville: University of Virginia Press, 2003.
Simo, M. *100 Years of Landscape Architecture: Some Patterns of a Century*. Washington, D.C.: ASLA Press, 1999.
Simo, M. *Sasaki Associates: Integrated Environments*. Washington, D.C.: Spacemaker Press, 1997.
Simon, J. *Détournement des Grandes Paysages: The Future of our Built and Natural Environment*. Paris: Collection amenagement des éspaces libres, No. 20.
Simonds, J. *Garden Cities 21: Creating a Liveable Urban Environment*. New York: McGraw-Hill, 1994.
Simonds, J. *Landscape Architecture: A Manual of Site Planning and Design*. New York: McGraw-Hill, 1983.
Simonds, J. *Landscape Architecture: The Shaping of Man's Natural Environment*. New York: McGraw-Hill, 1961.
Simonds, O. C. *Landscape Gardening*. New York: Macmillan, 1920.
Snow, M. *Modern American Gardens: Designed by James Rose*. New York: Reinhold, 1967.
Solomon, B. *Green Architecture and the Agrarian Garden*. New York: Rizzoli, 1988.
Sovkin, M., ed. *Variations on a Theme Park: The New American City and the End of Public Space*. New York: Moonday Press, 1992.
Space for Living: Landscape Architecture and the Allied Arts and Professions, IFLA. Amsterdam: Djambatan, 1961.
Spence, J. *Polymetis*. London, 1747.
Spens, M. *The Complete Landscape Designs and Gardens of Geoffrey Jellicoe*. London: Thames and Hudson, 1994.
Spirn, A. *The Granite Garden: Urban Nature and Human Design*. New York: Basic Books, 1984.
Spirn, A. W., ed. "Nature, Form, and Meaning." Special issue, *Landscape Journal* 7, no. 2 (1988).
St-Denis, B. "Just What Is a Garden?" *Studies in the History of Gardens and Designed Landscapes* 27 (2007): 61–76.
Steele, F. *Design in the Little Garden*. Boston: The Atlantic Monthly Press, 1924.
Steele, F. "Private Delight and the Communal Ideal." *Landscape Architecture* 31 (January 1941): 69–71.
Stiegler, B. *Technics and Time, 1: The Fault of Epimetheus*. Stanford, CA: Stanford University Press, 1998.
Stoddart, G. *Planificacion Ambiental Contemporanea: 22 realizaciones de arquitectura Paisajista*. Sartenejas, Venezuela: Universidad Simón Bolívar, 1999.
Streatfield, D. *California Gardens: Creating a New Eden*. New York: Abbeville Press, 1994.
Strong, R. *The Artist and the Garden*. New Haven, CT: Paul Mellon Centre for Studies in British Art, Yale University Press, 2000.
Summers, D. "Real Metaphor." In *Visual Theory*, ed. Norman Bryson and Keith Moxey. London: Polity, 1991.

Sustainable Landscape Design in Arid Climates. The Aga Khan Trust for Culture. Washington, D.C.: Dumbarton Oaks, 1996.

Sustainable Urban Landscapes: The Surrey Design Charrette, University of British Columbia. Vancouver: University of British Columbia Press, 1996.

Suzhou: Shaping an Ancient City for the New China, EDAW / Pei Workshop. Washington, D.C.: Spacemaker Press, 1988.

Tacha, A. *Dancing in the Landscape*. Washington, D.C.: Editions Ariel, Graystone Publishing, 2000.

Tankard, J. *The Gardens of Ellen Biddle Shipman*. New York: Sagapress, 1996.

Tankard, J. *Gardens of the Arts and Crafts Movement*. New York: Harry N. Abrams, 2004.

Tankard, J., and M. Wood. *Gertrude Jekyll at Munstead Wood*. Gloucestershire, Stroud: Bramley Books, Sutton Publishing, 1998.

Tate, A. *Great City Parks*. New York: Spon Press, 2001.

Taylor, A.D. *The Complete Garden*. New York: Garden City Publishing, 1921.

Teuscher, H. *Programme d'un Jardin Botanique Idéal*. Montreal: Montreal Botanical Garden, 1940.

Teyssot, G. *The American Lawn: Surface of Everyday Life*. New York: Princeton Architectural Press, 1999.

Thomas H. Mawson 1861–1933: The Life and Work of a Landscape Architect. Lancaster, UK: University of Lancaster, Visual Arts Center, 1978.

Thompson, G., and F. Steiner, eds. *Ecological Design and Planning*. New York: John Wiley, 1997.

Thompson, W. *The Rebirth of New York City's Bryant Park*. Washington, D.C.: Spacemaker Press, 1997.

Thoreau, D. *The Main Woods*. New York: Harper and Row, 1987.

Timms, P. *The Nature of Gardens*. St. Leonards, NSW, Australia: Publisher, 1999.

Tishler, W., ed. *American Landscape Architecture: Designers and Places*. Washington D.C.: The Preservation Press, 1989.

Tishler, W. *Midwestern Landscape Architecture*. Urbana: University of Illinois Press, 2000.

Todd, F. *Esthetic Forestry*. Montreal: Witness Printing House (hand-corrected proof, 23 pages).

Tooley, M., ed. *Gertrude Jekyll, Artist, Gardener, Craftswoman: A Collection of Essays to Mark the 50th Anniversary of Her Death*. Witton-Le-Wear, UK: Michaelmas Books, 1984.

Torres, A. *Isamu Noguchi: A Study of Space*. New York: The Montacelli Press, 2000.

Transforming the Common Place: Selections from Laura Olin's Sketchbooks. President and Fellows of Harvard College. Cambridge: Harvard University Graduate School of Design, 1996.

Treib, M., ed. *The Architecture of Landscape 1940–1960*. Penn Studies in Landscape Architecture. Philadelphia: University of Pennsylvania Press, 2002.

Treib, M. "Constructing Significance." *Landscape Australia* 16 (1994): 27–31.

Treib, M. "Design Vocabulary II: WATER." *Landscape Architecture* 77, no. 1 (1987): 72.

Treib, M, ed. *Modern Landscape Architecture: A Critical Review*. Cambridge, MA: MIT Press, 1993.

Treib, M. "Must Landscapes Mean? Approaches to Significance in Recent Landscape Architecture." *Landscape Journal* 14 (1995): 47–62.
Treib, M. *Noguchi in Paris: The UNESCO Garden.* New York: United Nations Educational, Scientific, and Cultural Organization; San Francisco: William Stout Publishers, 2003.
Treib, M, ed. *Thomas Church, Landscape Architect: Designing a Modern California Landscape.* San Francisco: William Stout, 2003.
Treib, M. "Woodland Cemetery: A Dialogue of Design and Meaning." *Landscape Architecture* 76 (1986): 42–49.
Treib, M., and D. Imbert. *Garrett Eckbo: Modern Landscapes for Living.* Berkeley: University of California Press, 1997.
Trulove, J. *The New American Garden: Innovations in Residential Landscape Architecture, 60 Case Studies.* New York: Whitney Library of Design, 1998.
Tschumi, C. *Mirei Shigemori: Modernizing the Japanese Garden.* Berkeley, CA: Stone Bridge Press, 2005.
Tuan, Y.-F. *Space and Place. The Perspective of Experience.* Minneapolis: University of Minnesota, 1977.
Tunnard, C. *The City of Man.* New York: Charles Scribner's Sons, 1953.
Tunnard, C. *Gardens in the Modern Landscape.* London: The Architectural Press, 1938.
Tunnard, C. *A World with a View: An Inquiry into the Nature of Scenic Values.* New Haven, CT: Yale University Press, 1978.
Uglow, J. *A Little History of British Gardening.* New York: North Point Press, 2004.
Vaccarino, R., ed. *Roberto Burle Marx, Landscapes Reflected.* New York: Princeton Architectural Press, 2000.
Vacherot, J. *Parcs et Jardins. Albums d'Études. Précédé de la 2e édition de Les Parcs et Jardins au Commencement du Xxe siècle.* Paris: Librairie Octave Doin, 1925.
Valentien, O. *Neue Gärten.* Ravensburg: Otto Maier Verlag, 1949.
Van Valkenberg, M. *Built Landscapes: Gardens in the Northeast.* Brattleboro, VT: Brattleboro Museum & Art Center, 1986.
Verey, R. *Good Planting.* London: Frances Lincoln, 1990.
Visôses de Paisagen: Landscape Sights. Edited by Guilherme Mazza Dourado. An exhibition on Contemporary Landscape Architecture in Brazil. Rio: Brazilian Association of Landscape Architecture, 1997.
Von Baeyer, E. *Rhetoric and Roses: A History of Canadian Gardening 1900–1930.* Markham, ON: Fitzhenry & Whiteside, 1984.
Von Maltzahn, K. *Nature as Landscape: Dwelling and Understanding.* Montreal and Kingston, ON: McGill-Queen's University Press, 1994.
Vroom, M. *Lexicon of Garden and Landscape Architecture.* Basel: Birkhäuser, 2006.
Walker, P. *Minimalist Gardens.* Washington, D.C.: Spacemaker Press, 1997.
Walker, P., and M. Simo. *Invisible Gardens: The Search for Modernism in the American Landscape.* Cambridge, MA: MIT Press, 1994.
Wallace, D. *Metropolitan Open Space and Natural Process.* Philadelphia: University of Pennsylvania Press, 1970.
Waugh, F. *Rural Improvement.* New York: Orange Judd, 1914.

Waugh, F. A. *Landscape Gardening: Treatise on the General Principles Governing Outdoor Art; with Sundry Suggestions for their Applications in the Commoner Problems of Gardening.* New York: Orange Judd, 1910.

Waymark, J. *Modern Garden Design Innovation since 1900.* London: Thames and Hudson, 2003.

Weddle Heinemann, A. E., ed. *Techniques of Landscape Architecture.* London: Heineman; New York: Elsevier, 1967.

Weilacher, U. *Between Landscape Architecture and Land Art.* Basel: Birkhäuser, 1999.

Weilacher, U. *In Gardens: Profiles of Contemporary European Landscape Architecture.* Basel: Birkhäuser, 2005.

Weilacher, U. *Syntax of Landscape: The Landscape Architecture of Peter Latz and Partners.* Basel: Birkhäuser, 2007.

Weilacher, U. "Versprechen statt fertiger Antworten." In *Schweingruber Zulauf,* ed. Heinz Wirz. Lucerne: Quart, 2006.

Weilacher, U. *Visionary Gardens: The Modern Landscapes by Ernst Cramer.* Basel: Birkhäuser, 2001.

Weiss, A. *Unnatural Horizons: Paradox & Contradiction in Landscape Architecture.* New York: Princeton Architectural Press, 1998.

Weller, R. *Room 4.1.3: Innovations in Landscape Architecture.* Penn Studies in Landscape Architecture. Philadelphia: University of Pennsylvania Press, 2005.

Westmacott, R. "The Gardens of African-Americans." In *The Vernacular Garden,* ed. J. Hunt and J. Wolschke-Bulmahn. Washington, D.C.: Dumbarton Oaks, 1993.

Whiteson, L. *The Watts Towers.* Oakville, ON: Mosaic Press, 1988.

Whyte, W. *The Last Landscape.* Garden City, NY: Doubleday, 1968.

Wiepking-Jurgensmann, H. *Die Landscaftsfibel.* Berlin: Deutsche Landbuchhandlung, 1942.

Wolschke-Bulmahn, J., ed. *Nature and Ideology: Natural Garden Design in the Twentieth Century.* Dumbarton Oaks Colloquium on the History of Landscape Architecture 18. Washington, D.C.: Dumbarton Oaks, 1997.

"The World of Dan Kiley." *Japan Landscape* 17 (1991): 92–95.

Wrede, S., and W. Adams. *Denatured Visions: Landscape and Culture in the Twentieth Century.* New York: The Museum of Modern Art, 1991.

Yahalom-Dan Zur, L., et al. *Point of View: Four Approaches to Landscape Architecture in Israel.* Tel Aviv: The Genia Schreiber University Art Gallery, 1996.

Yeatman, R. J., and W. C. Sellar. *Garden Rubbish.* London: Methuan, 1936.

CONTRIBUTORS

Anita Berrizbeitia is professor of landscape architecture at the Graduate School of Design, Harvard University. She is the coauthor with Linda Pollak of *Inside/Outside: Between Architecture and Landscape* (Rockport Publishers, 1999), has edited a study of works by the American landscape architect Michael Van Valkenburgh, and authored her own book, *Roberto Burle Marx in Caracas: Parque del Este 1956–1961* (University of Pennsylvania Press, 2005).

John Dixon Hunt is emeritus professor of the history and theory of landscape at the University of Pennsylvania and the editor of *Studies in the History of Gardens and Designed Landscapes*. He is the author of various books and articles, most recently a book on the gardens of Ian Hamilton Finlay, *Nature Over Again* (Reaktion Books, 2008), as well as *The Afterlife of Gardens* (Reaktion Books, 2004), *The Venetian City Garden* (Birkhäuser, 2002), and *A World of Gardens* (Reaktion Books, 2012). He is currently working on a book about the role of history in contemporary landscape architecture.

Peter Jacobs is a professor of landscape architecture at the University of Montreal. He served on the Senior Fellows committee on gardens and landscape studies at Dumbarton Oaks and as a professor at Harvard's Graduate School of Design. He has lectured widely in North America, Europe, and Latin America and is the recipient of the A.H. Tammsaare Environment Prize, the Canadian Society of Landscape Architects (CSLA) President's Prize, and the Governor General's medal on the occasion of the 125th anniversary of Canada's Confederation.

Michael Jakob is a professor in history and theory of landscape at hepia (Geneva) and professor of comparative literature at Grenoble University. He has written on landscape theory, aesthetics, the history of vertigo, contemporary theories of perception, and the poetics of architecture and on landscape architecture and its relations with time and industrial infrastructure. His most recent publication, as co-editor, is reflection of one hundred landscape paintings, 100 Paysages: Exposition d'un genre. Among his most recent publications: and Architecture du paysage (Gollion: Infolio 2012), Mirei Shigemori e il nuovo linguaggio del giardino gaipponese (Verbania: Tarara, 2012).

David Leatherbarrow is a professor of architecture.at the University of Pennsylvania. He has published widely on both the history and theory of architecture and the relations of landscape to built work, including *Uncommon Ground: Architecture, Technology, The MIT Press, 2000* and *Topographical Stories: Studies in Landscape and Architecture* (University of Pennsylvania Press, 2004). *Architecture Orientated Otherwise*, NY Princetonton Archietcural Press, 2009.

Michael Leslie is a professor of English at Rhodes College. He chaired the Committee of Senior Fellows in Landscape at Dumbarton Oaks and has published on early modern culture and the intersections between literature, art history, history of science and agriculture, and garden history. Founder of the Hartlib Papers Project and co-editor of *Culture and Cultivation in Early Modern England: Writing and the Land*, his most recent publications are editions of two plays by the largely forgotten seventeenth-century playwright Richard Brome, *The New Academy* and *The Weeding of Covent Garden*. This information is totally unnecessary for online editions.

Dennis McGlade is a fellow of the American Society of Landscape Architects, an honorary fellow of the Kew Guild, Royal Botanic Gardens, Kew, and a partner at OLIN, Philadelphia. A distinguished plantsman, he contributed to the book *OLIN Placemaking* Monacelli Press, 2008 on the firm's wide-ranging, international practice.

Laurie Olin is a well-known landscape architect, founder of Hanna/Olin, now the OLIN (Philadelphia), and practice professor at the University of Pennsylvania. He is the author of *Across on Open Field: Essays drawn from English Landscapes* (University of Pennsylvania Press, 2000) and joint author of books on the gardens of Vizcaya An American villa and its makers (University of

Pennsylvania Press, 2007) in Florida La Foce a garden in Tuscany (University of Pennsylvania Press, 2001). Both books were published by the University of Pennsylvania Press in 2006 and 2001 respectively.

Udo Weilacher is a landscape architect who has taught at the University of Karlsruhe, ETH Zurich, and the University of Hanover and, now, as professor of Landschaftsarchitektur und industrielle Landschaft at the Technical University of Munich. He is the author of distinguished books that include *Between Landscape Architecture and Land Art* (Birkhäuser, 1999), *Visionary Gardens. Modern Landscapes by Ernst Cramer* (Birkhäuser, 2001), *In Gardens. Profiles of Contemporary European Landscape Architecture* (Birkhäuser, 2005), and *Syntax of Landscape. The Landscape Architecture by Peter Latz and Partners* (Birkhäuser, 2007).

INDEX

Italics indicate pages with illustrations.

Abrahams, Garey, 59
Addison, Joseph, 120
Alaska, 197
allotments, *see* victory gardens
Amsterdamse Bos (Amsterdam), 2, 96
André, Édouard
   L'Art des Jardins, 15, 18
Antonioni, Michelangelo
   Blow-Up, 173–6, 179
arbitrary, 13–35
Arnold, Matthew, 3
Aronson, Shlomo, 49, 54
arts and crafts movement, 65, 68, 78
Asia and Asian gardens, 40, 48, 50, 51, 53, 63, 163
   see also Japanese gardens
Asplund, Erik Gunnar, 55
Atget, Eugène, 165–69
Auden, W. H., 131
Australasia, 2, 47, 55, 76

Balmori, Diana, 45
Banks, Joseph, 159
Barcelona, Spain, 48, 49
Barfield, Owen, 131
Barragán, Luis, 45, 186–90, *187*

Barthes, Roland
   Camera Lucida, 145, 146
Barton, Cheryl, 55
Bassani, Giorgio
   The Garden of the Finzi-Continis, 153–56, *157*, 158,
Battery Park (New York City), 49
Baudelaire, Charles, 173
Bauhaus, 49
Bava, Henri, 52
Beaux Arts design, 19–20
Belvedere Courtyard (Vatican), 172
Benjamin, Walter, 167
Berri Square (Montreal), 49
Berrizbeitia, Anita, 9
Billington, Jill
   New Classics Gardens, 121
Birkenhead, 3
Biron Cemetery, 55
Bonnefoy, Yves, 145
Bourgainville, Louis de, 159
Brazil, 18, 42, 49, 50, 55, 205
Breuer, Marcel, 198
Brodber, Erna
   Jane and Louisa Will Come Home Soon, 158–9

Bryant Park (New York City), 48, 51, 123, *124*
Bunyan, John, 149
Bürgi, Paolo, 127
Burnett, Frances Hodgson
 The Secret Garden, 144
Bye, A. E., 43, 83

Cabot, Francis, 41
California, 76
Calvino, Italo
 Marcovaldo, 156–8
Cardada, 127, *128*
Cartier-Bresson, Henri, 169
Carver, Humphrey, 38
Casares, Bioy, 174
Castello (Florence, Italy), 118
Castle Howard (Yorks, England), 118
Central Park (New York City), 95–6, 97, 163
Chacel, Fernando, 50
Chevreal, Michel-Eugène (colors in gardens), 68
Church, Thomas, 6, 41, 43–4, 121
CIAM, *see* International Congress of Modern Architecture
Citizen Kane, 72–3
Clément, Gilles, 49
Coleridge, Samuel Taylor, 150, 172–3
Collins, Belt, 54
Corajoud, Michel, 46
Corner, James, 122
cottage gardens, 64
Cran, Marion, 76
Crowe, Sylvia, 38
Czerniak, Julia, 30

Dante (Alighieri), 149, 155
Deering, James, 43
Delvaux, Paul, 174
Descombes, Georges, *32*
Désert de Retz (Chambourcy), 118
Dickinson, Emily, 156
digital representations, 34, 179
Downing, Andrew Jackson, 95

Duisberg-Nord Landscape Park (Germany), 2, 30, 131, 203–5, *204*
Dumbarton Oaks (Washington, D.C.), 43, 70–71
Duncan, Isadore, 10
Du Ponts
 and their gardens, 72–3

Eckbo, Garrett, 14, 15, *16*, 18, 19, 20, 21, 31, 41, 44, 53, 121, 122
 ALCOA Forecast Garden, 201–3, *202*, 205
Eisenman, Peter, *34*, 195–98, *196*
Eliot, T. S., 134, 141–2, 144, 145–6, 148, 149
Encke, Fredrich August (Fritz), 96
Englische Garten (Munich), 3, 94–5, 99, 123
Ermenonville (France), 3
Etruscan necropolis (Cervetri), 153, 195
Evans, Hugh
 Evans and Reed Nursery, 76
Exposition Internationale des Arts Décoratifs et Industriels Modernes (1925), 121, 201

Farrand, Beatrix, 43, 70
Faulkner, William
 and *The Sound and the Fury* 148
Finlay, Ian Hamilton, 8, 41, 127, 132, 136
 Finlay's Little Sparta, 127
 Fleur de l'Air, Provence, 136, *137*
Foerster, Karl, 78
Freidberg, Paul, 49
French Revolution, 94
Freshkills (New York City), 3, *19*

Gainsborough, Thomas, 177–8
garden shows and festivals, horticultural shows, 58, *59*, 99, 100
Generalife Gardens (Granada), 139, 149
Giedion, Sigfried, 99
Ginner, Charles, 165
Girot, Christophe, 127

Goethe, Johann Wolfgang von
  Elective Affinities, 164, 171, 175
Gordon, Caroline
  The Garden of Adonis, 146–8, 150
Greenaway, Peter
  The Draughtman's Contract, 176–8, 179
Groundswell Exhibition (2005), 123
Guevrekian, Gabriel, 122, 168, 173
Guillonet, Octave Victor, 167
Gustafson, Kathryn, 74

Haag, Richard (Rick)
  Gas Works Park (Seattle, Washington), 48, 54, 123, 131
Haffner, Jean-Jacques, 122
Halprin, Lawrence, 25, 49, 51, 60, 134
Hamburg, Germany, 97, *98*
Hanover, Germany, 99, 100
Harbers, Guido, 99
Hargreaves, George, 30–31
Hearst, W. R., 172
Hervé, Lucien, 169
Hirschfeld, Christian Cay Laurenz, 94
Homer, 136
Horticulturist, 95
Hough, Michael, 48, 53
House Beautiful, 122
Hubbard, Henry and Kimball, Theodora
  An Introduction to the Study of Landscape Design 15, *16*, *17*, *18*
Hurtwood, Lady Allen of, 53
Husserl, Edmund, 117

Ibsen, Henrick, 174
Industrial Revolution, 71
International Congress of Modern Architecture (CIAM), 99
International Federation of Landscape Architects (IFLA), 100–1
Invalidenpark (Berlin), 127, *128*
Irwin, Robert, 52
Israel, 49, *52*, 55, 57

Jackson, J. B., 46
Jacobs, Peter, 3

Jakob, Michael, 7
James, Geoffrey, 135
Japanese gardens, 55, 121, 134, 199–200
Jarman, Derek, 126, 170–71
Jekyll, Gertrude, 38, 40, 41, 68–70, *69*, 71, 74, 121
Jellicoe, Sir Geoffrey, 55
Jencks, Charles
  The Garden of Cosmic Speculation, 126–7
Jensen, Jens, 48, 75, 122
Johnson, Lawrence, 72
Jones and Jones, 52

Kafka, Franz, 153
Kandinsky, Wassily, 41
Karavan, Danny, 57
Kelsall, Malcolm, 117, 132
Kenna, Michael, 169
Kertesz, Andre, 169
Kienast, Dieter, 11
Kiley, Dan, 6, 9–10, 15, 18, 19, 20, 41, 44, 51, 52, 121
Kincaid, Jamaica
  My Garden 158–60
Kipling, Rudyard, 142–4
Klee, Paul, 164, *165*, 167
Kliass, Rosa, 49
Koolhaas, Rem, 21

Lagrange, Jacques, 173
land art, 5–6
Lang, Fritz
  Metropolis 171–2, 179
Lange, Willy, 77–78
Lartigue, Jacques-Henri, 169
Lassus, Bernard, 3, 5–6, 44, 50–1, 58–9, 125, *126*, 131
Latz, Peter, 1, 2, 30, 123, 124, 131, 203–5, *204*
Laurens, Henry, 191
Leatherbarrow, David, 4, 11
Le Corbusier, 190–95
Léger, Fernand, 191
Leopardi, Giacomo, 175

Leslie, Michael, 7
Lin, Maya, 55
Lloyd, Nathaniel, Daisy, and Christopher, 41, *73*, 74
Louis XIV, 91
Lowry, Malcolm
  Under the Volcano, 148–52, 159
Lutyens, Edwin, 68, *69*, 70, *73*, 74
Lynch, David
  Blue Velvet, 178
Lynch, Kevin, 20, 21, 22
Lyotard, Jean-François, 142

McGlade, Dennis, 2
McHarg, Ian, 21–2, 31, 122
Mahoney, Charles, 165, *166*
Mallet-Steven, Robert, 122
Marville, Charles, 169
Marx, Roberto Burle, 28, 41, *42*, 50, 181–86, *184*
  24 Rue Nungesser et Coli, Paris, 191, *192*
  Unité d'Habitation, Marseilles, *194*
  Villa Cook, 190
Maurières, Armand, 136, 138
meaning in gardens, 117–40
Mediterranean climate, 76, 135–9, 168, 193
Mexico, 45, 46, 65, 189, 203
Michelangelo, 181
Migge, Leberecht, 98–9
Millenium Park (Chicago), 74
Milton, John
  Paradise Lost 148, 149, 150
Moholy-Nagy, Lâasziâo, 41
Monet, Claude, 68, 166–7, 170
Montreal Botanical Gardens, 56
Moore, Robin, 53
Morei, Shigemorei, 55
Morris, William, 65
Morton, Margaret, 45
Museum of Modern Art, New York, 51

National Museum of Australia, 56, 57, 135
Neutra, Richard Joseph, 189

Nicholson, Harold, 41, 72
Noguchi, Isamu, 49, *52*, 198–200, *199*

Oberlander, Cornelia, 51
Olin, Laurie, 2, *34*, 49, 52, 60, *124*, 130, 195, *196*
Olmsted, Frederick Law, 25, 40, 95–6, 163
Olympic Park (Seattle, Washington), 3
Ossart, Eric, 136, 138
Ozenfant, Amédée, 191

Page, Russell, 54, 122, 131,
Paris
  Bois de Boulogne, 96
  Buttes Chaumont, 96
  Palais Royal, 48
  Parc Bercy, 2
  Parc Citroen, 49
  Parc La Villette, 7, 8, 21, 131
  Tuileries, 48, 51, 123
  UNESCO gardens, 198–200, 205
peace gardens, 57–8
Pedregal Gardens (Mexico City, Mexico), 186–90, *187*
Pellicer, Carlos, 188
Peto, Harold, 70, *71*
Petrarch, 170
plantings, 64–91
Plossu, Bernard, 169
Poe, Edgar Allen, 172
Porcinai, Pietro, 28–9
Portugal, Armando Salas, *187*, 188
Pratolino (Tuscany), 134
Proust, Marcel, 145
Provence, France
  Le Jardin de l'Alchimiste, 136, *138*
  Le Jardin de la Noria, 138, *139*
  see also Finlay, Ian Hamilton
Public Works Authority, 44

Réol, Marie Marguerite, 167
Repton, Humphrey, 6, 163
Resnais, Alain
  Last Year at Marienbad, 174–5, 179

INDEX

Riley, Robert, 11, 129, 133
Rio de Janeiro (Museum of Modern Art), 181–86, *184*
Rivera, Diego, 187
Robbe-Grillet, Alain, 174
Robinson, William, 38, 65–67, 68, 71, 74, 121, 131
roof gardens, 51–2, 182, 193–94
Rose, James, 14, 15, 18, 19, 20, 41
Ruskin, John, 65

Sackville-West, Vita, 41, 72
Sáenz, Benjamin Alíre, 154
Sarig, Gideon, 52
Sasaki, Hideo, 20–21, 26, 53, 54
Sasaki, Yoji, 9–10,
Scarpa, Carlo, 55
Schjetnam, Mario, 46
Schreber, Daniel Gottlob Moritz, 77, 96
Schumacher, Fritz, 97, *98*
Schwartz, Martha, 3–9, 29–30, 58, 126
Sckell, Friedrich Ludwig von, 95
sculpture gardens, 51, 52
   Parco di Celle, Pistoia, Italy 52
   Storm King, New York State 52
   see also Museum of Modern Art, New York
Sessions, Kate Olivia, 76
Shaftesbury, Third Earl of, 120
Shepheard, Sir Peter, 122
Simon, Jacques, 59, 60
Smith, Ken, 126
Solomon, Barbara, 60
Sonnfist, Allan, 48
Sooley, Howard, 170
Southern Agrarians, 146
Southern Living, 122
Spencer, Stanley, 165
Spenser, Edmund
   The Faerie Queene, 147–8, 150
Steele, Fletcher, 11, 38, 43, 121, 122,
Steele, Richard, 120
Stein, Clarence, 44
Stein, Gertrude, 5
Stevens, Mallet, 201
Stiegler, Bernard, 200

Stone, Edward T., 54
Stoppard, Tom
   Arcadia, 3, 160
Stourhead, England, 118
Stowe, England, 3, 118
Strand, Paul, 169–70
Sudek, Josef, 169
Sullivan, Chip, 60
Sunset Magazine, 122

Tati, Jacques
   Mon Oncle, 173–4, 179
Teyssot, George, 178
Theodor, Elector Karl, 94
Thoreau, Henry David, 37
Todd, Frederick G., 55
Treib, Marc, 129–30
Tschumi, Bernard, 131
Tunnard, Christopher, 38
Turkey
   plants from, 63
types of gardens, 37–61

use and meaning in gardens, 93–116

Valentien, Otto, 100
Valkenburgh, Michael van, 31, 53
Vaughn, Don, 49
Vaux, Calvert, 163
Vaux-le-Vicomte, France, 172
vernacular gardens, 46–7, 125–6
Vera, Paul and André, 68, 122
verbal representations of gardens, 8, 141–60
Versailles, France, 91, 118
victory gardens, 77, 96
Vierny, Sacha, 174
Vietnam Memorial (Washington, D.C.), 132
Villa d'Este (Tivoli), 118
Villa Lante (Viterbo), 118
Virgil
   The Aeneid, 149
visual representations of gardens, 161–179
Volkspark (Berlin), 97
Voltaire (François Marie Arouet), 158

Walker, Peter, 25, 26–8, 49
Washington Mall (Washington, D.C.), 55
Waugh, Frank, 38
Weilacher, Udo, 6, 7
Weller, Richard, 56
Wells, H. G., 65
Wexner Center for the Visual Arts (Columbus, Ohio), 195–98, *196*, 205
Wharton, Edith, 70
Whitman, Walt, 118
Williams, Asselin, and Akaoui, *see* Montreal Botanical Gardens
Williams Square (Dallas-Fort Worth, Texas), 49
Woodland Cemetery (Stockholm), 5, 129

Woolf, Virginia, 141
World Wars, 20, 43, 64, 67–8, 77, 82, 84, 85, 98, 121, 141, 142, 146, 149, 152, 193
Worlitz, Germany, 3
Wright, Frank Lloyd, 75, 187
Wright, Henry, 44

Xochimilco Ecological Park (Mexico City), 46

Yeats, W. B., 142
Yorkville Park (Toronto), 135
  Downsview, 3

Zion, Robert, 49

www.ingramcontent.com/pod-product-compliance
Lightning Source LLC
Chambersburg PA
CBHW080536300426
44111CB00017B/2753